# SELF ANALYSIS AND SELF KNOWLEDGE

Other Books by Dr. Mishra Are:

1. *Fundamentals of Yoga*, Doubleday & Co., Garden City, N.Y.
2. *Textbook of Yoga Psychology*, Doubleday & Co., Garden City, N.Y.
3. *Isha Upanisad*, Yoga Society of Dayton
4. *Kena Upanisad*, Yoga Society of Syracuse
5. *Dynamics of Yoga Mudras*, Yoga Society of New York

# SELF ANALYSIS AND SELF KNOWLEDGE

Based on ĀTMA BODHA of Shankaracharya
(Translation and Commentary)

by

SHRI RAMAMURTI MISHRA

Published by
CSA Press, Lakemont, Georgia 30552

Library of Congress Catalog Card Number 77-89867
Standard Book Number 0-87707-190-X

Printed for the publisher by
CSA Printing & Bindery, Lakemont, Georgia 30552

This book is humbly dedicated to the memory of my beloved Mother, Shrimati Sarasvati, and Father, Shriram Mishra, whose Spiritual love, guidance, and dedication created a divine home atmosphere in which was fertile field to sow seeds of Self Discovery.

## ACKNOWLEDGMENTS

SELF ANALYSIS AND SELF KNOWLEDGE was completed in 1961, when I was working in the Military Hospital, Montreal, Canada. Since then this book has gone through revolutionary changes. It was edited and checked by Shrimati Ann Adman, Professor and Head of the Department of English, Illinois University. The book was so large that I was advised to publish it in two volumes. It was sent to various publishers, and they advised condensation. Later it was condensed by Shrimati Shanti Devi. After that it was revised by George Leone, Vice President of Alcon Laboratories, Inc., in Fort Worth, Texas.

Now this book is ready for release, and I am obliged to express my thanks and acknowledgment to all friends who have contributed their services. I thank Shrimati Ann Adman for the first checking; Shrimati Shanti Devi for revision, condensation, and allitteration; Shrimati Anasuya Devi for further rechecking; Vyasananda for rewriting the Sanskrit, and Bharati Devi for the final checking of the Sanskrit; and ultimately I thank George Leone for taking all responsibility for publication of this book.

SHRI RAMAMURTI

TABLE OF CONTENTS

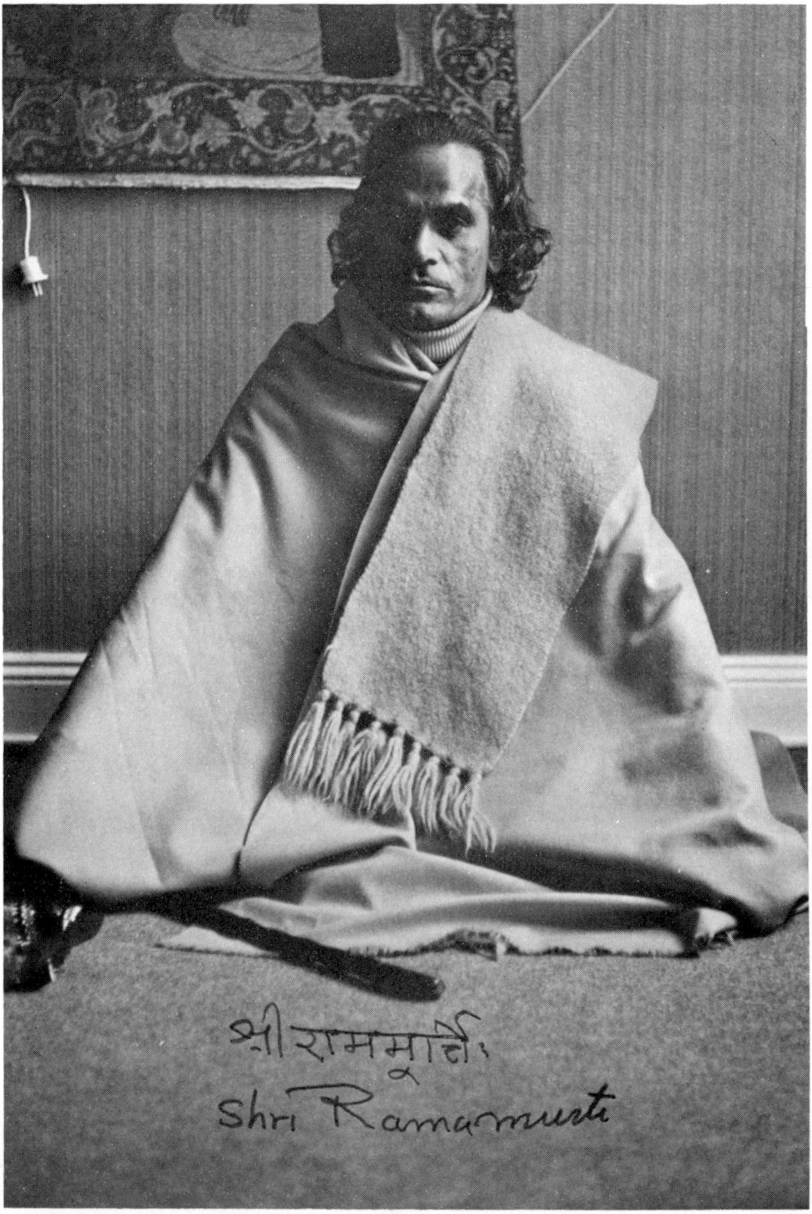
श्रीराममूर्तिः
Shri Ramamurti

Shri Bhagavandas, Guru of Shri Ramamurti

Ramamurti
श्री राममूर्ति:
SHRI Ramamurti

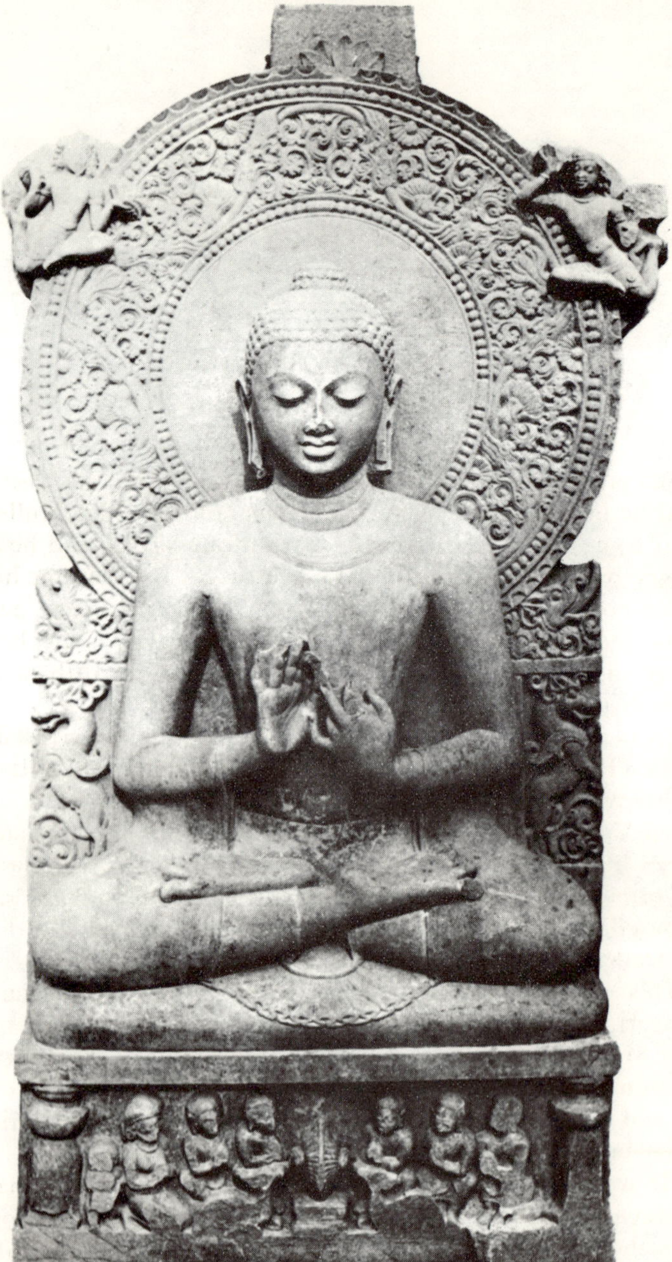

## SHANKARACHARYA

Shankara was born in 788 A.D. at Kaladi on the west coast of India; he left his body in 820 A.D., according to Max Muller. At the age of 8, he was already Master of the four Vedas, and he had won mastery over all scriptures by the age of 12. By the time he was 16, he had completed his commentary on the Upanishads, part of the Vedas, and had written innumerable hymns to all Gods; he had also written many other books. ATMA BODHA is one of those books on which this commentary is based.

Shankara is pictured as a solitary ascetic thinker, as well as being completely immersed in practical work. He belonged to the learned and hardworking sect of Brahmins of Malabar. In his youth he attended Vedic School under Govinda, the pupil of Gaudapada, world-famous philosopher. By a very early age, Shankara had mastered the four principal Vedas. He was filled with devotion, and as a sannyasin, wandered from place to place teaching and engaging in discussions with leaders of other schools of thought.

This great sage established four monasteries: the main one at Shringeri in Mysore Province, the others at Puri in the East, Dvaraka in the West, and Bhadrinath in the Himalayas. His devotion and filial affection for his mother caused him to go against the rules of sannyasins, and to perform her funeral rites, thereby incurring serious community opposition.

He was 32 years of age when he left his body at Kedarnath in the Himalayas. Shankara was a prophet dedicated to lead a people along the paths of virtue. His greatest achievement in the field of speculation is the Advaita system of philosophy.

This is a very short introduction to Acharya Shankara. The

readers are advised to see authoritative history written by various historians. Because of his supreme and sublime virtue, devotion, and divine service to all humanity he has been regarded as the incarnation of Lord Shiva to teach man unconditional unity with the Absolute.

## EXPLANATORY NOTES

Throughout this book, the words nādam, śabda-Brahman, sound current, third eye, saguṇa Brahman, and OM are used. They should not confuse the meditator. They all mean the Self. OM is the mantric and technical name of I AM. No doubt, here and there, these terms are used in the dualistic sense, but it is necessary in the state of avidyā, ignorance, to use them in that way. Worship would be impossible without dualism, but at the end we realize that a foreign God cannot be worshiped, and that He whom we worshiped as the omnipresent, omnipotent, and omniscient God is our real Self; thus, throughout this book, whenever a reader finds these words, he should understand that it is the devotional way of Self-analysis.

The paths of devotion, Karma Yoga, and knowledge are not absolutely distinct from one another because ultimately they lead to the same goal. Yet these paths are followed distinctly by mind because the current of mind is protonic, electronic, and neutronic in nature. According to its current, the mind changes the channel of its movement. The same meditator sometimes goes through devotion, sometimes through universal service, sometimes through meditation and Samādhi, and other times through investigation: "Who am I?"

## THE SANSKṚT ALPHABET

### VOWELS

| | | | | | |
|---|---|---|---|---|---|
| अ A | आ Ā | इ I | ई Ī | उ U | ऊ Ū |
| ए E | ऐ AI | ओ O | औ AU | अं AṀ | अः AḤ |
| | ऋ Ṛ | ॠ Ṝ | ऌ LṚ | ॡ LṜ | |

### CONSONANTS

| | HARD Simple | HARD Aspirate | SOFT Simple | SOFT Aspirate | Nasal |
|---|---|---|---|---|---|
| GUTTURALS | क Ka | ख Kha | ग Ga | घ Gha | ङ Ṅa |
| PALATALS | च Ca | छ Cha | ज Ja | झ Jha | ञ Ña |
| CEREBRALS | ट Ṭa | ठ Ṭha | ड Ḍa | ढ Ḍha | ण Ṇa |
| DENTALS | त Ta | थ Tha | द Da | ध Dha | न Na |
| LABIALS | प Pa | फ Pha | ब Ba | भ Bha | म Ma |

| | | | | |
|---|---|---|---|---|
| SEMI VOWELS | य Ya | र Ra | ल La | व Va |
| SIBILANTS (hard) & ASPIRATE (soft) | श Śa | ष Ṣa | स Sa | ह Ha |
| COMPOUND CONSONANTS | क्ष Kṣa | त्र Tra | ज्ञ Jña | |

### EXAMPLES FOR COMBINATION OF LETTERS

CONSONANT-VOWEL COMBINATIONS:

क् KA क KA का KĀ कि KI की KĪ कु KU कू KŪ कृ KṚ कॄ KṜ

के KE कै KAI को KO कौ KAU कं KAṀ कः KAḤ कॢ KḶ

CONSONANT COMBINATIONS:

ग्य GYA त्व TVA ष्ट ṢṬA ङ्क ṄKA ञ्ज ÑJA द्भ DBHA ह्न HNA प्र PRA र्क RKA

SPECIAL CONSONANT COMBINATIONS:

क्त KTA क्र KRA त्त TTA द्म DMA श्च ŚCA श्र ŚRA ह्म HMA ह्य HYA

## PRONUNCIATION OF TRANSLITERATED WORDS

### VOWELS

| | | | | | |
|---|---|---|---|---|---|
| A | अ | But | E | ए | Café (French) |
| Ā | आ | Father | AI | ऐ | My |
| I | इ | Bid | O | ओ | Beau (French) |
| Ī | ई | Seed | AU | औ | Now |
| U | उ | Put | AṀ | अं | Resonant Nasal |
| Ū | ऊ | Cool | AḤ | अः | Emphasized Aspirate at end of a word |
| Ṛ | ऋ | Trilled "RR" (Spanish) | | | |

### CONSONANTS

| | | | | | | | | |
|---|---|---|---|---|---|---|---|---|
| K | क् | Kite | Ṭh | ठ् | Light-hearted | M | म् | Mother |
| Kh | ख् | Lake house | Ḍ | ड् | Door | Y | य् | Yes |
| G | ग् | Give | Ḍh | ढ् | Adhesion | R | र् | Pero (Spanish) |
| Gh | घ् | Big house | Ṇ | ण् | End | L | ल् | Love |
| Ṅ | ङ् | Sing | T, Th | त् थ् | Tongue to | V | व् | V or W |
| C | च् | Church | D, Dh | द् ध् | Teeth | Ś | श् | Shut |
| Ch | छ् | French-horn | N | न् | Near | Ṣ | ष् | Similar to above but softer |
| J | ज् | Joy | P | प् | Pine | S | स् | Sun |
| Jh | झ् | Hedgehog | Ph | फ् | Up-hill | H | ह् | Home |
| Ñ | ञ् | Angel | B | ब् | Bird | Jñ | ज्ञ् | Nasalized 'gy' or 'jy' |
| Ṭ | ट् | Jet* | Bh | भ् | Abhor | | | |

* For Ṭ, Ṭh, Ḍ, Ḍh, Ṇ - Tongue to roof of mouth

## SUTRA NO. 1

तपोभिः क्षीणपापानां शान्तानां वीतरागिणाम् ।
मुमुक्षूणामपेक्ष्योऽयमात्मबोधो विधीयते ॥१॥

TAPOBHIḤ KṢĪṆAPĀPĀNĀṀ ŚĀNTĀNĀṀ VĪTARĀGIṆĀM.
MUMUKṢŪṆĀM APEKṢYO' YAM ĀTMABODHO VIDHĪYATE.

| | | |
|---|---|---|
| तपोभिः | Tapobhiḥ | By self-discipline |
| क्षीण-पापानाम् | Kṣīṇa-Pāpānām | Endowed with purity |
| शान्तानाम् | Śāntānām | Endowed with tranquillity |
| वीतरागिणाम् | Vītarāgiṇām | Free from personal like & dislike |
| मुमुक्षूणाम् | Mumukṣūṇām | Having intense desire for liberation |
| अपेक्ष्यः | Apekṣyaḥ | Having in view |
| अयम् | Ayam | This |
| आत्म-बोधः | Ātma-Bodhaḥ | Self-analysis, Self-knowledge |
| विधीयते | Vidhīyate | Is composed |

This *Self-knowledge (Ātma-Bodhaḥ)* is composed for those who have purified their hearts by *Tapaḥ*, Self-discipline; whose hearts abound in tranquillity; whose minds are free from the pairs of opposites, such as personal love and hatred; and who have intense desire to experience *Brahman* as their own Self.

This SELF-KNOWLEDGE (*ĀTMA-BODHAḤ*) is composed to enlighten the mind of those who are endowed with purity, simplicity, tranquillity, unmateriality and intense desire for freedom. The word *tapaḥ* here means the control of the motion of the sensory and motor organs. Proper use of the motion of the sensory and motor organs means prevention of wrong use, and application to right use. When the darkness of sin is thus removed, the mind is equipped for the process of enlightment.

Tranquillity of the mind is disturbed by material happiness and unhappiness, which create attachment to agreeable objects and aversion to disagreeable objects. When, through Self-analysis, one realizes that the realm of reality is entirely beyond material happiness and unhappiness, then one finds peace in one's heart. Due to such tranquillity of mind, one is unperturbed by neither favorable nor unfavorable situations.

*Vītarāga* is interpreted here as unmateriality; that is, the freedom of the Self from the congestion or covering of matter. Bondage of the Soul is due to its association with matter and material forces; liberation is the expulsion of matter from the Soul. Freedom is obtained by preventing an influx of additional matter and by completely expelling the matter and material forces with which the Soul already has become mingled.

The presence of material forces can be recognized in the form of wishes, imagination, aims, psychosexual and other desires. These passions and cravings, called *rāgaḥ* and *vāsanāḥ*, are constantly entering the mind where they are transformed into psychological forces. These are the driving forces that propel psychic energy; and, according to motivation, they have two purposes and two results. These driving forces may be constructive with constructive results and spiritual strength, or they may be destructive with destructive results and matter converging in the Soul. Through Self-analysis and spiritual motivation, these psychological forces drive psychic energy toward the attainment of spiritual liberation from the bondage of matter and material forces. Matter and energy are merely different aspects of the same thing. An electron is matter; its constant motion is atomic energy. As matter and energy can be neither created nor destroyed but merely altered in form, so the Soul can be neither created nor destroyed but merely altered in form. When psychic energy is withdrawn from a destructive path, and directed onto the constructive path, then unmateriality is present. This means freedom of the Self from the congestion or covering of matter.

*Mumukṣu* means having intense desire to obtain liberation. When one has this intense desire for freedom, then the psychological forces with their aims, wishes, and desires will be sublimated in the process of Self-analysis.

Freedom is classified in four groups, which include innumerable subclasses and subdivisions:

a. *Artha* is economic freedom, the primary freedom without which a man is helpless and hopeless. This economic freedom includes individual, domestic, national and international classes of freedom.

b. *Kāma* is physical and mental freedom. A man must be free from physical and mental diseases, worries and anxieties, and must have the capacity and maturity for proper physical and mental enjoyment. As long as a man is physically or mentally unfit, he can enjoy neither material prosperity nor Self-analysis. A sound body and sound mind are the basic substance for both material and spiritual progress and prosperity.

c. *Dharma* is the freedom of moral, ethical, and spiritual forces to overcome immoral, unethical, and corporeal forces. *Dharma* is any activity which uplifts the mind, thus including all religious and social sciences, the opening of various institutions, and the service of all living beings. It is especially in the service of humanity as the worship of the Supreme.

d. *Mokṣa* is spiritual freedom, the freedom of spirit from matter. One must know himself and his relation to the Universe. He must identify himself with *Ātman*, *Brahman*, which is One-without-a-second. Without realizing this identity, he will not win victory over matter and attain liberation from death. *Mokṣa* includes all subclasses of metaphysics and philosophy.

These are the four legs of the table of Self-analysis. If any one of them is lacking or impaired, one cannot have the ideal table of life. For example, a man who has economic freedom (wealth), but who lacks physical and mental vigor, is diseased. A man who has economic freedom and physical and mental health, but who lacks the moral and ethical principles of life, lives on the animal level although he has a human form. If a man has economic freedom, physical and mental freedom, moral and social freedom, but has no knowledge of Self, then he fails to achieve the goal of human life.

Therefore, the seeker desiring liberation, the ideal man for Self-analysis, must attain a state of equilibrium in all the *puruṣārtha catuṣṭayam*.

Four qualifications of the seeker are described here. The genuine seeker of truth must practice adequate and proper discipline. By direct personal experience he should realize that the Self of man is identical with Supreme Consciousness. To know *Brahman* means to become *Brahman*. Intellectual understanding must be followed by actual transformation of the life of the seeker. Philosophy is not merely a subject for amusing conversation or debate; it must become the way of the life force. For this reason, the following qualifications are extremely important as instruments of Self-analysis:

1. *Nitya-anitya vastu-viveka*

   This is discrimination between the real and the unreal, an intuitive conviction of the mind that *Brahman* alone is absolutely real substance, and that all other things of the Universe are interdependent and conditionally real, and that they last only as long as their conditions last; therefore, from the viewpoint of the Absolute, all transient things are unreal and illusory. The seeker of truth must come to know discrimination between unchanging reality and transient things.

2. *Ihāmutra phala-bhoga-virāgaḥ*

   Renunciation of sensory pleasures and of the enjoyment of temporal and material rewards here and in other worlds is *virāgah*.

3. *Śama-damādi-ṣaṭ-sampattiḥ* - the six treasures

   a. *Śama*. Holding the mind steadfastly on *Brahman*, after having detached it from destructive sense objects by continually observing their defects is called *śama*, displacement and sublimation of psychic energy. This brings calmness.

   b. *Dama*. Self-discipline and direction of sensory and motor organs away from their destructive activities is called *dama*. This brings self-control.

   c. *Uparati*, self-withdrawal. The motion of the mind (including the sensory and motor organs) being unaffected by external objects is called *uparati*. It brings power to withdraw from material objects and to center on the Self.

   d. *Titikṣā*. Bearing all afflictions without a reaction formation for personal revenge is called *titikṣā*, tolerance. It removes anxieties, frustrations and lamentations from life. It brings understanding of the real situation and of the Self.

e. *Śraddhā*. This is insight and judgment of truth as truth and of untruth as untruth. Faith is here united with practice and philosophy.

f. *Samādhānam*. Constant concentration of consciousness on Supreme Consciousness is called *samādhānnam*. It brings equanimity to the Self.

4. *Mumukṣutvam*

Intense desire to free one's self from matter and material forces by means of Self-analysis is called *mumukṣutvam*. Self-knowledge, which is realized through Self-analysis, is the direct cause of liberation.

The seeker of truth, equipped with the above described qualifications, is an ideal man for the Analysis of Self.

## SUTRA NO. 2

**बोधोऽन्यसाधनेभ्यो हि साक्षान्मोक्षैकसाधनं ।**
**पाकस्य वह्निवज्ज्ञानं विना मोक्षो न सिध्यति ॥२॥**

BODHO' NYASĀDHANEBHYO HI SĀKṢĀN MOKṢAIKASĀDHANAM.
PĀKASYA VAHNIVAJ JÑĀNAṀ VINĀ MOKṢO NA SIDHYATI.

| | | |
|---|---|---|
| बोधः | Bodhaḥ | Knowledge (of the Self) |
| अन्य-साधनेभ्यः | Anya-Sādhanebhyaḥ | Compared to auxiliary causes |
| हि | Hi | Indeed |
| साक्षात् | Sākṣāt | Direct |
| मोक्ष-एक-साधनम् | Mokṣa-Eka-Sādhanam | One cause for liberation |
| पाकस्य | Pākasya | For cooking |
| वह्निवत् | Vahnivat | As fire |
| ज्ञानम् | Jñānam | Knowledge |
| विना | Vinā | Without |
| मोक्षः | Mokṣaḥ | Liberation |
| न | Na | Not |
| सिध्यति | Sidhyati | Accomplished |

Cognition of the Self, *Brahman*, is the direct cause of enlightenment and liberation from ignorance. All other causes are auxiliary; just as fire is the direct cause of cooking food, while all other causes are auxiliary.

As fire is the direct cause of cooking, and all other causes of cooking are secondary and indirect, so in the same way the practice of austerities, rituals, donations, charities, ethical and moral preparations are secondary and indirect causes of liberation, but the knowledge of the Self is the direct cause of liberation.

The purpose of meditation is removal of mental and physical diseases, and purification of *cittam*, mindstuff, by removing the material covering from it.

Consciousness in man (which is called individual soul), Cosmic Consciousness (which is called God), and *nirvāṇam* consciousness (which is called *Brahman*) are identical. Ignorance residing in an individual soul creates the sense of separation, dualism, multiplicity, and ultimately bondage and suffering. When the Self is realized through concentration, contemplation and meditation, then the sensation of suffering and bondage disappears in the same way as the perception of a dream disappears upon awakening. Self-knowledge is neither created nor obtained; it is realized. Liberation is the direct identification and realization of the Self principle, which is existent from Eternity, although it is hidden from direct perception, when one is in the state of ignorance. When the material coverings are removed from *cittam* ('I Am') through Self-analysis, then the Soul is liberated. It remains where it is, what it is and eternally has been, the first principle of the entire manifested and unmanifested Universe. Hence, liberation is not a property imposed on consciousness, but the inherent nature of consciousness, as light is the inherent nature of the sun. Since the self principle in man is by inherent nature eternal and immortal, it cannot be the effect of any antecedent cause. Knowledge is the cause of liberation. Realization and the attainment of Self-knowledge mean the rediscovery of Self-knowledge, which is ever-present.

Action which leads to material gain and prosperity is called *avidyā*; however pure and sublime, it can neither destroy ignorance nor produce the environment conducive to liberation. Action which leads to Self-analysis is *vidyā*.

Self-analysis does not mean discovery of this or that; it means discovery of the discoverer. By discovering the Self, one discovers the total Universe to be the radiation of the Self.

## SUTRA NO. 3

अविरोधितया कर्म नाविद्यां विनिवर्तयेत्।
विद्याविद्यां निहन्त्येव तेजस्तिमिरसङ्घवत् ॥३॥

AVIRODHITAYĀ KARMA NĀVIDYĀṀ VINIVARTAYET.
VIDYĀVIDYĀṀ NIHANTYEVA TEJAS TIMIRASAṄGHAVAT.

| | | |
|---|---|---|
| अविरोधितया | Avirodhitayā | Not being opposed to (ignorance) |
| कर्म | Karma | Action |
| न | Na | Not |
| अविद्याम् | Avidyām | Ignorance |
| विनिवर्तयेत् | Vinivartayet | Destroys |
| विद्या | Vidyā | Knowledge |
| अविद्याम् | Avidyām | Ignorance |
| निहन्ति | Nihanti | Destroys |
| एव | Eva | Verily |
| तेजः | Tejaḥ | Light |
| तिमिरसङ्घवत् | Timirasaṅghavat | As dense darkness |

All good and virtuous actions are done and should be done for the purification of the mind, in which the full reflection of *Brahman* can be experienced; however, all such actions cannot lead one to direct Self-realization because they are not in conflict with ignorance. Only the knowledge of the Self removes *karmas* and ignorance, as light removes darkness. All virtuous actions must be done for the purification of the heart, but no one should understand or regard them as the final cause of liberation. When the mind is purified by virtuous actions and universal service, then the Self is cognized directly by the light of the Self.

Any action that leads to material covering and that is performed with the consciousness of the doer, any action done for selfish motives, cannot remove the covering of ignorance from the human soul, for this type of action is identical with ignorance. That Self-knowledge which is obtained through Self-analysis alone destroys ignorance, just as sunlight destroys the dense darkness of night.

Any action which leads to material covering is called *karma*. The motion of consciousness that leads to Self-analysis is called knowledge. Here the terms ignorance, knowledge and action are not used in the specific sense but in a general sense. Any knowledge other than Self-knowledge is called ignorance. Any action that leads directly to Self-analysis and Self-knowledge is called knowledge.

Identity with *Brahman*, One-without-a-second, is the knowledge. All other knowledge is included in the general term "Ignorance." The sense of multiplicity is the result of ignorance; the sense of oneness is the result of knowledge.

If the Self is omnipresent, omniscient and omnipotent, why is there the sensation and perception that the Self is finite, ignorant, and limited to the body?

## SUTRA NO. 4

परिच्छिन्न इवाज्ञानात्तन्नाशे सति केवलः ।
स्वयं प्रकाशते ह्यात्मा मेघापायेंऽशुमानिव ॥४॥

PARICCHINNA IVĀJÑĀNĀT TANNĀŚE SATI KEVALAḤ.
SVAYAṀ PRAKĀŚATE HYĀTMĀ MEGHĀPĀYEN' ŚUMĀN IVA.

| | | |
|---|---|---|
| परिच्छिन्नः | Paricchinnaḥ | Limited |
| इव | Iva | As if |
| अज्ञानात् | Ajñānāt | Due to ignorance |
| तत्-नाशे | Tat-nāśe | On the destruction of that |
| सति | Sati | Being |
| केवलः | Kevalaḥ | Alone |
| स्वयम् | Svayam | By itself |
| प्रकाशते | Prakāśate | Reveals, shines |
| हि | Hi | Verily |
| आत्मा | Ātmā | The Self |
| मेघ-अपये | Megha-Apāye | When clouds are removed |
| अंशुमान् | Anśumān | The sun |
| इव | Iva | Like |

This Self, the I-principle, seems to be limited and bound by the individual name, form and body. The cause of this limitation and bondage is ignorance of one's own real Self. When, by means of meditation, ignorance is nullified, then the self-evident, self-existent Self is cognized as omnipresent, omniscient, and omnipotent in the same way as the real nature of the sun is realized when clouds are removed from the path of the seer.

Omnipresent, omniscient, and omnipotent consciousness feels a sense of limitation in the body on account of ignorance. Due to ignorance of his real nature, man has hypnotized himself with wrong suggestions. As a consequence of this hypnotic dream he feels himself limited in knowledge, in power, and in existence. When this ignorance is overcome through Self-analysis, the Self, which is the real existence of man, which is omnipresent, omniscient, and omnipotent, reveals itself and the reality of the Universe in the same way that the sun reveals the real nature of the world when clouds disappear.

The body is a transmitter and receiver through which consciousness transmits and receives conscious and unconscious energy. The body is like television, where programs of the Self are manifested. Self-analysis is dehypnotism. It removes the hypnotic trance from consciousness. A man feels birth, eating, sleeping, anxiety, suffering, decay, death; these experiences are part of the hypnotic trance of individual consciousness. The real Self is birthless, deathless, unchanging reality. *Ātman* is pure Consciousness, immortal and Self-luminous. By the light of the Self this entire manifested and unmanifested Universe is illumined.

On a cloudy day the ignorant think that the sun is covered by clouds, however, clouds and millions of planets collectively would be turned into nothingness if they tried to touch the sun. Likewise, ignorance cannot touch the human Soul. Actually the clouds cover the people, not the sun. In the same way, due to ignorance, it is the mind that is overpowered by matter and material forces, not the Self; hence in ignorance one feels the sensations of birth, suffering, decay and death.

Knowledge is identical with the Self. As the rays of the sun cannot be separated from the sun, so knowledge cannot be separated from the Self. One may contend that apparently there is dualism between sunrays and the sun, between Self-knowledge and the Self. The philosophical statement that knowledge and the Self are identical seems to be contradicted. The answer follows.

## SUTRA NO. 5

अज्ञानकलुषं जीवं ज्ञानाभ्यासाद्विनिर्मलम् ।
कृत्वा ज्ञानं स्वयं नश्येज्जलं कतकरेणुवत् ॥५॥

AJÑĀNAKALUṢAṀ JĪVAṀ JÑĀNĀBHYĀSĀD VINIRMALAM.
KṚTVĀ JÑĀNAṀ SVAYAṀ NAŚYEJJALAṀ KATAKAREṆUVAT.

| | | |
|---|---|---|
| अज्ञान-कलुषम् | Ajñāna-kaluṣam | Stained by ignorance |
| जीवम् | Jīvam | The embodied soul |
| ज्ञान-अभ्यासात् | Jñāna-Abhyāsāt | From the practice of knowledge |
| विनिर्मलम् | Vinirmalam | Pure |
| कृत्वा | Kṛtvā | Having made |
| ज्ञानम् | Jñānam | Knowledge |
| स्वयम् | Svayam | Itself |
| नश्येत् | Naśyet | Disappears |
| जलम् | Jalam | Water |
| कतक-रेणु-वत् | Kataka-reṇu-vat | As the powder of the Kataka nut |

Education is the collection of information and it remains as the dual force in the meditator because he must memorize such information frequently. When this knowledge is transformed into experience, the duality of this knowledge disappears; then experiential, pure Consciousness shines forth in the same way as the natural purity of cloth shines after being cleaned with detergent. Self-discipline, devotion, and spiritual knowledge from the outside are like purifying substances to the mind. When the mind is purified, pure Consciousness is vividly experienced; thus, learning and education are an indirect cause of knowledge, while true knowledge is the direct perception of Reality.

The knowledge of dualism is as important in the state of ignorance in the conditional world as the knowledge of nondualism is in the state of *samādhi* in the unconditional state, *nirvāṇam*. Through long, constant, zealous, faithful and repeated practice, knowledge of the Supreme is manifested in the embodied Soul, which is already oriented to dualistic knowledge. When Supreme Knowledge is incarnated in its full brilliance, dualistic knowledge disappears, just as chemical substances disappear after cleaning the cloth, when it is rinsed in pure water.

Intellectual knowledge of nondualism or intellectual identity with *Brahman* is not real nondualism or real identity with *Brahman*. It itself exists as dualistic knowledge, but it acts as a catalyst to remove other forms of knowledge, just as detergent removes soil from cloth so that the soil can be washed away in clean water; likewise, after destroying other forms of knowledge, intellectual identity with *Brahman* also disappears when the real and natural experience of identity with *Brahman* arises.

An ordinary man has dualistic knowledge about himself and the Universe around him. When he reaches the higher state of *samādhi*, he experiences identity and Oneness with the Supreme. When he comes out of that state, he again feels the multiplicity of knowledge. He wonders why he does not maintain a continuation of identity with the Supreme when out of *samādhi*. As long as ignorance is not fully destroyed, dualistic knowledge will remain with the embodied Soul. Residual dualism will remain in the human mind in proportion to the quality and quantity of ignorance.

Omnipresence and omniscience without omnipotence are worse than death and ignorance. If God were omnipresent and omniscient without being omnipotent, then the sufferings of God would be greater than those of the individual soul; and if it were so, it would be better for individual souls to remain self-enclosed individuals with their limited suffering than to rise to the state of Godhood, where burdens and suffering of the Universe are waiting to devour them. Meditation is the concentrated process of Self-analysis through which Supreme Consciousness is incarnated in the embodied Soul.

Identification is an inherent power of *cittam*, mindstuff. When *cittam* identifies with matter and material forces, duality and multiplicity become the driving forces of *cittam*. When identification of material forces is removed through Self-analysis, and identity of *cittam* with *Brahman* is realized, dualistic individual consciousness is transformed into Supreme Consciousness.

As an ignorant man as the head of the government in a country would destroy himself and his country, so would an ignorant person, who obtained non-dualistic knowledge of *Brahman* without having purified his mind through Self-analysis, be a menace to himself and others. As long as identification with the darkness of the vicious circle of ego and egocentric desires is not completely overcome by the light of identification with the Supreme, dualistic knowledge will remain with the human soul to protect him from the world and the world from him.

Contraction and expansion of Consciousness depend on the driving forces of ego-consciousness. The more ego brings material attachment to the embodied Soul, the more driving forces lead his consciousness outward, the more his consciousness is contracted, and the more dualistic knowledge increases its force; vice versa, the more Consciousness is expanded, and dualistic knowledge decreases its force.

Dualistic knowledge is thus a protective mechanism in the state of ignorance, a demon in the punishment of evil activity, a detective in the process of Self-analysis, and *Saguṇa Brahman* in worship. It is God in reward for virtuous activities and it is *nirvāṇam* in liberation.

Individual consciousness, due to increasing dualism, is splitting into a multiplicity of components and is covered with physical, chemical, biochemical, biological, and psychological forces that take the form of skin, flesh, blood, bones, and various other tissues. Individual consciousness, due to decreasing dualism, reaches beyond the above-mentioned forces and physical consciousness and realizes Oneness with the Supreme. As a matter of fact, Consciousness neither contracts nor expands, it remains as it is—but the contractions and expansion of the ego mechanism seemingly brings the phenomena of contraction and expansion over Consciousness.

## SUTRA NO. 6

संसारः स्वप्नतुल्यो हि रागद्वेषादिसङ्कुलः ।
स्वकाले सत्यवद्भाति प्रबोधे सत्यसद्भवेत् ॥६॥

SANSĀRAḤ SVAPNATULYO HI RĀGADVEṢĀDISAṄKULAḤ.
SVAKĀLE SATYAVAD BHĀTI PRABODHE SATYASAD BHAVET.

| | | |
|---|---|---|
| संसारः | Sansāraḥ | The sense-perceived Universe |
| स्वप्न-तुल्यः | Svapna-tulyaḥ | Like a dream |
| हि | Hi | Indeed |
| राग-द्वेष-आदि- | Rāgadveṣādi | Attachments and aversions |
| संकुलः | Saṅkulaḥ | Full of |
| स्व-काले | Sva-kāle | In its own duration |
| सत्य-वद् | Satya-vad | Like truth, real |
| भाति | Bhāti | Appears |
| प्रबोधे सति | Prabodhe-sati | On awakening |
| असत् | Asat | Unreal |
| भवेत् | Bhavet | Is |

This *Sansāra*, the sense-perceived Universe, is similar to the Universe of dreams. Hate and Love, pain and pleasure, subjects and objects of the dream world and the waking state are much alike. A dream is not realized as a dream so long as one is dreaming. Its dream quality is experienced only after one has awakened. Life is a waking dream; it may be called a cosmic dream. The dream quality of this waking life cannot be realized as long as one's real "I" is not awakened.

The aim of Self-analysis is to proceed from analysis of the individual self to the reality of the one Absolute Self. The mind and body cannot be separated from each other, and as a whole they are technically called the individual, nor can the individual and the Universe be separated from each other. The individual depends on Universal forces for accommodation to eating, sleeping, breathing, etc. It is not, in any sense, independent from the Universe: hence, it is called individual (in - not, - divisible). Only for the purpose of study do we classify body and mind as individual and the Universe separately as a unit, but these classifications are figurative and descriptive. In reality, they are inseparable.

Every individual has a principle of Self-determination which is named Self or Soul. Every living being has a soul. All souls are fundamentally identical in nature. The physical organisms in which these souls are incorporated are responsible for differences. Therefore, in Self-analysis the following factors are important:

1. Constitutional factor;
2. Situational and environmental factors;
3. Developmental factors, and
4. Factors from previous births.

Behind every phenomenon, whether a man is laughing, weeping, feeling, thinking, waking, dreaming, sleeping, in birth or death, one principle is common: that is Consciousness.

Consciousness is awareness. This awareness can be subjective or objective, determinant or indeterminant. When it is determinant, it is aware of something. When it is indeterminant, it is aware of nothing. From the viewpoint of awakening, awareness of somethingness or of nothingness has equal meaning. Without awareness, there is no existence; without consciousness, one can neither see nor experience. Even to notice the absence of something requires the presence of consciousness or cognition, as a person, awakening from sound sleep, feels that he slept well and saw no dream. In this experience, one's consciousness exists as a witness. In positive and negative awareness, the presence of the person who experiences that awareness is inevitable although he does not pay attention to his own existence. In the same way, the common principle, consciousness, which is the center of individual as well as Universal Existence, is present as a witness behind every phenomenon, mental or physical.

This witnessing reality is described in three fundamental principles:

1. Consciousness;
2. Existence;
3. Bliss, Reality.

This is *Sat-Cit-Ānanda*. Every witnessing element must have these three basic principles to observe phenomenon. Without consciousness, he cannot be aware of the facts. Without existence, he cannot be present there; and unless he is in normal condition he will color every fact by his own prejudice, belief, tradition and habit. Every individual soul has these—consciousness, existence, and the inherent principle of reality.

According to the evolution of existence, consciousness, and reality (bliss), the following four states are important in Self-analysis:

1. Waking state. Here one deals with objective and subjective consciousness and individual and universal phenomena are more systematic and realistic than in dreamland.

2. Dreaming state. In dreams also, subjective and objective consciousness work, but individual and universal phenomena are spontaneous, instantaneous, and not systematic as in the waking state. Dream experiences are a projection of the individual mind.

3. Sound sleep. Here there is oneness of individual and universal phenomena, but without consciousness, i.e. in ignorance. Due to ignorance one has only the sensation of nothingness. Subjective and objective distinctions are lost here. In the philosophical sense, this is union with *Brahman* through *māyā*, ignorance.

4. *Turīya* state. This is the state where one is united and identified with *Brahman* through *vidyā*, knowledge. In this state also there is no subjective and objective consciousness. The subject in this state, the "I" is impersonal and all-inclusive, beyond subject and object.

Every state is real in its own reality. The three previous states are real conditionally. The fourth state, *turīya*, is unconditionally real. Symbolism depends on certain conditions to express hidden reality. Waking, dreaming, and sound sleep are symbols dependent on conditions to express the motion of reality according to the quality and quantity of the evolution of reality in these three states. These symbols have great meaning and must be understood properly through Self-analysis. As long as we do not understand their meaning, so long they will be repeated again and again. When a condition is removed, that particular state becomes unreal. The waking state is real as long as one is in the waking condition, but when one is dreaming, the waking state becomes unreal for that person who is dreaming. The same explanation applies to dreaming and sound sleep. All states are symbols except *turīya*; it alone is operating unconditionally in every state. *Turīya*, which is real, is expressed through various states or symbols. The other three states depend on *turīya*; it depends on nothing but itself. From the viewpoint of *turīya* all other states are unreal. It alone is ultimate Consciousness, Existence, Reality and Bliss. This unreality of the three other states from the viewpoint of Absolute Consciousness is philosophical, and has its own significance. Every higher experience reduces the lower experience to the point of unreality. One reality is expressing its existence through different indications.

Every experience involves the process of perception. For perception there must be:

1. Subject;
2. Object;
3. Instrumentation;
4. Medium, the internal and external environment.

When perception is right but the interpretation is wrong, the result is illusion. Hallucination is false perception. Delusion is false belief, which does not depend even on perception. These have great symbolic meaning, and unless these expressions are understood, life force will compel the individual to stop progress. These three mechanisms—delusion, illusion, and hallucination—are operating in the human mind. We want to change misinterpretation to right interpretation. false perception to right perception and false belief to right faith. Behind every state is reality and this should be realized through Self-analysis. Phenomena of the waking and dreaming states are both dreamlike in quality, but the reality on which they depend is beyond dreams. This does not mean that these dreamlike states are nothingness, nor does it indicate negligence of duty and responsibilities; rather, dreams give us the insight to understand things as they really are.

Both *Brahman* and the world, unity and multiplicity, the unconditional and the conditional, immortality and mortality, eternity and non-eternity, reality and appearance cannot be real from the same standpoint. If both were equally real, knowledge of the manifoldness of the world could not be transcended by the knowledge of unity, eternity, and divinity. There would be no reason to seek *Nirvāṇam*, liberation, if both were equally real. The doctrine of world scriptures stating that deliverance comes through knowledge would have no meaning if multiplicity and unity were equally real.

The illusoriness of the phenomenal world of the waking state is thus explained by Shaṅkarācārya, "The phenomenal World of the waking state, full of love and hate and the rest, is unreal as a dream. It seems to be real as long as one is ignorant of one's reality. It becomes unreal when one identifies with one's reality."

From the standpoint of *Brahman*, the world of the waking state is as illusory as the dream world is from the standpoint of the waking state. Objective phenomena stand over against subjective phenomena and any change of experience in the subject will bring a change in experiencing the object. Whatever is perceived is object, and it is conditional and unreal. The Consciousness which perceives, but itself is not perceived, is unconditional and real. Whatever is the object is conditional; therefore, its reality is conditional. From the viewpoint of Absolute Consciousness, whatever is object and whatever is conditional is subject to dissolution: *Yad dṛśyam tad nāśyam*.

The waking state and dream state are objects of consciousness; hence they are unreal. The definition of reality is "that principle which is not contradicted in past, present, or future"—*Trikālābādhyam satyam*. The states of waking, dreaming, and sound sleep are contradicted by one another. These states are collectively contradicted by the experience of identity with the Supreme. Because they are Self-contradictory, they are not Ultimate Reality. The phenomenal world is a waking dream. The states of waking and dreaming are passing through cause and effect, space and time, and they are not Self-explanatory. The real consciousness is obscured by them. In the state of Supreme Consciousness, *nirvāṇam*, all these states, with cause and effect, space and time, merge into a single unity, *turīya*, or the Supreme. Phenomena that were present yesterday but absent today and tomorrow are unreal. The real is that which is present at all times. It is that Supreme Consciousness which eternally was, is and shall be.

## SUTRA NO. 7

तावत्सत्यं जगद्भाति शुक्तिकारजतं यथा ।
यावन्न ज्ञायते ब्रह्म सर्वाधिष्ठानमद्वयम् ॥७॥

TĀVAT SATYAM JAGAD BHĀTI ŚUKTIKĀRAJATAṀ YATHĀ.
YĀVAN NA JÑĀYATE BRAHMA SARVĀDHIṢṬHĀNAM ADVAYAM.

| | | |
|---|---|---|
| तावत् | Tāvat | So long as |
| सत्यम् | Satyam | True and real |
| जगत् | Jagad | Sense-perceived universe |
| भाति | Bhāti | Appears |
| शुक्तिका-रजतम् | Śuktikā-rajatam | In the mother-of-pearl shell silver |
| यथा | Yathā | Like |
| यावत् | Yāvat | As long as |
| न | Na | Not |
| ज्ञायते | Jñāyate | Is realized |
| ब्रह्म | Brahma | Brahman |
| सर्व-अधिष्ठानम् | Sarva adhiṣṭhānam | Substratum of all |
| अद्वयम् | Advayam | One-without-a-second |

This sense-perceived Universe appears to be tangible and eternally real as long as the substratum, *Brahman*, pure Consciousness, is not realized. In the same way, the appearance of silver in a mother-of-pearl shell appears to be real as long as the true nature of that shell is not perceived.

The illusion of silver in an oyster shell appears to be real only as long as the oyster shell is not thoroughly examined. The perception of a mirage is accepted as real as long as the place where it appears is not examined and recognized properly. Likewise, the world of the waking state, with subjective and objective experiences and sensations, full of multiplicity, appears to be real as long as the nondual Self, *Brahman*, which is the central foundation of all existence, is not analyzed, recognized, and identified properly. In the state of waking, dreaming and sound sleep, in addition to changes in the process of physical, chemical, biochemical, and biological forces, there are remarkable changes in the processes of action and reaction of psychological forces. In sound sleep, psychological forces are in a state of equilibrium. Due to equilibrium, the result of action and reaction and sensation and perception is nullification, as in a tug-of-war when two opposing groups exert equal force on a rope. Though both sides are in extreme action, no action is perceived. Likewise, in sound sleep, due to the balance of opposing driving forces of the mind, the witness-consciousness of the sleeper is aware of nothing. This nothingness which is felt and experienced in sound sleep means the nothing which has no relationship to anything in manifestation.

A "thing" is "that which is conceived, spoken of, or referred to as existing as an individually distinguishable entity, specifically:

a. Any single entity distinguished from all others; as, everything in the Universe;
b. A tangible object as distinguished from a concept, quality, etc.; as, a book is a thing and its color is a quality;
c. An inanimate object;
d. An item, detail, etc.; as, not a thing has been overlooked;
e. That which is represented, as distinguished from the word or symbol that represents it."

According to this definition, sound sleep is beyond things but not beyond existence, otherwise a man in sound sleep would be accepted as dead. This is contrary to popular experience. A thing is manifestation; and absence of a thing means only nonmanifestation, not absence of reality. Manifestation is part of existence; it is not the totality of existence. Noumenon and phenomenon are two aspects of existence. Things belong to the realm of phenomena or manifestation. So, in sound sleep, due to the equilibrium of Cosmic forces, one reaches beyond the state of manifestation or phenomena.

Psychic forces which present the private mental world of the dream state are in harmony with the Cosmic law in the waking state, which is common to all. Consider carefully when a dream is over, "What is that which is left with you, and what is that which you lost?" All subjective and objective phenomena of the dream world are apparently lost, except the creator of the dream world with the memory of creation, i.e. consciousness. This consciousness is a witness which is beyond the subjective and objective creation and beyond the perception, sensation, and feeling of the dream.

The process of evolution and involution, as well as the law of conservation of energy and matter is operating in all states whether it be waking, dreaming or sound sleep. The appearance and disappearance of dream phenomena are the processes of evolution and involution, respectively, in the dream world. The dream world and its perception, sensation, and feeling are not lost; they are in a state of involution when one is awakened. They can be experienced and perceived again when the same conditions are present in the dreamer. This is why certain dreams are repeated over and over again. When a dream is over, the dreamer has lost nothing because consciousness, which is the substratum, the basic foundation, the creator of the dream, and which perceives everything but itself is unperceived and changeless, remains with the dreamer when he is awakened.

Similarly, in the state of *samādhi*, when one is metaphysically awakened and identified with *Brahman*, the waking state with all its relations goes into involution and the consciousness of the waking state is transformed into *Brahman* Consciousness, just as the creation of the dream experience is transformed into consciousness of the waking state with all its relations.

As dreamers when awakened are able to understand the symbolic meanings of the dream and their application to improve the standard of waking life, so when meditators are spiritually awakened in the state of *samādhi* through Self-analysis, then they are able to examine the symbolic meaning of waking life and its application to the understanding of Ultimate Reality. In comparison with *Brahman* Consciousness, both waking and dream states are symbols, while identity with *Brahman* is Reality.

Dreams will be repeated if their meaning, application, message, and mission are not utilized by the dreamer to improve his standard of life; likewise, birth and death will be repeated if their meaning, application, message, and mission are not utilized by the seeker of truth. The waking state is systematic and chronological; the dream state is spontaneous and instantaneous. Dreams are the creation of the dreamer, but their significance, message, and application cannot be understood so long as the dreamer is dreaming. It is the waking state which discloses the meaning of dreams to the dreamer. Similarly, it is metaphysical awakening which explains the meaning, application, and significance of waking phenomena. When the seeker is awakened, the perception of waking phenomena and their multiplicity becomes illusion but their symbolic meaning becomes important to overcome the influence of ignorance, which is the process of death.

There is no creation and destruction of the Universe in a real sense. Whatever we perceive as the appearance of creation and destruction is really the process of evolution and involution. All production is the development and transmission from potential existence to actual existence. The process of evolution is the passage from the implicit to the explicit. All destruction is envelopment. It is transition from actual existence to potential existence. The process of involution is the passage from explicit to implicit, the disappearance of effect into its cause. There is no such thing as annihilation. Past and future states are not destroyed; they can be perceived by the enlightened mind.

Due to inadequate perception of a rope, one identifies the rope with a snake by one's own projection in accordance with previous experience. In this perception the rope itself remains unchanged and unseen although it is the basis of the illusory perception. The existence and perception of the illusory snake would be altogether impossible without the rope as the basic foundation of the illusion, but when the rope is recognized and identified as such, the illusory perception and existence of the snake disappear. In the same way, when *Brahman* is recognized, realized, and identified, the illusory characteristics of the Universe disappear.

Pure Consciousness alone is true existence and reality in the Absolute sense. The existence, consciousness, and reality of the multiple universe are false, although they are true in the sense of relativity. To a knower of *Brahman*, everything is *Brahman*. What appears to a perceiver as multiplicity of the world in the sense of relativity, to a Self-realized man is nothing but *Brahman* because he has overcome the sense of relativity. The phenomenal characteristics of the Universe of name and form, individuality and multiplicity, are superimposed upon *Brahman* through ignorance of the nature of Reality.

## SUTRA NO. 8

सच्चिदात्मन्यनुस्यूते नित्ये विष्णौ प्रकल्पिताः।
व्यक्तयो विविधास्सर्वा हाटके कटकादिवत् ॥८॥

SACCIDĀTMANYANUSYŪTE NITYE VIṢṆAU PRAKALPITĀḤ.
VYAKTAYO VIVIDHĀS SARVĀ HĀṬAKE KAṬAKĀDIVAT.

| | | |
|---|---|---|
| सत्-चित्-आत्मनि | Sat-cit-ātmani | On the embodiment of pure existence and consciousness |
| अनुस्यूते | Anusyūte | All pervading |
| नित्ये | Nitye | Eternal |
| विष्णौ | Viṣṇau | On Lord Visnu |
| प्रकल्पिताः | Prakalpitāḥ | Projected by imagination |
| व्यक्तयः | Vyaktayaḥ | Manifested forms |
| विविधाः | Vividhāḥ | Manifold, various |
| सर्वाः | Sarvāḥ | All |
| हाटके | Hāṭake | On gold |
| कटक-आदिवत् | Kaṭaka-Ādivat | As bracelets and other ornaments |

The basic and fundamental substratum of this Universe is Lord *Viṣṇu*, the omnipresent one, who is *Sat-Cit-Ānanda*, Eternal Existence-Consciousness-Bliss. Names and forms of objects of the Universe Universe are superimposed on this omnipresent Consciousness in the same way as names and forms of the various golden ornaments are superimposed on gold.

Individuality and multiplicity of the Universe exist in the mind of the perceiver, in the plane of relativity, while the essence of multiplicity of the Universe is *Sat-Cit-Atman, Brahman,* whose Nature is omnipresent, omniscient, and omnipotent. In the same way, behind the various names, forms and multiplicity of gold products such as rings, necklaces, bracelets, etc., the reality is gold, which is unchanged.

Philosophically and etymologically the word "Universe" means the turning and existence of one Eternal principle behind the various names and forms of the world. (Unus, one + versus, past participle of *vertere*, to turn.) Otherwise the name should be given "multiverse."

All philosophical study depends on two principles, the principle of the Absolute and the principle of relativity. From the principle of the Absolute, *Brahman* is Eternal Existence, Eternal Consciousness, and Eternal Reality. It is One-without-a-second. The state in which this identity is realized is called *Nirvāṇam*. All names and forms of the Universe are false and illusory from the Absolute standpoint.

The principle of relativity represents the theory of relativity, which means that things are real in their relationship, and if the relationships are changed, then the things are changed. According to this theory, one entity is examined from the standpoint of its relationship with other entities in cause and effect, time and space. Consider generations of men in cause and effect. With his son, a man is a father, but with his own father, he is the son. Consider space. The same city may be to the east, west, north, and south—according to its relationship to other cities. Consider time. Any one point in time includes the past, present and future. One and the same point in time is the present to the present generation; it is the future to the past generations; and the past to the generations to come.

Relativity is as old as the manifestation of the Universe. It begins with the manifestation of phenomenon and ends in noumenon. In the relative world nothing is true without some relationship, and therefore nothing exists permanently and absolutely.

The principle of relativity presents the following four stages for Self-analysis: 1) Theory of dependent origination; 2) Theory of *karma*; 3) Theory of constant change; and, 4) Theory of nonexistence of Soul, and Souls as independent entities among all other relative entities.

1) The theory of dependent origination indicates the conditional existence of things. There is a spontaneous and universal law, causation, which conditions the appearance of all events, physical and mental. This law is called *dharma*, and it works automatically without the help of any individual conscious guiding factor.

According to this theory, whenever an event occurs, it becomes the cause of another event, which is called the effect in the relative sense. The law of Universal causation is the basis of Eternal continuity, of becoming. In the world of relativity, including all states of manifestation, every existence is a transformation. Whatever has a cause must perish. Whatever is born, brought into being and organization, contains within itself the inherent seed of dissolution. A thing is only a force, a cause, a condition which is transformed into matter and its motion. In the presence of a cause, an effect arises; and in the absence of the cause, the effect does not arise.

Nothing happens fortuitously; the whole world is conditioned by causes. Nothing exists without a cause, nor does it appear without leaving some effect. Thus the theory of relativity presents the middle path, which avoids the two extremes of eternalism and annihilism in the relative world. Eternalism means that some reality eternally exists as an independent entity among other entities of the relative world. Annihilism means that something existing can be annihilated or can cease to be. The Absolute has no relativity and, vice verse, relativity has no Absolute characteristic in its realm. Here, being and becoming cannot stand independently. Relativity is eternal becoming, and the absolute is Eternal being. There is no firm and permanent resting place in relativity. When we analyze any single entity from the standpoint of relativity, it becomes multiple. On the other hand, when we analyze from the viewpoint of the Absolute, it becomes One-without-a-second.

From the standpoint of relativity a man is father, son, husband, brother, brother-in-law, friend or enemy to different men. From the viewpoint of the Absolute we know through Self-analysis that he is not an element among the elements, an atom among atoms, a molecule among molecules, a compound among compounds, or a mixture among mixtures. He is neither the sensory organs nor the motor organs, neither the nervous system, brain, mind, intellect, nor Nature itself.

Yet all these above-mentioned entities depend upon his integrity, unity, and existence. His real Existence is not a thing among all other things of the Universe. He has no multiple existence in his individuality, and ultimately he is realized as One-without-a-second, the fundamental Existence, Consciousness, and Reality. Thus, by conclusion, we come to know that the same entity is *Brahman* in the Absolute sense and multiple in the sense of relativity.

2) The law of *karma* is an aspect of the principle of relativity. According to the law of *karma*, the past existence of a man was in accordance with his former pasts. His present existence is the effect of his whole past, and his future existence will be the effect of

his present existence. This includes all actions and reactions, whether they are chemical, mechanical, physical, or metaphysical.

Any action or reaction is *karma*. Every entity of the organic or inorganic world is under the direct control of *karma*. Every motion, whether it be organic or inorganic, physical or mental, is the result or the effect of prime force or ultimate force on matter. Force on matter is called *karma*.

3) The law of Universal change and impermanence indicates that, in the realm of relativity, whatever exists arises from some condition, and is therefore impermanent, that all things are subject to decay. "This, too, shall pass away" may be applied to subjective and objective experiences. Whatever exists arises from causes and conditions, and disappears upon disappearance of the conditions. Whatever begins, must also end; that which is high shall be laid low; where meeting is, parting follows; where birth is, death is sure to supervene.

If all were not eternally impermanent in the relative plane, a man would be helpless and hopeless. If body, mind, sensation, perception, and present consciousness were permanent in this plane, the sufferer would suffer eternally. There would be neither dynamism nor evolution in the Universe. This type of world would be static, without growth or possibility of change.

Mind is more important than body because it can adapt itself to change immediately, while the body requires more time. Those who cannot adapt to change are called inadequate personalities; a man who can adapt easily to change is a well-adjusted person. He is not disturbed by the advent of any change; death and birth are received with equanimity.

The electromagnetic theory of matter has brought about a revolution in the general concept of the nature of physical reality. It is not static; it is radiant energy, constantly in motion and change.

Mind energy can change in a moment. The world of sense and science is a constant stream of being and becoming. From one moment to the next, a person may become something entirely different through mind energy. Birth and death on the physical plane may take a long time, but a constant rotation of births and deaths is going on every moment on the plane of the mind. Old ideas are dying; new ideas are being born in the same moment in psychic energy. The ceaseless flux of being and becoming is called the world; this world is in the mind.

Awareness of change takes time. Hair and nails are growing and being trimmed all the time, yet a person continues to think that he has the same hair and nails. The motion of electromagnetic waves of light is changing constantly from the sun to the earth, or in the light of a lamp, yet it seems to a perceiver as though he has been perceiving the same light all the while.

Change is an Eternal force operating in all states of life—waking, dreaming, and sound sleep; and all this change causes matter to move. The mind of ordinary man cannot recognize the changes because it has a threshold of limitation in perception of both higher and lower changes. To examine a man while he is running fast or moving slowly, the examiner would have to move at a speed equal to that of the runner. The observer must move at a speed equal to the speed of that which he examines.

The mind must be trained to move slower than the slow and faster than the fast; only then can one observe and check the results. If the mind can run faster than the speed of light, faster than the speed of electromagnetic waves, and slower than metabolic changes in cell physiology—only then can it notice the changes going on in Nature.

When the mind is trained by the disciplines of Self-analysis, concentrating one's consciousness on the stream of sound current *nādam*, it runs faster than the fast and moves slower than the slow. It becomes greater than the great and smaller than the small. In consequence of this Self-discipline, the mind can notice any change.

Change is a constant becoming without beginning and without end. There is no static moment when becoming may attain to Absolute being in the realm of relativity. No sooner does one conceive it by the attributes of name and form than it has changed into something else. By shutting their eyes to successive events the ignorant think of things rather than of processes in this Absolute flux. By an artificial attitude they make sections in the stream of change and call them things. Identity of object and subject, in relativity, is unreality. Out of Universal conditions and relations, people build a seemingly stable and undivided world. Substance and quality, whole and part, cause and effect are mutually involved and cannot be separated; yet in a descriptive and figurative sense, they are described separately. This is unreality. Origination and cessation, persistence and discontinuance, unity and plurality, coming and going, etc., are relative conceptions which are regarded as Absolute by the ignorant.

Things are not existent in themselves; they operate only in the world of appearance and disappearance. As long as one searches for the Absolute in the limited and relative plane, so long one is subject to ignorance, which is the cause of misery. By realizing the truth of things, one realizes that it is absurd to regard as Eternal and Real the isolated phenomena of the incessant series of transformations. Life is a continuous movement.

According to the quality and quantity of speed of change, *yogins* have classified Nature in five phenomenal states: solid, liquid, gaseous, light and cosmic rays, and *ākāśam* (ether). These depend on conditions of velocity and speed of *tanmātras*; when conditions change, the states are changed. For instance, if atomic motion of the solid state is increased, the solid will be transformed into a liquid.

4) The theory of the nonexistence of Soul, and Souls as independent entities among all other relative entities, means that the Absolute does not exist in the relativity. Ultimate Reality is *Viṣṇu*, omnipresent, omniscient, omnipotent, and all-inclusive. The Absolute and the relative are opposed to each other in Nature as day and night. The experience of a beginner in meditation is like day. When the driving forces of selfishness move between his individuality and Reality after meditation, then he experiences the night of relativity in much the same way as the part of the earth turned away from the sun is in shadow.

Really speaking, there is neither sunset nor sunrise because the sun is shining perpetually; yet, due to the motion of the Earth, when our horizon comes between us and the sun, we have night. In the same way, ultimate Reality shines eternally in the realm of the Absolute. Yet according to the motion of *cittam* towards or retreating from Self-realization, the day and night of its presence and absence are felt. As the sun is the Ultimate Cause, without which there would be annihilation of the world, so *Brahman* is the Ultimate Cause, without which there would be complete annihilation of this relative plane. To present permanent Souls, or other permanent entities in the realm of relativity, would be to present day and night together. This is contrary to truth and experience. The relative and absolute cannot be present in the same plane. If a man knows God, then either he is beyond the law of relativity and has become Infinite, or God has become finite. No being, including prophets, angels, teachers, masters and other incarnations, is an exception to the law of change in realm of relativity.

Man is both Absolute and relative, but not at the same time. Absoluteness and relativity are not created but realized, because they are eternally present everywhere.

Here is the conflict and contradiction. A man wants to be Absolute, to be Eternal, yet he does not want to lose his individuality and his ego-consciousness. He does not want to realize Eternity as it is. Instead he wants to create eternity in his own way. He is trying to do something which even God cannot do. Wonderful is man's imagination of Reality. It is truly said that God created man in His own image; but in turn, man created God in his own image.

"I am Alpha and Omega." Here the word "I" is not relative. It is beyond the grammatical use, and it means Absolute Alpha and Omega, not a particular relative person in a particular body. This "I" includes all three persons of grammar—I, you, he—yet it is beyond them. Thus the theory of relativity in philosophy is important, and one should bear in mind that the same word may have many meanings in different relationships. On the other hand, a word has no meaning without relationships.

These are the forms of existence:

1. *Pratibhāsika* is existence and appearance which disappears through right perception; for example, the perception of a snake in a rope.

2. *Vyavahārika*, which includes:
   a. *Asti*, Existence;
   b. *Bhāti*, Reality;
   c. *Paryaya*, conditional existence;
   d. *Nāma*, names or terms;
   e. *Rūpa*, forms.

   From the practical standpoint, multiplicity of the world and duality of Souls is true until *Brahman* is realized. Existence and Reality (see above) belong to *Brahman*. The next three, conditional existence, names, and forms, belong to relativity.

3. *Pāramārthika*. From the standpoint of the Absolute, the multiplicity and individuality of the phenomenal world are altogether illusion. The Absolute has Eternal Existence, Consciousness, Reality, and Bliss—*Sat-Cit-Ānandam*.

   "By identity with the Absolute, the entire world

becomes known." Here *Chāndogya Upaniṣad*, Chapter VI, verses 4,5,6 presents the following three examples:

"Just as, my dear, by knowing one lump of clay, all that is made of clay becomes known, the modification being only a name and form from the practical viewpoint, arising from speech, while the Ultimate Truth is that it is just clay.

"By knowing one nugget of gold all that is made of gold becomes known, the modification being only a name and a form from the practical viewpoint, arising from speech, while the Ultimate Truth is that it is just gold.

"By knowing one pair of nail scissors, all that is made of iron becomes known, the modification being only a name and form from the practical viewpoint, arising from speech, while the Ultimate Truth is that it is still just iron. So, my dear, names and forms of the world are from the practical viewpoint, arising from speech, while the Ultimate Truth is that it is just *Brahman* (Consciousness)."

An effect is identical with its cause. The reality behind the effect is the same as the cause itself. Hence, the Universe is nothing but *Brahman*, because it is the Ultimate Cause of the Universe. The names and forms, variety and multiplicity, individuality and unity, are from the practical viewpoint in the realm of relativity, arising from speech, Ultimate Truth is that the Universe is *Brahman*.

How can one establish identity with the Supreme? Identity with the Supreme is inherent in the Nature of one's Consciousness. When this Oneness is realized, the multiplicity, which is superimposed on Oneself, disappears.

## SUTRA NO. 9

यथाकाशो हृषीकेशो नानोपाधिगतो विभुः ।
तद्भेदाद्भिन्नवद्भाति तन्नाशे केवलो भवेत् ॥९॥

ATHĀKĀŚO HṚṢĪKEŚO NĀNOPĀDHIGATO VIBHUḤ.
ADBHEDĀD BHINNAVAD BHĀTI TANNĀŚE KEVALO BHAVET.

| | | |
|---|---|---|
| यथा | Yathā | As |
| आकाशः | Ākāśaḥ | Space |
| हृषीकेशः | Hṛṣīkeśaḥ | Governing Consciousness |
| नाना-उपाधि-गतः | Nānā-upādhi-gataḥ | Associated with distinguishing conditions, various physical, mental and traditional habits |
| विभुः | Vibhuḥ | All-pervading |
| तत्-भेदात् | Tat Bhedāt | On account of these differences |
| भिन्नवत् | Bhinnavat | Diverse and different |
| भाति | Bhāti | Appears |
| तत्-नाशे | Tat-Nāśe | When these are destroyed |
| केवलः | Kevalaḥ | One alone |
| भवेत् | Bhavet | Becomes |

As the all-pervading space seems to be diverse and distinct on account of its association with various objects that are different from one another, so the omnipresent Self, the "I"-principle, seems to be diverse and different in every body on account of its association with various bodies, which are different from one another. As the all-pervading space becomes one space on the destruction of limitations, so the omnipresent Self becomes one on the destruction of the identities of these bodies.

Omnipresent, omniscient, and omnipotent *Brahman*, which is One-without-a-second, appears to be diverse to the seeker who is in the state of ignorance, on account of his association with various *upādhis*, which are multiple, innumerable, and diversified. When through Self-analysis, all *upādhis* of multiplicity and individuality are overcome in the state of *samādhi* or *nirvāṇam*, the seeker feels identity with the Supreme, and feels Oneness with the entire Universe through Supreme Energy, which is the Life Force of all organic and inorganic beings.

As all-pervading *ākāśa*, space, seems to be divided by various *upādhis*, such as the space within a drum, and the space within a jar, and the space limited by a building, these limitations apparently present different characters of space. When these limitations, *upādhis*, are removed, then the oneness and continuity of space is realized. Likewise, the psychophysiological mechanism–body, senses, and mindstuff–presents an apparent limitation of Consciousness; Consciousness seems to be qualified, and even a product of the psychophysiological mechanism. Everyone knows that television and radio programs are not products of the receiving sets, but that they are ethereal and present everywhere in the atmosphere. They are only manifested through these mechanisms, not limited by them. Likewise, Consciousness is omnipresent, omnipotent, and omniscient, and it is only manifested through the mechanical unity of body, mind, and Senses. When this Self, "I Am," is realized through Self-analysis, and the limitation of the psychophysiological organism is overcome, then the Oneness of Consciousness is realized.

*Brahman* is One-without-a-second; all that is sensed and perceived is nothing but *Brahman*. Persons only have a sense of multiplicity and individuality due to various *upādhis*. *Upādhi* is a thing which imparts its own property to another object placed in its vicinity; it is true conditionally. For example, a red flower makes a crystal placed over it look like a ruby by imparting to the crystal the flower's redness. (*Upa*, juxtaposition + *ādhi*, incorporation, reflection). *Upa samīpa vartini adadhāti saṁkrāmayati svīyam dharmam iti upādhiḥ*.

The incorporation of *upādhi* is in one's subjective experience, and the reflection of *upādhi* is in one's objective experience. The flower above has *upādhi*; the all-pervading *ākāśa* appears to have dimensions and forms when circumscribed in a jar or in a house because of *upādhi*. *Upādhi* is, therefore, a conditional and environmental factor, which individually and collectively bestows upon a thing distinctive character for the time being.

Wherever there is smoke, there is fire. The existence of smoke depends on fire by means of certain conditions, *upādhis*. We cannot say that wherever there is fire there is smoke because the existence of fire is not conditional upon the existence of smoke. Fire can exist either with smoke or without smoke. Although smoke is produced by fire, the specific and immediate cause of smoke is the presence of moist fuel. There is, therefore, an invariable concomitant, *vyāpti*, between moist fuel and smoke. Smoke is the effect and cannot exist without wet fuel.

The existence of microcosm and macrocosm, individuality and Universality, with *Brahman* is like the existence of smoke with fire, due to various *upādhis*. As smoke is a transformation of fire due to damp fuel, so the microcosm and the macrocosm are transformations of *Brahman*, due to *avidyā* and *māyā*, individual and Universal forms of *upādhi*. Here it is necessary to understand the difference between the pervader and the pervaded. In the above illustration, smoke is pervaded and fire is the pervader. From the viewpoint of substance, smoke and fire are pervaded and substance is the real pervader. Substance is that in which quality and action exist inherently.

There are nine fundamental substances: five states of Nature, *prakṛti*, mind, Soul, time, and space. (This is Vaiśeṣika philosophy.) Space is substance devoid of action. Action presents union and separation. Wherever there is fire there is substance, because substance is the pervader, but it is not true to say that wherever there is substance there is fire, because fire is pervaded by substance. Thus substance can exist even where there is absence of fire, as fire can exist where there is absence of smoke. The pervader occupies the greater area, and the pervaded occupies the lesser area. Substance occupies the greatest area.

Likewise, the microcosm is pervaded and the macrocosm is the pervader, but *Brahman* is the Real and Ultimate Pervader. The individual and the Universal occupy a great and a greater area, but *Brahman* occupies the greatest area. *Brahman* exists wherever the indivdual and the Universal exist, and it exists in their absence as *Nirvāṇam*. The world is traced in *Brahman* due to *upādhi*. Wherever there is a world, there is *Brahman*; but when *Brahman* is realized in its pure form and, in the absence of *upādhi* , there is neither separate existence of individuality (*avidyā*) nor Universal Existence (*māyā*). In short, superimposition of the property of *Prakṛti*, Nature, on *Puruṣa*, Self, is *upādhi* because Eternal *Puruṣa* which has no birth, death, pain, or suffering, experiences the above phenomena. Incorporation of the property of *Brahman* into individual consciousness and into *prakṛti* is called knowledge, *vidyā*.

From the subjective and objective viewpoint, *upādhi* is 1) individual, called *avidyā*, nescience and 2) universal, called *māyā*, illusion.

From the viewpoint of manifestation of Consciousness there are four classes of *upādhi*:

1. *Upādhi* in the waking state is subjective and objective where the individual is a member of the external world, though he is not the creator of the external world.

2. *Upādhi* in the dream state is also subjective and objective; but here the individual is not only a part of the dreamland creation, rather he is the real creator.

3. *Upādhi* in the state of sound sleep is called *kāraṇopādhi*, causal state, where no subjective or objective worlds exist for the sleeper. It is union with *Brahman* through causal *upādhi*.

4. The religious, scientific, and philosophical *upādhi* exist where the seeker and the Self-analyst have some fantasy and fanciful ideas regarding the microcosm and macrocosm. It exists until the *turīya* state, identity with *Brahman*, is realized.

The first three *upādhis* are the major part of material life. The fourth *upādhi* is spiritual in nature. Therefore, Self-analysis is the process where one deals with waking, dreaming, and sound sleep phenomena simultaneously. While the Self-analyst is out of all these three states of *upādhi* in meditation, he should be careful not to play the part of actor or agent. He should be an impartial judge, observer, and witness.

In meditation one is neither sleeping, dreaming, nor, technically, waking. In the waking state all sensory and motor organs are united with the external world, while in meditation they are focused on ideas and symbols. The meditator is in the state of Consciousness which is called, *turīya*, the fourth state of Consciousness. In this state the Self-analyst wants to overcome all destructive driving forces, whether they are from waking, dreaming, or sound sleep states. In the beginning every meditator has the experience of falling asleep. This is the first manifestation of *yoganidrā* which comes from the causal state, and which is a sign of success for beginners.

Due to wrong thinking one loses sleep, and ultimately is overpowered by sleep, suffering, and darkness. In opposition to wrong thinking, meditation is a process of serious constructive thinking. Unlike in wrong thinking, the student may fall asleep in the beginning of his meditation. Ultimately, however, through the process of Self-analysis he overcomes sleep, suffering, and ignorance, and attains enlightenment. This falling asleep in the beginning, then, is the first manifestation of *yoganidrā*, and is a part of meditation in the beginning.

Subjective *upādhi* due to which one does not understand one's own real Nature is called *avidyā* ignorance regarding one's Self. Subjective *upādhi* due to which one does not understand the real Nature of the Universe around oneself is called *māyā*, ignorance regarding the Reality of the Universe. As *jīvātman*, individual Soul, and *Paramātman*, Cosmic Soul, are ultimately One, so are *avidyā* and *māyā* one. Due to the force of *upādhi*, the mind sees individuality and multiplicity in what is really one.

It is common that one sees the objective world according to one's own experience. Any change in subjective experience inevitably brings a change in objective experience. *Yogis* have discovered that investigation of the individual soul naturally brings investigation of the Cosmic Soul.

*Māyā* is the absence of recognition of Reality. It is neither yours nor mine, but it is an impersonal force, which imparts itself to individual consciousness immanently and transcendentally. When we open our eyes on things which are already created, which we perceive but do not create and make, this is ignorance of reality regarding the objective world. This is objective *māyā*. When we dream, we see and perceive things already created by our subconscious mind, but still we do not know how and why dreams are created. Our subconscious mind has created them, but the conscious mind does not know how. This is subjective *māyā*, which is *avidyā*.

*Upādhi* or *māyā* is the material cause of the Universe; thus, it cannot be only subjective ignorance. The two, *avidyā* of individual existence and *māyā* of Universal Existence arise together, reside together, and fall together; thus even *avidyā* is dependent of *Brahman*. It cannot be said that the objective phenomena of Nature are the product of individual consciousness any more than the subjective phenomenal Self is the product of Nature. Both mentalism and materialism are products of *upādhi*.

From the viewpoint of progressive experience in Self-analysis, for the purpose of description, there are four stages of Reality:

1. External phenomenon is perceived, and from this perception subtle, internal Reality is inferred in the same way as from the sign of smoke the unknown reality of fire is inferred.

2. In further meditation and investigation of Self, when the seeker is united with *Brahman* through his Consciousness, internal reality, noumenon, *Brahman* is perceived and realized directly and the external world is inferred.

3. In further advanced meditation, one feels the external world to be nothing but a projection of his own mind. The external world is perceived as one's own identity. This is called subjective idealism or mentalism.

4. In the Ultimate Experience of *samādhi*, the seeker reaches beyond the subjective-objective experience, and experiences this Ultimate Force as One-without-a-second. There is not even a trace of relativity left. Hence, there is complete annihilation of the material universe. From the negative viewpoint this is called *śūnyavāda*, voidness. From the viewpoint of the Absolute, this is called *Brahman* or *pūrṇavāda* (fullness). It is complete and perfect in itself. All three relative states are merged in the fourth. So long as this completeness is not realized, there will be no satisfaction in life and no real happiness.

The environmental energy which conditions the outer world also conditons the inner world. One fundamental force, through *upādhis*, is splitting into subjective and objective aspects, and presenting the phenomena of relative force, energy, matter, motion, and consciousness. *Upādhi*, by presenting the sense of duality, protects the subjective-objective world on the relative plane in the state of ignorance. By presenting union and identity with the Supreme, it protects the seeker in the state of *samādhi*. Thus *upādhi* renders possible the cognition of *Brahman*.

Reflection of *Brahman* in *māyā* is *Īśvara*, God, and in *avidyā* it is *jīvātman*, individual soul. As the difference between *māyā* and *avidyā* is only descriptive and not real, so the difference between *Īśvara*, God, and *jīvātman*, individual soul, is descriptive and unreal. Through meditation and Self-analysis, identity between *Īśvara*, God, and *jīvātman*, individual soul, is descriptive and unreal. Through meditation and Self-analysis, identity betwen *avidyā* and *māyā* is recognized. *Brahman* exists whole and undivided, even in the smallest object. The appearance of duality is due to individual intellect which operates through the mechanism of cause and effect, time and space. We perceive multiplicity of the Universe due to the *tanmātric* motion, vibration of Nature. Ultimate Reality is *Brahman*.

*Māyā* (*upādhi*) has two inherent powers that are operating simultaneously: 1) Covering power (*āvaraṇam*) and 2) Projection power (*vikṣepa*). By the power of covering, it covers the True Nature of the Self, and by the power of projection it projects the Universe of the senses.

Projection is the manifestation of the Universe externally, while introjection is incorporation of the properties of *māyā* on *Brahman* internally. The result of this internalization is an apparent covering of the essential Nature of *Brahman*. For example, the perception of a snake in a rope in semi-darkness is a projection, which is positive in nature. The reality of the rope is covered; this is negation of reality. Thus covering and projection operate simultaneously. When the real nature of the rope is recognized, the projection of a snake into the rope disappears.

In the process of projection, one will project according to one's previous memory, experience, and association. When a man has conquered all projections and coverings of *māyā* by Self-analysis, he will not perceive erroneous illusions of multiplicity of the world on *Brahman*. To overcome the coverings and projections of *māyā* on *Brahman*, one has to overcome the coverings and projections of *avidyā* on one's own Consciousness.

## SUTRA NO. 10

नानोपाधिवशादेव जातिवर्णाश्रमादयः ।
आत्मन्यारोपितास्तोये रसवर्णादिभेदवत् ॥१०॥

NĀNOPĀDHIVAŚĀDEVA JĀTIVARṆĀŚRAMĀDAYAḤ.
ĀTMANYĀROPITĀS TOYE RASAVARṆĀDIBHEDAVAT.

| | | |
|---|---|---|
| नाना-उपाधि- | Nānā-upādhi | Different conditionings |
| वशात् | Vaśāt | Due to the control |
| एव | Eva | Only |
| जाति-वर्ण- | Jāti-Varṇa | Birth, color |
| आश्रम-आदयः | Āśrama-Ādayaḥ | Class, position, etc. |
| आत्मनि | Ātmani | Upon the Self |
| आरोपिताः | Āropitāḥ | Are superimposed |
| तोये | Toye | On water |
| रस-वर्ण-आदि | Rasa-varṇa-ādi | As taste, color |
| भेदवत् | Bhedavat | And other differences |

Birth, death, class, creed, gender, and nationality belong to the body. Since the Self, I, is identified with the body, the characteristics of the body are superimposed on the Self in the same way as qualities of color and flavor are superimposed on water.

On account of the identification of One's Consciousness with *upādhis* such as class, creed, color, country, east, west, infancy, youth, adulthood, old age, etc., which are superimposed on *Ātman*, one feels the duality and multiplicity of the world in the same way as one perceives in a mixture such as water the characteristics of color and flavor. The multiplicity is superficial appearance only: they belong to the body and not to the Soul. As water is tasteless and colorless, so is the Soul beyond all characteristics which belong to the realm of Nature.

Every apparent, finite existence is turned into infinite Existence when it is investigated fully and completely. "That is perfect; this is perfect. The perfect comes out of the perfect. Taking the perfection from the perfect, the perfect itself remains."

This fullness is hidden, due to defective perception which gives a finite appearance to what is already Infinite. When defective perception is checked by right perception, this fullness is realized. Reality and unreality cannot stand together. When *Brahman* is recognized and identified, *māyā* disappears. The multiplicity of the world is then transformed into *Brahman*; hence the world is *Brahman*. The question of multiplicity, subjectivity, and objectivity arises only when the world of experience is accepted as Reality in itself and by itself in its relative form. When the fullness of the Absolute Reality is realized, all names and forms of the relative world disappear into one Existence–*Brahman*.

## SUTRA NO. 11

पञ्चीकृतमहाभूतसंभवं कर्मसञ्चितम् ।
शरीरं सुखदुःखानां भोगायतनमुच्यते ॥११॥

PAÑCĪKṚTAMAHĀBHŪTASAṀBHAVAṀ KARMASAÑCITAM.
ṠARĪRAṀ SUKHADUḤKHĀNĀṀ BHOGĀYATANAM UCYATE.

| | | |
|---|---|---|
| पञ्चीकृत- | Pañcīkṛta- | Of the five great elements |
| महाभूत- | Mahābhūta- | (Solid, Liquid, Gas, Light, |
| संभवम् | Sambhavam | Ether) - a collection |
| कर्म-सञ्चितम् | Karma-Sañcitam | Result of previous karma |
| शरीरम् | Ṡarīram | The gross body |
| सुख-दुःखानाम् | Sukha-Duḥkhānām | Of pleasure and pain |
| भोग-आयतनम् | Bhoga-Āyatanam | Medium of experiencing |
| उच्यते | Ucyate | It is said |

The gross body is the product of the five great elements—solid, liquid, gas, light and ether—and it is the result of previous *karmas*. The purpose of this body is to experience pain and pleasure, which are the result of one's *karmas*, and to experience relative knowledge. By means of this body, one should serve the Universe as though serving the Supreme, and thus experience the Real form of One's own Self.

The gross body, which is determined by past *karmas*, which are produced by constitutional, developmental, and environmental factors, and which is a conglomeration of the five states of Nature: solid, liquid, gaseous, light, and ether—is the medium through which Consciousness experiences pain and pleasure in the waking state.

Now the center of interest is shifted from different bodies to the

Self of man. The gross body (*sthūla śarīram*), the subtle or astral body (*sūkṣma śarīram*), and the causal body (*kāraṇa śarīram*) arising out of *prakṛti*, Nature, are tested and examined critically and found to be passing and changeful, and not the permanent essence of Self. These are merely outer coverings which conceal an inner, permanent Reality, which cannot be identified with any of these bodies. Though consciousness of all these bodies is grounded in, manifested by, and dependent on the Self, the real Consciousness is pure, simple, and Absolute. This Infinite, conscious Reality, *satyam jñānam anantam* is the real Self of man. It is identical with the Self of all beings, *sarva-bhūtātman*. In the relative sense it is called *Ātman*; in the Absolute sense it is called *Brahman*. The keen-sighted, with the help of sharp, penetrating intellect, by means of Self-analysis perceive this Self concealed in all these bodies. The highest knowledge, *parā vidyā*, is Self-realization attained by removing body-consciousness of identity.

The functional and structural unit of a gross body, which includes protoplasm as the medium of life, is called a cell. The human body consists of several hundred trillion cells of hundreds of types. These cells are grouped according to the same types into tissues; amd a group of different types of tissue is called a system. A group of the same type of tissue is called an organ. This body is moved as the result of forces, including physical, chemical, biochemical, biological, hormonal (called *ojas*) and psychological. This gross body operates in the waking state. The Consciousness operating through an individual entity is called *vaiśvānara*, Cosmic Consciousness, because this Consciousness leads the individual in diverse ways to enjoyment of the experience of the Cosmos, the external Universe (*virāt*).

Atoms, elements, molecules, and compounds through the five states of nature: solid, liquid, gaseous, light, and either—are intermingled in the gross body; hence it is called *pañcikṛta mahābhūta sambhavam*, intermingling of the five states.

The gross body is the product of:

1. Influence of previous incarnations;

2. Constitutional influences from parents;

3. Developmental, anatomical, psychological, and physiological factors (including the chronological development of *cittam*, mindstuff);

4. Environmental and situational factors.

The gross body is the medium through which consciousness experiences pain and pleasure in the waking state. This medium is influenced by *karmas*. There are three types of *karmas*. From the viewpoint of relativity, those *karmas* which have passed away are called *bhukta karmas*. Those whose actions are going on are called *prārabdha karmas*. Those whose operations will come in the future are called *sañcita karmas. Bhukta karmas* are done; they do not need any control. Present *karmas* are difficult to control; they can be controlled only by pure mind, that is to say by knowing their true meaning and operation. Future *karmas* can be controlled easily by careful and vigilant Self-analysis. As past, present, and future states are three different aspects of the One Reality—time, so the three types of *karmas* are one.

## SUTRA NO. 12

पञ्चप्राणमनोबुद्धिदशेन्द्रियसमन्वितम् ।
अपञ्चीकृतभूतोत्थं सूक्ष्माङ्गं भोगसाधनम् ॥१२॥

PAÑCAPRĀṆAMANOBUDDHIDAŚENDRIYASAMANVITAM.
APAÑCĪKṚTABHŪTOTTHAṀ SŪKṢMĀṄGAM BHOGASĀDHANAM.

| | | |
|---|---|---|
| पञ्च-प्राण- | Pañca-prāna- | The five pranas |
| मनो-बुद्धि- | Mano-Buddhi- | The mind and intellect- |
| दश-इन्द्रिय- | Daśa-Indriya- | Five sensory and five motor organs |
| समन्वितम् | Samanvitam | Combined with |
| अपञ्चीकृत-भूत- | Apañcīkṛta bhūta | The rudimentary elements |
| उत्थम् | Uttham | Formed or produced from- |
| सूक्ष्माङ्गम् | Sūkṣmāṅgam | The subtle body |
| भोग-साधनम् | Bhoga - Sādhanam | Instrument for experience |

The subtle body consists of the five senses, the five classes of *prāṇa*, *manah* (mind), *ahaṁkāra* (ego), *buddhi* (superego), and the five motor organs. The subtle body also is the product of the five elements in their subtle form. The purpose of the subtle body is to become the instrument for experiencing the subtle Universe as in dream, imagination, and image forming; and to become free from the subtle imprints of *karma* in the mind.

The subtle body, which includes the combined forces of five *prāṇas* plus *manah* (mind), *ahaṁkāra*, or Self-consciousness, and *buddhi* (intellect or Superconsciousness), and the five sensory and five motor organs, and which consists of the combined forces of the five pure states of nature, is the medium through which Consciousness experiences pleasure and pain of the psychic world in the dream state.

*Prāṇa* is called the primal force of the Universe, and it includes all forms of energy. This prime force generates motion in the matter of the body. In general, *prāṇa* includes all centripetal and centrifugal forces operating in the body and in the Universe. For descriptive purposes there are five classes of this prime force:

1. *Prāṇa* is the force which sets cardiovascular and respiratory systems in motion;

2. *Apāna* moves products out of the body, and it includes all outward or centrifugal motions of the body;

3. *Udāna* is the force of articulation, speech, singing, transmission and reception, and crying;

4. *Samāna* includes chemical, biochemical, and biological forces and transformation of matter into physical energy and–vice versa–physical energy into physical matter;

5. *Vyāna* is the force which deals with reflex actions of the body and magnetic pressure.

This subtle body is called the astral body; its dynamic forces are predominantly psychic forces. It has the power of infinite expansion and contraction. When consciousness operates through the subtle body, it is called *taijasa*, radiation. Cosmic Consciousness, which is the subject in the waking state, cognizes material objects in the waking state. *Taijasa*, the radiant psychic consciousness, experiences mental states dependent on the predispositions and impressions left by the waking experiences. In this state, according to conditions of the subconscious mind, the psychic forces present their own world in the form of dreams. The dream phenomena are experienced as external, but they are realized as part of the internal psychic world when one is awakened; likewise, waking phenomena are experienced as external but they, too, are realized as part of the internal world, when one is awakened; likewise, waking phenomena are experienced as external but they, too, are realized as part of the internal world, when one is enlightened through *samādhi*. Dream phenomena are called subtle in contradistinction to the objects of the waking state, which are external and gross.

The five sensory organs are sight, smell, hearing, taste, and touch. The five motor organs are hands, feet, tongue, excretory system, and reproductive system. *Manah* is the primary instinctual force of thinking, and is called the pleasure principle. *Ahaṁkāra*, the secondary thinking force, is the pleasure principle with reality. It is an executive force, and is developed out of *manah* in the relative plane. *Buddhi*, the principle of Ultimate Reality, is the judicial force of thinking. The principle, by which the evolution and involution of Nature are controlled, is called *buddhi. Buddhi* includes the process of accumulation, adaption, and assimilation.

*Manah*, *ahaṁkāra*, and *buddhi* collectively constitute one faculty which is called *cittam*. *Cittam* is the principle through which *citti*, consciousness, is manifested. The subtle body is predominantly ethereal, and belongs to the Nature of life, although other states of Nature, too, take part in the constitution of this body in the subtle form; hence this body is a product of *prakṛti*. The individual at the time of death leaves the gross body and goes to the next incarnation accompanied by this astral body.

## SUTRA NO. 13

अनाद्यविद्यानिर्वाच्या कारणोपाधिरुच्यते ।
उपाधित्रितयादन्यमात्मानमवधारयेत् ॥१३॥

ANĀDYAVIDYĀNIRVĀCYĀ KĀRAṆOPĀDHIR UCYATE.
UPĀDHITRITAYĀDANYAM ĀTMĀNAM AVADHĀRAYET.

| | | |
|---|---|---|
| अनादि - | Anādi | Beginningless |
| अविद्या | Avidyā | Ignorance |
| अनिर्वाच्याः | Anirvācyā | Indescribable |
| कारण - उपाधिः | Kāraṇa-upādhiḥ | The causal body |
| उच्यते | Ucyate | Is called |
| उपाधि - त्रितयाद् | Upādhi-tritayād | Than the three conditioning Bodies |
| अन्यम् | Anyam | Other |
| आत्मानम् | Ātmānam | The Self |
| अवधारयेत् | Avadhārayet | One should understand |

The causal body is the product of *Prakṛti*, *Māyā*. It operates during dreamless sleep, coma, and death. The purpose of this body is to bring the mind into the state of *Prakṛti*, thoughtlessness. These three bodies, gross, subtle, and causal, are called *upādhis*, limitations, and they belong to the ego. The real Self, I, is beyond these three bodies.

The causal body is the product of *avidyā*, ignorance, which is endless, beginningless, and inexplicable in relative terms. The Consciousness which operates through all these states of *upādhi* such as waking, dreaming, and sound sleep is beyond them all.

The states of waking, dreaming, and sound sleep are conceived as waves in the ocean of Supreme Consciousness which pervades these states, but also remains beyond them. In it—all that is, has been, or shall be—are united. In terms of theology, it presents the panorama of panentheism (*pan*, all + *en*, in + *theos*, God) but not pantheism; all is not equal to God, but all is in God, who is greater than all.

The causal body operates all the time, but its full manifestation is in sound sleep. In sleep, one does not desire anything and does not see any dream whatsoever. The consciousness operating in this state is called *prajñā*, mass of cognition. It is full of Bliss, experience, and is aware of nothing but itself, although this experience is through *avidya*, ignorance.

In the waking state consciousness is predominantly moving outward; in the dream state, it is moving inward. In the state of deep sleep, the conscious energy enjoys peace and has no awareness of anything outward or inward except its own motion. The transitory character of identity with *Brahman* in sound sleep shows that it is not real identification through Self-knowledge because in sound sleep the external and internal worlds are not overcome, but are only in abeyance.

In the waking and dreaming states, consciousness is perceptual, while in sound sleep it is conceptual. The phenomena of manifestation lapse in the state of sound sleep into a mass of cognition. All sensations and perceptions of the day, due to indiscrimination, become a mass of darkness at night in deep sleep. No desire, no thought remains. All impressions have become one. Only knowledge and bliss are left. The temporary loss of duality has led to the view that this is the state of union with *Brahman*. Consciousness in sound sleep is called *prajñā*, because it is not aware of variety. Sound sleep is the gateway to cognition of the other two states of consciousness known as dream and waking.

In the waking state, consciousness is bound by the sense of perception; it moves in the Cosmic world, i.e., outside. In the dream state it has freedom to create its own world from the material of the waking world, producing pleasure and pain, delight and oppression out of itself. In dreamless sleep, Consciousness is liberated from the relative world of cause and effect, space and time. In the three states, it is the one Consciousness alone. *Eka eva tridhā smṛtaḥ*.

No one has seen light, but it is light by which the world is seen. If material particles, which themselves are seen only in the presence of light, are removed from the pathway of light, then light cannot be perceived. In the same way, no one has seen the real Nature of Consciousness. Whatever is perceived in the presence of Consciousness or in the light of Consciousness is the world of *prakṛti* and its *upādhis*, waking and dreaming. If these states are removed as in sound sleep and death, the real Nature of Consciousness cannot be recognized. If one recognized the processes of one's own sound sleep and death, then to that one it is neither sound sleep nor death.

That which is designated as *prajñā* when seen from the viewpoint of cause and effect, space and time, is the cause of All, the knower of All, the inner controller of All, and the source of All. It is the beginning and the end of All states. When it is viewed from the standpoint of the Absolute, it is free from all phenomenal relationships, and is described as *turīya*. Hence the distinction between God and the Absolute, *Īśvara* and *Brahman*, *prajñā* and *turīya*, is eliminated.

These bodies are the best media to study the magnetic influence of pure Consciousness, just as an electroscope is the instrument to indicate the flow of electricity. Happiness and unhappiness, pleasure and pain, health and disease, knowledge and ignorance, life and death, Eternity and mortality, have not been seen tangibly by anyone, but their flow, direction, quality, and quantity are experienced, sensed, and perceived by constant action and reaction, constructive and destructive changes in the mind and body. As electricity is beyond the electroscope, although it influences the electroscope by its electronic motion, so pure Consciousness is beyond the three bodies although all these bodies are in a constant magnetic influence of Consciousness, immanently and transcendentally.

How are these bodies related to Consciousness, *jīvātman*? How is the world related to *paramātman*? Are conscious Spirit and unconscious Nature two separate entities? Is unconscious Nature dependent on and a product of conscious Self? Or is it independent? Is conscious Self dependent on and a product of unconscious Nature? Who is the creator of unconscious *prakṛti* and of conscious *puruṣa*? If Ultimate Reality is One. then why do people see multiplicity in the world? What is the relationship between unity and multiplicity? How can the Absolute have become many? How can *Ātman*, which is nothing but *Brahman*, identify itself with these perishable bodies, senses, mind and ego?

Some believe that the Creator is God, who created the world out of Nature and matter, in the same way as a carpenter creates pieces of furniture out of wood. The difficulty is that, like a carpenter, God then would be an External power.

If we accept that God created the world out of *prakṛti*, Nature, which is Real, then the question arises, "Who created *prakṛti*?" If both *prakṛti* and God are Real and Eternal, and if any addition to God and other realities be admitted, God would cease to be the All-inclusive Reality, and duality would descend upon us. By this argument, God would lose his Infinity.

Or if we accept that, due to the influence of God, every entity of unreality is transformed into Reality, there will be no freedom. Freedom can be obtained only from that which is foreign to its real and inner Nature. Freedom cannot be obtained from its real and inner Nature. If we accept freedom from its real Nature, that would mean annihilation of that thing, and reality would be proved illusion.

Some believe that God himself has become the world, and the real cause of the Universe is not outside the universe. This is the difficulty of pantheism which means that everything is God. One cannot distinguish this relationship of identity from atheism.

Some believe that God created the world out of nothing, but the main philosophical difficulty in this view is that God would then be out of the Universe. Something cannot come out of nothing. If God be accepted as penetrating this Universe, a product of nothingness, then the Universe of nothingness is illusion. If the Universe be accepted as Real, then God becomes the Universe. In this case he would be matter, not God.

If God created the world out of nothing, this world would be nothing but illusion because, according to the principle of cause and effect, the effect is always according to its cause; thus the world would be nothing because its cause is nothing.

Some believe that this Universe is a product of Nature, and that there is no such thing as God, and that conscious and unconscious phenomena are stages and aspects of Nature. But this view cannot explain the most beautiful arrangement and mathematical involution and evolution of the Universe because we do not see any creation in the world without a conscious Creator. If a chair cannot be made without a conscious carpenter, then how can this complicated Universe of Cosmic forces, constantly moving electrons, intrinsically dancing and ungraspable atoms be created without a conscious Creator?

It is difficult to reconcile all these questions and answers about the creation of the Universe and its relationship with its Creator.

All these and like views and their solutions seem to the unprejudiced thinker to be out of joint. If the world be Real, how can it disappear on the realization of Self? The knowledge of Reality can dispel only the unreality, which is appearing as Reality, but not that which is really Reality. Reconciliation lies in understanding the terms *avidyā* and *māyā*. If both the world and God were Real, liberation from the world and identity with God would be impossible because one Reality cannot be changed into another. If they can be interchanged, their duality and disappearance are apparent only and their identity is real. If the world is appearance and illusion, like an object in a dream or a mirage, then the present reality of the world and its disappearance on the knowledge of Absolute Reality is intelligible.

Due to the opposite natures of Consciousness and unconsciousness, there will be neither union nor identity of God and Nature. If Nature be conceived as Real, but within God, and the world be conceived as a real transformation of Nature, we face a serious dilemma. The question would arise whether Nature is part of God, or identical with the whole of God. If Nature be accepted as a part of God, then we are compelled to accept that Spiritual substance is composed of parts as material substance is. So it would be difficult to separate Spirit from matter, and Spirit would be liable to dissolution as material substance is.

According to natural law, whatever has parts is liable to disintegration. If the alternative that Nature is the whole of God be accepted, then by the transformation of Nature into matter and the material world, God is wholly reduced to matter and the world, and there is no God left beyond the world after creation. Without a change in the cause, there can be no change in the effect; and if change is in the real Nature of God, then change would be accepted as Reality. In this case, whether God's change be in part or in entirety, God could not be a permanent and unchanging Reality. He would cease to be God, and we should be faced with materialism. Neither pure materialism nor pure theism can solve this dilemma. The condition of union and identity is impossible between two opposite things.

These difficulties are reconciled and solved by *vivarta vāda*. According to *vivarta vāda*, change is real from the viewpoint of relativity, but from the viewpoint of the Absolute, it is apparent, hence unreal. Illusory modification of any substance is called *vivarta vāda* and real modification is called *pariṇāma vāda*. In semi-darkness the appearance of a snake in a rope is called *vivarta vāda*. The transformation of milk into curd is called *pariṇāma vāda*. *Vivarta vāda* and *pariṇāma vāda* are the two aspects of *satkārya vāda*, which means that the effect is the evolution of the cause, and that the cause is the involution of the effect. That is to say, there is no real difference between cause and its effect. Cause is potentiality, and effect is actuality. According to *satkārya vāda*, there is neither creation nor destruction; there is rather only evolution and involtion. The appearance of the world in *Brahman* is *vivarta vāda*, which is illusory. The process of the attribution of something, where is does not exist, is called *adhyāsa*. In short, all illusions are projections, *adhyāsas*. The world is projected, *adhyāsta*, on *Brahman* by imagination (ignorance of the Reality of *Brahman*), in the same way as a serpent is projected onto a rope by ignorance of the real Nature of the rope; thus this ignorance, *māyā*, is the cause of creation.

*Māyā,* the magical force of creation, is indistinguishable from the Supreme. Supreme Nature is the Supreme Energy of Supreme Consciousness, and cannot be separated from it, just as light and heat are the real Nature of fire, and cannot be separated from it. It is by this Energy that the Supreme has produced the wonderful world. The appearance of multiplicity in the subjective-objective world is taken as real by the ignorant, but the wise, through Self-analysis, see nothing but *Brahman*, the One-without-a-second. *Māyā* means, generally, ignorance regarding the Cosmos. On account of this ignorance, *Brahman*, pure Consciousness, is imagined as the Creator of the Cosmos. *Avidyā* means, generally, ignorance regarding one's own Reality on account of which one feels oneself as an individual soul, *jīvātman*, an entity separate from the rest of the Universe. Due to ignorance one imagines oneself as an individual soul and *Brahman* as the Universal Soul.

*Māyā* and *avidyā* cannot be known and removed by *māyā* and *avidyā* even as the dense darkness of night cannot be known and removed by darkness. As darkness is known and removed by the present of light, so also *māyā* and *avidyā* are known and removed by the light of the Self.

When and why ignorance comes into individual consciousness cannot be explained, *anirvacanīya*, in the relative plane through Self-analysis in *samādhi* through the language of the Self, *Brahmavidyā*.

The detached and independent Nature of the Supreme can be illustrated as follows: The world of electrons, atoms, and elements can be compared to a nation. The five states of nature and *tanmātras* can be compared to the states within a nation. The mind and the sensory and motor organs are the vice-president and congress or parliament. *Ahaṁkāra* is the executive office, the president; *buddhi*, the intellect, is the supreme court; and the real *Ātman*, Self-luminous eternally.

In conclusion, Consciousness is analyzed through four stages: 1) waking; 2) dreaming; 3) sound sleep; 4) *turīya*.. The waking and dreaming states have the similarity of subjective-objective multiplicity. The dream state is spontaneous and instantaneous; the waking state is systematic and chronological. Sound sleep and *turīya* have a similarity in union and identity with *Brahman*. In sound sleep there is union with *Brahman* through ignorance, *māyā*, and in *turīya* there is union and identity with *Brahman* through self-knowledge. Both states, *turīya* and sound sleep, present a sense of perfection, although in sound sleep it is due to ignorance, and in *turīya* it is the result of Self-knowledge. It is common experience that an ignorant man understands himself to be perfect, and he is complacent. The more he learns, the more he realizes his ignorance and begins to feel a sense of imperfection in himself. This is the beginning state of Reality. When he completes Self-realization and is enlightened with the light of *Brahman*, he becomes one with *Brahman*, and because he becomes *Brahman*, he is perfect as *Brahman*.

Classification of bodies into waking, dreaming and sound sleep states is only descriptive. When the body is operating in one state, the other two states are working in harmony. In the waking state, the gross body is predominant in operation; in the dream state the subtle body is predominant; and in the sound sleep state, the causal body is predominantly operating. Thus there is no real separation among these three bodies, except for description.

## SUTRA NO. 14

पञ्चकोशादियोगेन तत्तन्मय इव स्थितः ।
शुद्धात्मा नीलवस्त्रादियोगेन स्फटिको यथा ॥१४॥

PAÑCAKOŚĀDIYOGENA TAT TANMAYA IVA STHITAḤ.
ŚUDDHĀTMĀ NĪLAVASTRĀDIYOGENA SPHAṬIKO YATHĀ.

| | | |
|---|---|---|
| पञ्च-कोश-आदि- | Pañca - kośa - ādi | With the five sheaths |
| योगेन | Yogena | On account of association |
| तत्-तन्मयः | Tat-tanmayaḥ | Identical with that |
| इव | Iva | Like |
| स्थितः | Sthitaḥ | Appears |
| शुद्ध-आत्मा | Śuddha-Ātmā | Pure Consciousness, Self |
| नील-वस्त्र-आदि- | Nīla-Vastra-ādi | Blue cloth, etc. |
| योगेन | Yogena | By association with |
| स्फटिकः | Sphaṭikaḥ | A crystal |
| यथा | Yathā | As |

In addition to the limitations of the three bodies, there are five limiting sheaths—the sheaths of matter, Energy, Consciousness, Intelligence, and Bliss. All five sheaths are the product of Cosmic Energy. Pure Consciousness, in association with these five sheaths, appears to be identified with them, as a crystal appears to be endowed with the color of cloth with which it is in contact.

The description of *Ātman* as Eternal Existence, Consciousness, and Reality seems to be only a concept and faith because, practically, in daily life, individual existence and consciousness seem to be dependent on eating and sleeping. This indicates that individual consciousness is the product of physical, chemical, biochemical, and biological forces. According to the principle of causality, the effect is nothing but the extension and development of its cause; therefore, this consciousness is nothing but these forces. However, *Ātman* is beyond biological life and psychological consciousness. Due to the reflection of Supreme Consciousness through these mechanisms, it seems to be a product of them in the same way as a television program seems to be the product of the television set; but this is a misunderstanding due to ignorance of the real Nature of Supreme Consciousness and Supreme Light.

These forces present five sheaths: *Pañca-kośādiyogena.* On account of reflection in the five sheaths, pure Consciousness appears to be identified with them in the same way that, due to the reflection of colors in a crystal, a crystal appears to be identified with them. In reality, pure crystal and pure Consciousness respectively are beyond colors and sheaths. Biological life and psychological consciousness are neither fundamental nor Eternal in the Absolute sense. Self-consciousness or ego-consciousness, which is the executive and leading dynamo of organic life, belongs to the realm of relativity, and passes through constant change of cause and effect, space and time; hence, substantiality and simplicity cannot be attributed to the present individual consciousness.

Individual consciousness is a complex structure and systematic unity of the conscious experiences of an individual soul. It is defined and determined by bodily states and sheaths. The body, with its sensory and motor organs, with the three states of waking, dreaming, and sound sleep, and the five sheaths, enters into unity and identity with pure Consciousness and presents mathematical Unity and Continuity. This individual consciousness increases and decreases according to evolution and involution of the bodily states and sheaths. It is not the Ultimate cause of its own Existence and Consciousness; therefore, it cannot be accepted as pure, substantial, Eternal, and simple Consciousness in its present form. The unchangeable Essence, *Brahman*, the underlying foundation of all individual egos, is beyond bodies and sheaths, beyond suffering, decay and death.

Pure, eternal, and unchanging Consciousness appears as finite, individual soul due to the relationship of *ātman* to the *upādhis* of the body, including the sensory and motor organs and the five sheaths. These *upādhis* are inexplicable in the realm of relativity; therefore the relationship between psychological, finite consciousness and the metaphysical, infinite Consciousness can be understood only through Self-realization.

The five sheaths which enshrine and reflect the light of pure Consciousness are:

1. *Annamaya kośa*, the physical and material covering which reflects the consciousness of physical force;

2. *Prāṇamaya kośa*, which is electrical magnetic pulsation and vibration. It is all motions; includes chemical, biochemical and biological forces;

3. *Manomaya kośa* includes psychological forces, and reflects the consciousness of mentalism. In this sheath, everything appears to be made of thought. Everywhere the ocean of thought is perceived, and everything is perceived in the ocean of thought and feeling;

4. *Vijñānamaya kośa* reveals the constitution of Consciousness. This is the state of the revelation of Supreme Consciousness in the relative plane;

5. *Ānandamaya kośa* reflects the Ultimate Reality of *Puruṣa* and *Prakṛti*, Supreme Consciousnesss and Supreme Nature, as well as beatific Bliss.

The gross body consists of the physical sheath. The subtle body includes *prāṇamaya*, *manomaya*, and *vijñānamaya* sheaths. The causal body consists of *ānandamaya* sheath. These five sheaths are purely descriptive for the purpose of Self-analysis; there is no hard and fast line to separate one sheath from the other. They are interdependent, interpenetrating, and from one to five consecutively, they are inclusive. For example, the fourth sheath includes the first, second, and third. From fifth to first they are consecutively exclusive. For example, the third sheath excludes the fourth and fifth but includes the first and second. Through meditation one progresses chronologically from one sheath to the next, melting, as it were, one into the next highest, until the highest peak is reached in the sheath of Bliss.

As the infinite Cosmic space seems to be limited by the walls of a jar, and as a pure crystal seems to be contaminated by the red or blue color with which it is associated, so does the pure *Ātman* appear to have borrowed the qualities of the five sheaths with which it is associated. As to children, space appears to be stained with dust, color, etc., so to the ignorant, the Self appears to be bound or tinted with sin, depression, frustration, or other things. When the limitations on space are removed, space remains unmoved. When bodies and sheaths are born or die, the Self remains unmoved.

It is common experience of every conscious being that one has no memory of one's birth or residence during pregnancy in the embryonic state. Speaking of the birthdate, we mean the date when the body was born. That which is born will die, but so long as the birth of the Self is not indicated and verified, the question of its death is irrelevant; thus the memory and fear of death are baseless, for they belong to the body, not to the Self. The Self is reflected through the body as a program is reflected through a television set. In a court, so long as a charge is not proved against a person, the question of conviction is irrelevant; therefore, as long as one has no knowledge and memory of one's birth, one has no reason to expect and fear death.

The five sheaths are the five planes of consciousness, existence, and reality in the realm of relativity. Absolute Consciousness, Existence, and Reality are beyond them, although they are immanent, All-pervading, the inner controller and inner foundation of them. When, through Self-analysis, all the five relative planes of Consciousness are realized as identical with Supreme Reality, and when the dualism of the five sheaths which apparently seem to be dividing Absolute Reality are overcome through meditation, concentration, and contemplation, that which remains as the non-reducible substratum and substance is *Brahman*. It is Self-illumined, Self-radiating, Self-shining, and Self-effulgent, Absolute Consciousness, Existence, and Reality. When the consciousness reflecting through the five sheaths is recognized as identical with conscious noumenon, *puruṣa*, and when all different sheaths, which are mechanisms reflecting *puruṣa*, are recognized as identical with *prakṛti* or *māyā*, unconscious noumenon; and when *puruṣa* and *prakṛti* are recognized as substance and quality, then the separating dualism disappears, and indefinable, everlasting *Brahman* is realized. The process of elimination of sheaths through discrimination is described in the following slokas.

## SUTRA NO. 15

वपुस्तुषादिभिः कोशैः युक्तं युक्त्यावघाततः ।
आत्मानमन्तरं शुद्धं विविच्यात्तण्डुलं यथा ॥१५॥

VAPUS TUṢĀDIBHIḤ KOŚAIR YUKTAṀ YUKTYAVAGHĀTATAḤ.
ĀTMĀNAM ANTARAṀ ŚUDDHAM VIVICYĀT TAṆḌULAṀ YATHĀ.

| | | |
|---|---|---|
| वपुः | Vapuḥ | Form |
| तुषादिभिः | Tuṣādibhiḥ | With husks, chaff, etc. |
| कोशैः | Kośaiḥ | With sheaths |
| युक्तम् | Yuktam | Identified |
| युक्त्या | Yuktyā | By investigation |
| अवघाततः | Avaghātataḥ | By thrashing |
| आत्मानम् | Ātmānam | The Self |
| अन्तरम् | Antaram | Within |
| शुद्धम् | Śuddham | Pure |
| विविच्यात् | Vivicyāt | One should separate |
| तण्डुलम् | Taṇḍulam | Rice |
| यथा | Yathā | As |

The Self, the I, is apparently identified with the three bodies and the five sheaths. Through investigation of the Self, "Who Am I?" one should discriminate and separate the pure and inmost Self, the "I AM," from all three bodies and five sheaths with which it is identified, in the same way as one separates a grain of rice from its husk without damaging it.

Through Self-analysis one should discriminate the pure and

inmost Self from the five sheaths which cover the real Nature of Ultimate Reality in the same way as one separates a rice kernel from the covering husk by striking it.

Reflection of the sun and moon in mirrors may produce innumerable images in different sizes, shapes, and colors, entirely different from one another, according to the conditions of the mirrors. Still the sun and moon are untouched and unchanged in their reflective processes.

So also the appearance of *Brahman* may produce multiplicity and changeability of images of *jīva* through different bodies and sheaths. The individual images and the individual souls are just the reflections. The Reality is the sun; the Reality is *Brahman*.

The theory of reflection presents the trinity of a reflecting substance, a reflective substance, and a reflection or image. As the sun is the reflecting substance, a mirror is the reflective substance, and the image is the reflection, so *puruṣa* is the reflecting substance, mind is the reflective substance, and *jīva* (individual soul) is the reflection or image.

Apparently the theory of reflection presents dualism in *Brahman* because without reflecting and reflective substances there would be no reflection or image; but this dualism is relative. When it is examined from the viewpoint of the Absolute, it presents the Oneness of *Brahman*. For example, in the case of the sun and a mirror and its image, the three seem to be relatively different from one another, but really the mirror and the image are nothing but other forms of the sun in the Absolute sense.

From the viewpoint of evolution, if the entire solar system is not other than the sun, how can mirrors and reflections be other than the sun? Multiplicity is relative and apparent; Unity is Absolute and Real. The theory of reflection indicates not only how one reality becomes multiple in relative planes without going into any change and modification in reality, but also shows how multiplicity is unity from the standpoint of evolution in the sense of the Absolute.

When a student directly recognizes *Brahman* as one Absolute Reality, his identification with sheaths and bodies disappears. Strangely enough, the whole process of Self-analysis apparently presents the picture of dualism of Self and non-self, *puruṣa* and *prakṛti*, mind and matter, metaphysics and physics. Without detaching Self from non-self in the relative plane, nondualism cannot be recognized in the sense of the Absolute. For example, a house and the dweller of the house are two different entities in the sense of relativity, but from the viewpoint of atoms and elements there is identity between the two in the Absolute sense. The dweller and the house are only two different conditons of arrangement of atoms and elements. Without detaching his reality from the house in the relative plane, the dweller cannot recognize his nondual Spirit. Identity between the dweller and his house is not Reality, but the identity of the dweller with *Brahman*, which includes the entire manifested Universe, is Reality.

It is wonderful to find in modern physics proof of a statement made by *Yogins*. In the famous textbook of modern physics, *The Nature of the Physical World* by Arthur S. Eddington, he writes, "There are two tables–duplicates of every object about me." (He means from the ordinary viewpoint and from the scientific one.) "One table is familiar to me . . . it is a commonplace object . . . it has extension; it is comparatively permanent; it is substantial . . . . Table number two is not belonging to the world previously mentioned–that world which appears . . . when I open my eyes . . . my scientific table is mostly emptiness. Sparsely scattered in that emptiness are numerous electric charges rushing about with great speed; but their combined bulk amounts to less than a billionth of the bulk of the table itself . . .

"There is nothing substantial about my second table. It is nearly all empty space, pervaded . . . by fields of force, but these are assigned to the category of 'influence,' not of 'things' . . . the attributes of the external world, except as they are reflected in measuring devices, are outside scientific scrutiny . . . the process, by which the external world of physics is transformed into a world of familiar acquaintance in human consciousness, is outside the scope of physics."

## SUTRA NO. 16

सदा सर्वगतोऽप्यात्मा न सर्वत्रावभासते ।
बुद्धावेवावभासेत स्वच्छेषु प्रतिबिम्बवत् ॥१६॥

SADĀ SARVAGATO' PYĀTMĀ NA SARVATRĀVABHĀSATE.
BUDDHĀVEVĀVABHĀSETA SVACCHEṢU PRATIBIMBAVAT.

| | | |
|---|---|---|
| सदा | Sadā | Always |
| सर्वगतः | Sarvagataḥ | All-pervading |
| अपि | Api | Although |
| आत्मा | Ātmā | The Self |
| न | Na | Not |
| सर्वत्र | Sarvatra | Everywhere |
| अवभासते | Avabhāsate | Shines |
| बुद्धौ | Buddhau | In the intelligence |
| एव | Eva | Only |
| अवभासेत | Avabhāseta | Should manifest |
| स्वच्छेषु | Svaccheṣu | In clear objects, like a mirror |
| प्रतिबिम्बवत् | Pratibimbavat | As the reflection |

The Self, the I AM, although it is All-pervading, is not cognized in everything. It is cognized only in *Buddhi*, Intelligence, in the same way as a reflection is seen clearly only in a mirror, although it is falling equally on every object.

*Ātman* is omnipresent, omniscient, omnipotent, and All-pervading Reality, but its omnipresence, omniscience, and omnipotence are not recognized without the enlightenment of *Buddhi*, Intellect.

Every object reflects every other object, but these reflections are perceived only in shining objects such as mirrors. As the reflection of ordinary objects is not perceived except in lustrous objects, so it is that *Ātman* is not recognized without the enlightenment of *Buddhi*.

This is in similitude to the operation of radio and television. Although scientifically we know that broadcast and telecast programs are everywhere present in the atmosphere, we cannot hear or see them unless and until we tune in our receiving sets by connecting them with and turning them on to the electrical power, which makes the tubes glow. This manifestation of the programs through receiving sets does not limit the actual programs in any sense; the studio performance is untouched and unaffected by the radio and television receivers. Even so, the omnipresent, omniscient, and omnipotent *Ātman*, being manifested only through *Buddhi*, Intelligence, is not diminished in its omnipresence, omniscience, and omnipotence by *Buddhi*.

Four factors, which include innumerable other factors, are involved in all knowledge:

1. Subjective consciousness, "I"—consciousness, *citti*;

2. Instrumentation, which includes psychological forces, senses, sensation and the sensory organs, motion, vibration, motor organs, and *cittam*-;

3. Object, that which is presented for analysis; and

4. Medium, the atmosphere. This environment, external and internal, is the vibration of the Supreme, *Ātman*. It is called atmosphere because it is the vibration of *Ātman*. Change in any one of these factors will inevitably bring a change in the other three factors.

*Cittam* is the psychological mechanism through which *citti*, Consciousness, is manifested. This *cittam* is classified in three divisions:

1. *Manaḥ*, the primary thinking principle. *Manaḥ* is mind-consciousness, the principle of pleasure and happiness; it operates like a parliament or congress with every organ having representation in the assembly.

2. *Ahaṁkāra* self-consciousness or ego-consciousness. *Ahaṁkāra* is the principle of pleasure and happiness presenting discrimination between reality and unreality, and eliminating unreality to avoid suffering in life. It operates like an executive officer such as a president or prime minister.

3. *Buddhi*, Super-Consciousness. *Buddhi* presents real happiness by discriminating between Ultimate Reality and conditional reality. *Buddhi* operates like the supreme court.

Ultimate Reality is One-without-a-second, pervading all objective and subjective phenomena, but knowledge in relativity is obtained through *cittam* only. All objective phenomena in the process of knowledge are synthesized and analyzed by *manaḥ* according to sensations given to the mind by sensory organs. In every sensation, environmental energy strikes the end organs, the receptive organs, and an impulse passes through the conductive system of nerves to perceptory organs in the brain, where psychic energy begins to synthesize and analyze the nature of these impulses according to previous experience.

The mind presents its experience to *ahaṁkāra*, self-consciousness, which distinguishes the real Nature of impulses from unreality, discriminates Self from non-self. *Ahaṁkāra* presents the analysis before *Buddhi*, which stamps final judgment for a valid experience, which is called knowledge.

Experience is a definite and unerring cognition of something, the result of action and reaction or modification, of *cittam*, which reflects consciousness, Self, in it. *Cittam* is unconscious energy which belongs to *Prakṛti*, Nature. Intelligence is Conscious Energy which belongs to *Puruṣa*. In the relative world *puruṣa* cannot perceive objects without the other three factors (medium, instrumentation, and object) although it is All-pervading and shining Eternally in every existence; thus, when forms are impressed on *cittam*, it reflects the light of the Self.

Perception is the direct cognition of an object through its contact with instrumentation. When an object such as a house comes within the range of our vision, there is contact between the house and our eyes. Through environmental energy the house produces certain impressions in our sensory organs, and these impressions are analyzed by the mind. After the action and reaction of *ahaṁkāra*, self-consciousness, *Buddhi*, Superconsciousness, becomes modified and is transformed into the house. *Buddhi* however, being the unconscious material principle, cannot know the house by itself, although the existence of the house is present in it. In the same way, electrical vibrations of a television program imitate the performers, although the vibrations themselves are unconscious of their own activity.

As *Buddhi* has an abundance of *Sattva* (purity), it accordingly reflects the consciousness of *puruṣa*, somewhat like a transparent mirror reflects objects and filters light. With the reflection of the Self's consciousness in it, the unconscious modification of *Buddhi* into the form of the house becomes illumined in the conscious state of reality, which we call perception. Just as mirror reflects the light of a lamp, and by this reflection manifests other objects, so the mechanism of *Buddhi*, being transparent, reflects the Consciousness of the Self, and illuminates other objects. The result of this reflection is called knowledge. The process of reflection is called perception. This reflection is mutual. Due to the reflection of *cittam* on *puruṣa*, the latter begins to feel itself a part of the phenomenal world. When there is a reflection of *puruṣa* on *cittam*, the former recognizes its identity with *Brahman*. This mutual reflection is the cause of liberation or bondage: liberation when *puruṣa* reflects on *cittam*, and bondage when *cittam* shadows *puruṣa*.

The process of Self-analysis and meditation is nothing but the reflection of *puruṣa* on *cittam*. When individual *cittam* is purified by concentration, contemplation, and meditation, it is transformed into Cosmic *Cittam*. It is this *Cittam* which reflects the Consciousness of the Supreme. *Cittam* has the Eternal power of transformation. In a lower plane it is transformed into lower life. In a higher plane, by higher knowledge, it is transformed into *Brahman*. When the entire *cittam* is transformed into the light of the Supreme, One attains liberation.

The world is only the reflection of *cittam*. *Cittam* should be purified by Self-analysis. Man is according to his *cittam*. By contact with matter, it becomes matter; by contact with *Brahman*, it becomes *Brahman*. Transformation and reflection are the inherent qualities of *Cittam*.

In the process of Self-analysis, a student should take the role of an impartial judge.

## SUTRA NO. 17

देहेन्द्रियमनोबुद्धिप्रकृतिभ्यो विलक्षणम् ।
तद्वृत्तिसाक्षिणं विद्यादात्मानं राजवत्सदा ॥१७॥

DEHENDRI YAMANOBUDDHIPRAKṚTIBHYO VILAKṢAṆAM.
TADVṚTTISĀKṢIṆAṀ VIDYĀD ĀTMĀNAṀ RĀJAVAT SADĀ.

| | | |
|---|---|---|
| देह- इन्द्रिय- | Deha-indriya | Body - senses |
| मनो- बुद्धि- | Mano-buddhi | Mind - intellect |
| प्रकृतिभ्यः | Prakṛtibhyaḥ | And Cosmic Energy (Nature |
| विलक्षणम् | Vilakṣaṇam | Different, distinct from |
| तत्- वृत्ति- | Tat - Vṛtti | Of their functions |
| साक्षिणम् | Sākṣiṇam | Witness |
| विद्यात् | Vidyāt | One should know |
| आत्मानम् | Ātmānam | The Self |
| राजवत् | Rājavat | Like a king |
| सदा | Sadā | Always |

Know for certain that *Ātman*, I AM, transcends the body, senses, mind, *buddhi*, and *prakṛti*. It is the witness of their functions; and, like a king, it is their ruler and controller. The Self pervades and interpenetrates the body, sense organs, mind, ego, and super-ego, and yet remains totally different from them. It is the Eternal subject and unchanging Consciousness.

*Ātman* should be realized beyond the phenomena of the body, sensory organs, motor organs, *cittam*, and *prakṛti*, (unconscious noumenon), as an impartial witness to their functions, or as an impartial king or judge.

As an impartial king follows his kingdom, or as a judge follows his legal duty in the court, without identifying with any party, or as a physician follows his patients, without identifying with them, so *Ātman* follows the functions of the body, senses, and mind without identifying with them.

Impartial subjective and objective analysis should be the basic principle of Self-analysis. In each individual existence there is Eternal Consciousness, immanent and transcendent, witnessing all internal and external phenomena.

One should examine one's mind and mental phenomena constantly, as a physician examines a patient. As a physician gains experience and insight into the problems of his patient and cures the patient of disease, so one should gain insight into one's own mind and mental problems, and should work out solutions. Going beyond the relationship of physician to patient, a Self-analyst should follow his mind day and night. There is disaster if a physician identifies with a patient, and understands himself to be the patient, or if a judge identifies with a party, and understands himself to be the party. In such case, the physician is not able to treat the patient, nor is the judge capable of making an impartial decision.

It is common psychological experience that we can advise others in their unfavorable situations, but when we are in a calamity, we need to seek understanding and help from others. This psychological experience is due to the different positions of witness and victim. As long as one is an impartial witness, one understands the situation well, and can help others accordingly. But in one's own calamities, one is not a witness because one has identified with the calamities; therefore, every meditator should understand his *Ātman* to be an impartial witness, observing the activity of his mind. He should not be a witness as a man on a highway, but a real witness as a physician in his office, a king in his kingdom, or a judge in his court.

As long as identification of *Ātman* with the matter of body, senses, and *cittam* continues, there will be no Self-analysis, and no elimination of suffering from life.

In every experience we have some sort of identification with the body and mind. According to that identification we interpret the action and reaction of others, and we feel happy or unhappy, successful or unsuccessful. When this identification is changed, one becomes happy to have right understanding and insight into Reality.

For example, we read in newspapers of innumerable deaths, still we do not feel that loss to the same degree as do those who are directly related to the victims. We deal with others' problems as philosophers, but we deal with our own problems as victims. This difference in our outlook is due to our position as a witness or as an agent.

However, this witness role should not be misunderstood or confused with one of indifference and insensibility to others' calamities with no heart or desire to help others. "Mine" and "Thine" express the attitude of an ignorant person; but the *Yogin* should understand the entire world as his own Soul. Wherever there is a feeling of possession, there is undue attachment and identification; and wherever there is a feeling of separation and distance, there is undue detachment, repulsion, or hatred.

What is the relationship between the witness Self and the individual self? Unchanging consciousness, which is the substratum of the phenomena of the gross and subtle bodies, and which is observing their effects without being affected by them in any way, is called the witness Self, *Sākṣin*. Pure Consciousness operating through the perceptual mechanism, *cittam*, with the five organs of action and perception, identifying with their phenomena, is called the individual self, *jīva*. When an aspirant realizes the presence of the witness Self, he has understanding and can overcome his identification with the body and mind. The witness Self is an impartial observer of the individual soul, which participates in relative life and its phenomena. The witness Self is Self-luminous, shining by its own light like the sun, illuminating the planets of sensory and motor organs in the body; thus, every individual soul has two aspects, one Real, the other unreal, that of *Sākṣin*, or impartial judge, and that of *abhimānın*, or enjoyer and active agent.

The individual self operates through the limitations of the senses, but the witness Self remains beyond the limitations of the senses, and uses them as instruments. The Ultimate Consciousness operating in an individual soul should be realized, recognized, and identified as witness Self. *Ātman*, Eternal Consciousness, operating in the individual soul, is called *jīva-sākṣin*, witness to individual phenomena. While operating in the Universe, Eternal Consciousness is called *Īśvara-Sākṣin*, witness to Cosmic phenomena.

## SUTRA NO. 18

व्यापृतेष्विन्द्रियेष्वात्मा व्यापारीवाविवेकिनाम्
दृश्यतेऽभ्रेषु धावत्सु धावन्निव यथा शशी ॥१८॥

VYĀPṚTEṢVINDRIYEṢVĀTMĀ VYĀPĀRĪVĀVIVEKINĀM.
DṚŚYATE' BHREṢU DHĀVATSU DHĀVANNIVA YATHĀ ŚAŚĪ.

| | | |
|---|---|---|
| व्यापृतेषु | Vyāpṛteṣu | While functioning |
| इन्द्रियेषु | Indriyeṣu | The senses |
| आत्मा | Ātmā | The Self |
| व्यापारी इव | Vyāpari iva | As if engaged, active |
| अविवेकिनाम् | Avivekinām | Of the non-discriminating people |
| दृश्यते | Dṛśyate | It is perceived |
| अभ्रेषु | Abhreṣu | Clouds |
| धावत्सु | Dhāvatsu | When moving |
| धावन् | Dhāvan | Moving |
| इव | Iva | Like |
| यथा | Yathā | Just as |
| शशी | Śaśī | The moon |

According to the condition of body, mind, and senses, the Self, I, appears to be either happy or unhappy, restless or tranquil, healthy or unhealthy. In the same way, the moon appears to be moving when clouds move across its path in the sky. The cause of the identity of "I AM" with the body, mind, and senses is ignorance of One's Real Nature. In its Real Nature, the Self is pure Consciousness and is Eternally unqualified with the characteristics of body, mind, and senses.

Some persons argue that daily practical experience indicates that *Ātman* is not merely a witness Self, but is a participant in activities of the daily life of an individual. This view is assumed only because of ignorance of the Real Nature of *Ātman* and *cittam*. The properties of *cittam* are superimposed on *Ātman*; hence *Ātman* appears to be passing through suffering, birth, and death. By analogy, one may say that the properties of clouds are superimposed on the moon, so that the moon seems to be moving when, relatively speaking, it is the clouds moving. Only knowledge of the Real Nature of the moon can dispel the illusion. So it is that only knowledge of the Real Nature of *Ātman* can free one from delusion.

Self is intelligent principle, pure Consciousness, pure Existence, and Reality. It is beyond material marks and characteristics, and free from the limitations of cause and effect, space and time, body and mind. No material change or activity, no thought or feeling, no pleasure or pain can reach to the realm of Self. It is *cittam* and not Self which is moving through pleasure and pain, etc.

Real Consciousness in association with *cittam* becomes something else such as national self, social self, domestic self, willing and thinking self, etc. All these are non-Self. On the happy and unhappy condition of *cittam*, the Self considers itself happy or unhappy in the same way that parents consider themselves lucky or unlucky, happy or unhappy in their children's successes or misfortunes. People suffer pain and enjoy pleasure in the relative plane because the experiencing Self in them has wrongly identified with the experienced objects.

## SUTRA NO. 19

आत्मचैतन्यमाश्रित्य देहेन्द्रियमनोधियः ।
स्वक्रियार्थेषु वर्तन्ते सूर्यालोकं यथा जनाः ॥१९॥

ĀTMACAITANYAMĀŚRITYA DEHENDRIYAMANODHIYAḤ.
SVAKRIYĀRTHEṢU VARTANTE SŪRYĀLOKAṀ YATHĀ JANĀḤ.

| | | |
|---|---|---|
| आत्म-चैतन्यम् | Ātma-caitanyam | I-Consciousness |
| आश्रित्य | Āśritya | Depending upon |
| देह-इन्द्रिय- | Deha-indriya | Body - senses- |
| मनो-धियः | Mano-dhiyaḥ | Mind-intellect |
| स्व-क्रियार्थेषु | Sva-kriyārtheṣu | In their respective activities |
| वर्तन्ते | Vartante | Operate |
| सूर्य-आलोकम् | Sūrya - ālokam | Light of the sun |
| यथा | Yathā | As |
| जनाः | Janāḥ | Men |

The body, senses, mind, ego, and super-ego operate in their respective functions because of the presence of the Self, I-Consciousness, just as men work in their respective fields in the presence of the light of the sun.

Body, senses, mind, ego, and intellect are engaged in their respective activities due to the magnetic influence of Consciousness, which is the intrinsic Nature of *Ātman*, just as all planets are in constant motion due to the magnetic gravitational force intrinsic to the sun. Planets borrow motion from the sun. Body, mind, and senses borrow Consciousness of *Ātman*. The motion of body, mind, and senses is unconscious, and it needs the guidance of conscious motion to reach a desired destination, just as the mighty but unconscious motion of an airplane needs the guidance of a pilot to reach an intended destination. There is thus a complementary relationship of the conscious guidance of *puruṣa* and the mighty power of unsconscious Nature. In the same way a crippled person with sight and a blind person with a whole body need each other's help.

As a plane left to its own motion will go into destruction, so does *cittam* left to its motion go into the suffering of birth and death.

A Self-analyst should understand clearly the union of the two energies. There is dualism of *puruṣa* and *prakṛti* in the relative plane, Although they are One in the Absolute sense. A meditator should try to unite them and lead his meditation from the relative to the Absolute. Understanding *puruṣa* will give not only liberation from suffering, but also the mastery of spiritual mind over matter and Nature.

Materialism, the philosophy that matter is the only reality, is the first obstacle in the way of Self-analysis. Matter seems to be the only reality because it alone is perceived. According to the materialistic viewpoint, the individual soul passes through birth and death, pain and pleasure. In this view, the Soul cannot be Eternal and changeless Reality. Birth and death, etc., belong to the individual body, not to the Soul.

## SUTRA NO. 20

देहेन्द्रियगुणान्कर्माण्यमले सच्चिदात्मनि ।
अध्यस्यन्त्यविवेकेन गगने नीलतादिवत् ॥२०॥

DEHENDRIYAGUṆĀNKARMĀṆYAMALE SACCIDĀTMANI.
ADHYASYANTYAVIVEKENA GAGANE NĪLATĀDIVAT.

| | | |
|---|---|---|
| देह-इन्द्रिय-गुणान् | Deha-indriya-guṇān | Qualities of body & senses |
| कर्माणि | Karmāṇi | Actions |
| अमले | Amale | Pure |
| सत्-चित्-आत्मनि | Sat-cit-ātmani | Self, pure Consciousness |
| अध्यस्यन्ति | Adhyasyanti | Superimpose |
| अविवेकेन | Avivekena | By lack of discrimination |
| गगने | Gagane | On the sky |
| नीलतादिवत् | Nīlatādivat | Blueness, etc. |

Due to ignorance of the Real Nature of the Self, one identifies the Self with the body, mind, and senses; and their activities are superimposed on the "I," which is pure Consciousness. This superimposition of the body on *Ātman*, "I," is similar to superimposition of blueness and concavity on the sky.

Having not perceived the Eternal Existence, knowledge, and Reality that is *Ātman*, the ignorant superimpose the material characteristics of the body on *Ātman*, just as blueness and concavity are imposed on the sky.

Dualism of Spirit and matter is inevitable in the relative plane.

The best way to escape dualism is to understand Self, and to eliminate the false identity of *prakṛti* and its products as *Ātman*. The Self does not contract or expand to occupy a smaller or larger body in which it is manifested. The Self is always All-pervasive, and is not limited to the body in which it is manifested. The relationship of mind, body, and Soul is so intimate that all mental phenomena are interpreted as experience of the Soul.

Our knowledge about the Universe and about our bodies is mere ideational picture and image. Phenomena, external things, are material in nature. Sense data and images of the mind are also material in characteristic because they arise from material things and are limited in their nature as are external things. The motion of sense data and images from the external world to the brain and the mind, and from the mind and brain to the external world, is called knowledge. Sense data and images come and go. They are prototypes and photographs of external things, composed of the subtlest matter.

Sense data and images of the mind could not appear as conscious if there were no Self, no principle of Consciousness, as the basic foundation of these images. *Ātman* is distinct from all these. It is a principle which has no change, no form, and which is like a beacon light to illumine the mute, pictorial panorama of the mind. The Self is Light. Although we speak of Self, we do not have a mental picture of ourselves as we have of other things; nevertheless, in all our knowledge, the Self is postulated, and we seem to know our Self. The Self cannot be found as an image of knowledge since it is an immanent, transcendent principle, which is behind and beyond the subtle matter of knowledge.

Our cognition, as long as it consists of mere forms of images, is simply compositions of subtle mind-substance, and thus is like a painted canvas surrounded by darkness. As the canvas is moved into the presence of light, images appear one by one as they are illuminated. So it is with our knowledge. The special characteristic of Self is that it is like a Light without which all Knowledge would be obscured.

Form and motion are characteristics of matter. As far as knowledge is only a limited form and movement of mind, it is the same as matter. These knowledge-forms are given life by virtue of the Conscious-principle, *Ātman*. The movement of matter occurs in the presence of this Self; thus, this Self must be identified. The material body and mind are illuminated as Consciousness by the Self, and they reflect all changes of knowledge and experience, material pleasure and pain, on the Self, in the same way as pictures are reflected on a screen. The screen itself goes through no change; only the pictures move, but without the screen they have no existence.

Each item of knowledge, in that it carries with it the awakening and enlivening of Consciousness, is the manifestation of the principle of Consciousness. Knowledge revelation is not an unveiling or revelation of a particular part of the Self; it is a revelation of the Self only as far as knowledge is pure awakening, pure enlivening, and pure Consciousness. The content and image of knowledge are not a revelation of the Self, but are a revelation of blind knowledge-stuff, which is matter. Self is beyond this revelation. A substance is not affected by the superimposition of other substances on it. As a rope does not become a snake by the mental projection of a snake upon it so *Ātman* is not affected by the superimposition of mind-body characteristics.

## SUTRA NO. 21

अज्ञानान्मानसोपाधेः कर्तृत्वादीनि चात्मनि ।
कल्प्यन्तेऽम्बुगते चन्द्रे चलनादि यथाम्भसः ॥२१॥

AJÑĀNĀN MĀNASOPĀDHEḤ KARTṚTVĀDĪNI CĀTMANI.
KALPYANTE' MBUGATE CANDRE CALANĀDI YATHĀMBHASAḤ.

| | | |
|---|---|---|
| अज्ञानात् | Ajñānāt | Due to ignorance |
| मानस-उपाधेः | Mānasa-upādheḥ | Of the limited mind |
| कर्तृत्वादीनि | Kārtṛtvādīni | Agency of actions, etc. |
| च | Ca | And |
| आत्मनि | Ātmani | On the Self |
| कल्प्यन्ते | Kalpyante | Are imagined, attributed |
| अम्बुगते | Ambu-gate | Reflected in the water |
| चन्द्रे | Candre | In the moon |
| चलनादि | Calanādi | Movements, agitations, etc. |
| यथा | Yathā | As |
| अम्भसः | Ambhasaḥ | Of the water |

Because of ignorance of the Real Nature of the Self, the functions of the body, mind, and senses are identified as those of the Self; thus, the condition of the body, mind, and senses is attributed to the Self, just as the movement of the moon's reflection in a river or the ocean is attributed to the moon instead of to the water.

Do notions such as "I am happy, I am unhappy"; and "I am doing this," indicate that *Ātman* is an active agent in all activities of life? Flowing water or a moving mirror may show by reflection an apparent motion of the sun or the moon. In reality, it is not the motion of the sun or moon which we see in the water or the mirror; it is the motion of the water and the mirror.

The sum and substance of the Universe is involved in the equation *Ātman* = *Brahman*. The word *Ātman* denotes the Ultimate Essence of the Universe. It also denotes life Energy, including the motions of breath and heart in man. The word *Brahman* is generally used to mean the Ultimate Essence of the Univese. The word *Ātman* generally denotes the inmost Essence of man. In the Ultimate sense the two are one and the same.

To investigate the inmost Essence, *Ātman* we cause the following media to reflect the Energy of *Ātman*.

1. *Annamaya Ātman*, the physical part of man;

2. *Prāṇamaya Ātman*, the vital breath and electro-magnetic part of man;

3. *Manomaya Ātman*, the conscious part of man;

4. *Vijñānamaya Ātman*, the intuitive part of man; and

5. *Ānandamaya Ātman*, the final Essence of man, the Blissful part of man, the Self which is pure Consciousness, Existence, Reality.

Fear is common experience. It can be removed only by analysis and realization of *Ātman*. The growing influence of fear indicates that man is neglecting to center his Existence in *Ātman*. The *Ātman*, free from hunger, thirst, sin, grief, old age, and death, whose desires and cognitions are true, that . . . is to be sought. He who knows the Self attains all worlds. All his desires are fulfilled.

The body is the center of manifestation of the deathless, bodiless Self in the same way as radio and television sets are the center of manifestation of the programs, which are present everywhere in the atmosphere. The embodied self is affected by pleasure and pain, etc. although these cannot touch the bodiless Self.

Due to our ignorance of Reality, characteristics of the body, mind and senses, and the *Ātman* are mutually superimposed. The property of matter is superimposed on *Ātman*, and the property of *Ātman* is superimposed on matter. *Ātman* pure Conscousness, the constant, changeless Essence of man, which is beyond the limits of subjective-objective phenomena, should be realized to overcome the subjective-objective psychosis.

The real and Ultimate Self is the Seer of All that is seen, the Hearer of All that is heard, and the Knower of All knowledge. It sees but is not seen, hears but is not heard, knows but is not known. The Self is the light of All lights. Bliss is not attributed to it; it is Bliss itself.

In meditation, a meditator realizes and examines all subjective phenomena as though they were objective phenomena; thus he has an opportunity to become aware of his mistakes and to correct them. A person may write subjective ideas; however, when he examines the writing, it is objective phenomena. Prior to writing, the ideas were subjective phenomena; after writing they have become objective phenomena, and the writer may be astonished to see mistakes in his own handwriting. In meditation, also, when the mind presents the state of conflict in inner life, one is amazed. Sometimes a person is terrified by the mental presentation, and may feel incredulous that this motion picture presented by the mind was once recorded by himself, and that he played the lead role in it.

The *Ātman* should be realized as limitless Existence. All limitation is full of pain. It is the Infinite alone that is highest Bliss. When a man receives this rapture, he is full of Bliss; for who could breathe, who could live, if that Bliss had not filled this Infinite *Ākāśam*, Ethereal Space. Man attains peace and Bliss when he recognizes this invisible support of All, the inexpressible *Ātman* as his own Self. Then his identification with the body and the material mind disappears.

The Self is nearer and dearer to us than any other relations, including our own body and mind. It is for it and by it that all relative manifestations, including body, mind, and all relations, appear near and dear to us. It is dearest, par excellence, our inmost *Ātman*.

In the state of *nirvānam* one realizes the supreme Bliss of *Ātman* as one's own Self, and the identification with a particular body and mind disappears from one's life. As long as one is not liberated and is in the relative plane, is there any logical or epistemological proof that birth and death, pain and pleasure, attachment and aversion belong to the body and mind, and not to one's inmost Essence, *Ātman*? The proof, which is realized and recognized in daily life by everyone, is explained in the next sloka.

## SUTRA NO. 22

रागेच्छासुखदुःखादि बुद्धौ सत्यां प्रवर्तते ।
सुषुप्तौ नास्ति तन्नाशे तस्माद्बुद्धेस्तु नात्मनः ॥२२॥

RĀGECCHĀSUKHADUḤKHĀDI BUDDHAU SATYĀṀ PRAVARTATE.
SUṢUPTAU NĀSTI TANNĀŚE TASMĀD BUDDHES TU NĀTMANAḤ.

| | | |
|---|---|---|
| राग-इच्छा- | Rāga-icchā | Attachment - desire- |
| सुख-दुःखादि | Sukha-duḥkhādi | Pleasure-pain-etc. |
| बुद्धौ सत्याम् | Buddhau satyām | When Intellect functions |
| प्रवर्तते | Pravartate | Exist |
| सुषुप्तौ | Suṣuptau | In deep sleep |
| न अस्ति | Na asti | Is not |
| तत्-नाशे | Tat-nāśe | At disappearance of it |
| तस्मात् | Tasmāt | Therefore |
| बुद्धेः | Buddheḥ | Of Intellect (Conscious Mind) |
| तु | Tu | Only |
| न | Na | Not |
| आत्मनः | Ātmanaḥ | Of the Self |

Attachment, detachment, love, hatred, pain, and pleasure are the products of mindstuff. They are born with the mind, they grow with the mind, and they disappear when the mindstuff disappears, as in dreamless sleep; therefore they belong to mindstuff and not to *Ātman*, Self, which is immanent, transcendent, and All-pervading.

Material attachment and detachment, happiness and unhappiness, pain and pleasure belong to *buddhi* (*cittam*), and not to *Ātman*, for in deep sleep, when the mind goes into potential existence, they are not perceived. If they belonged to *Ātman*, they would not cease to exist because *Ātman* is ever awake, ever existent. Disturbance of deep sleep is a great error. The enlightened person needs little sleep—because his mind is always resting.

There are two types of contact:

1. *Ordinary*, external, superficial, superimposed, and temporary, which can be removed and changed as easily as a man changes clothing. Clothing is in ordinary contact and can be removed or changed, or a man can live without clothing;

2. *Extra-ordinary*, internal, real, inherent, and Eternal contact, which cannot be removed or changed. To remove or change this type of contact would destroy one's whole existence. By analogy, heat and light have inherent contact with the sun. This is Eternal and cannot be changed. Heat and light are the intrinsic Nature of fire. To change them would mean the annihilation of fire.

The body, senses, and mind are not in extraordinary contact with *Ātman* because they are discarded at the time of death. Within any twenty-four hours, the mental and physical states also change. If mind-body phenomena such as pain and pleasure had essential contact with *Ātman*, as heat and light have with the sun, they could remain with *Ātman*; but psychological experience tells us that mental and physical states are changing. In sound sleep, *Ātman* exists, but mental phenomena do not; therefore, pain and pleasure, birth and death, belong inherently to the mind and body; but mind and body and all their phenomena are not inherently related to *Ātman*. Existence belongs to *Ātman*; hence it is continual with *Ātman* even in sound sleep. In sound sleep a man is not dead, but continues to exist; hence existence is intrinsic in *Ātman*.

In the state of anesthesia, pain is removed by anesthetic chemicals. The association of pain with psychic Energy is disconnected by disintegration of the sensation of pain from the body to the central nervous system. The ordinary examples of sedatives, tranquilizers, hypnotic, and anesthetic drugs indicate that pain and suffering belong to the physical existence of the body. The *Ātman* is beyond physical characteristics. When the whole body is in a state of trance, *samādhi*, every tissue is anesthetized to external and internal pain by the power of mind. By the electronic motion of *tanmātras*, all *karmas* are nullified and consumed. A man becomes free from mental and physical diseases and realizes the Blissful, shining, serene Nature of *Ātman*.

## SUTRA NO. 23

प्रकाशोऽर्कस्य तोयस्य शैत्यमग्नेर्यथोष्णता ।
स्वभावः सच्चिदानन्दनित्यनिर्मलतात्मनः ॥२३॥

PRAKĀŚO' RKASYA TOYASYA ŚAITYAM AGNER YATHOṢṆATĀ.
SVABHĀVAḤ SACCIDĀNANDANITYANIRMALATĀTMANAḤ.

| | | |
|---|---|---|
| प्रकाशः | Prakāśaḥ | Light |
| अर्कस्य | Arkasya | Of the sun |
| तोयस्य | Toyasya | Of water |
| शैत्यम | Śaityam | Coolness |
| अग्नेः | Agneḥ | Of fire |
| यथा | Yathā | As |
| उष्णता | Uṣṇatā | Heat |
| स्वभावः | Svabhāvaḥ | Intrinsic nature |
| सत-चित-आनन्द- | Sat-cit-ānanda- | Reality, Consciousness-Bliss |
| नित्य- | Nitya- | Eternity |
| निर्मलता- | Nirmalatā- | Purity |
| आत्मनः | Ātmanaḥ | Of the self |

As the Nature of the sun is light, the Nature of water is liquidity and coldness, and the Nature of fire is heat, so the Real Nature of the Self is Eternal Existence-Consciousness-Bliss.

The inherent Nature of *Ātman* is Existence, Consciousness, Reality, Eternity, purity, and Bliss, just as light is the intrinsic characteristic of the sun, as liquidity is intrinsic of water, and heat is intrinsic of fire.

Self-analysis is based on intuitive experience. It is beyond logical reasoning, although it does not contradict logic. It is the source of logical thinking. All willing, feeling, thinking, and reasoning originate from intuition. Intuition should not be confused with fanciful imagination, which is sometimes contrary to reason. Intuition is the direct perception of Reality and does not need logic. We need reasoning and inference when we proceed from a known sign to an unknown reality. For example, after seeing smoke, by use of reasoning, we infer the existence of fire; but to use smoke to prove the existence of fire, when fire is directly perceived, is a form of insanity. Logic is not needed in direct perception. Intuition is direct perception of Reality.

Everyone has direct and positive experience of that "I AM" on which depends all transactions of life. No one experiences "I am not." Does anyone need to prove logically that "I AM"? All logical thinking depends on "I AM" or the Self, but "I AM" does not depend on logic; for in dreamless sleep the mind with its logic is absent, but "I AM," or Self, is present always.

When the relationship between an effect and its material cause is carefully examined, one finds intuitively that the effect is nothing but an extension of its cause. Intuitive perception cannot show in a clay pot anything other than clay, nor in a gold ring anything other than gold. From the viewpoint of intuitive experience, it is unreasonable to think that the effect, the thing now produced, was absent before. Potentially it was always there in its material cause. Substance is changed from one form to another, but there is no annihilation of reality of the substance. The change is only in *nāma* and *rūpa*, name and form, not in the existing reality behind these names and forms.

Without understanding this principle, that nothing which did not exist previously can come into existence, one's further efforts toward Self-analysis will be fruitless. One must be prepared to accept all that logically and epistemologically follows from it. This theory is called *satkāryavāda*.

From the theory of *satkāryavāda* we come to know that matter and energy can be neither created nor destroyed, but they can be changed into various names and forms. This does not imply a change in reality. Self-analysts do not deny the perception of multiplicity of names and forms, but they do question the interpretation of the perception and its logical and philosophical significance.

A closer examination indicates that names and forms are nothing but another aspect and state of reality, and that they cannot be separated from reality even in part. They have no reality of their own, nor can any change in name and form transcend reality; hence the perception of multiplicity of names and forms cannot be interpreted as a change of reality. On the contrary, in spite of changes of name and form, a substance is recognized as an identical entity. For example, an individual entity passing through the various names and forms of infant, child, youth, adolescent, and oldster is recognized as an identical person. How would psychological identification be possible if the changes of name and form meant changes of reality? Therefore, the law of causality does not imply any change in reality. The panorama of the world is appearance only, like the appearance of a snake where there is only a rope, and cannot alter Reality, the *Ātman*. Our interpretation of the perception of change is a mental projection on reality. Our ignorance regarding the Nature of reality admits the perception of things that do not really exist.

From the viewpoint of Self-analysis, the following terms should be clearly understood: 1) Substance; 2) Quality; 3) Action; 4) Being; 5) Becoming; 6) Phenomenological phase; and 7) Existential phase. This may be called the philosophical existential approach.

A substance, *dravyam*, is that in which quality and action can exist inherently. Quality and action have no separate existence; they exist only in a substance. A thing must exist if it is to have any quality or action belonging to it. A substance is the substratum of quality and action, and it is the constitutive and material cause of other composite things produced from it. When a substance depends on something else, it is called compound.

A quality, by qualifying a substance, enlarges the meaning and narrows the application of the substance. Enlargement of meaning is necessarily accompanied by narrowing of application. This is a vital point in philosophy; for example, consider the word: "cow"; as long as its meaning remains unmodified, as long as no quality is indicated and added to it, "cow" can then be applied to an almost countless number of individual animals called by the general name of cow; but if we speak of a red cow, the meaning is amplified so that it has a limited application to red cows only. Observe that when we enlarge the meaning of cow by adding the red quality, we do not alter the meaning of cow. Red cow means all that cow means and more besides; but its application becomes narrow and limited to only one class of cows.

Thus we come to the conclusion that every determination is negation, every quality predicated of any substance is a sort of limitation imposed on it. In theistic language, it means that to predicate quality to God is to limit God; hence, from the real standpoint, God, the Ultimate substance, is indeterminate and cannot be described by any positive qualification. Indeterminate *Brahman*, when described by any positive qualification such as omnipresent, omniscient, and omnipotent, becomes the lower *Brahman*, God.

Substance has two categories: 1) Eternal, which is non-produced; and 2) Non-eternal, which is produced.

Anything which is the bearer of some quality is a substance. According to this definition of substance, a clay jar or a gold ring is substance; but from the practical viewpoint, we know that the quality of a jar or a ring has no separate existence from the jar or the ring; and also that the jar and the ring have no reality apart from their cause, the clay and the gold—which are the real substance. The jar and the ring are only forms of modification; however, as even clay and gold are liable to modification, but do not cease to remain clay and gold, neither of them can be called real substance. They are only more abiding forms of manifestation of some other substance, which persists through all modifications of clay and gold.

This substance is also present in the origin of clay and gold, and is present in what they become after dissolution. If all so-called substances are thus liable to modification, then the substance underlying all objects of the world would be that which persists through all forms of objects. Pure and simple existence, not of specific form, is the only substance which is common to all modifications and forms of objects. It is revealed in the perception of every phenomenon, whatever its nature. It can therefore be called the Ultimate and real substance, the material cause, and the central foundation underlying the reality of the phenomenal world.

Existence is common to all mental and physical states. Behind the changing states of mind and body, every state, idea, and image has its existence. Even an illusory perception, which presents difficulty in rational explanation, exists as an idea in the mind of the perceiver. Existence is thus one fundamental reality which stands through all internal and external, subjective and objective phenomena. The term "existence" comes from a Latin root, *ex sistere*, meaning literally: "to stand." It is real substance, existing eternally. All determinate subjects, objects, mental states, and other phenomena are its diverse manifestations.

There is relative existence and there is Pure, Absolute Existence. Pure Existence is the central Reality behind all subjective and objective, internal and external phenomena. It is without name and form—though appearing in various forms, unpartitioned and not partitionable—though all phenomenal parts and dimensions depend on it. It is infinite—though it appears in all finite forms. It is essence though it appears to precede essence. This Infinite, indeterminate Existence is the essence and material center of the entire phenomenal world. It is called *Brahman*.

Is this Absolute Existence conscious or unconscious? First we need to know the meaning, the nature, and the criterion of consciousness. A mental state is conscious, because its existence is self-revealing. When we perceive objectivity, its existence also reveals itself. The internal and external, subjective and objective, mental and material states have the power of appearing; thus Absolute Existence is of the Nature of Self-revealing Consciousness. By virtue of Self-revelation, Existence is distinguished from non-existence. Whatever is non-existent cannot appear and reveal Itself.

Two questions naturally arise: 1) Are there objects which exist, but do not appear; and 2) Are there objects which appear, but do not exist?

There are no objects which exist, but do not appear; however, the existence or appearance of subtle substance is hidden from an ignorant person. This is a defect in the perceiver; it is not non-appearance. Existence and appearance are identical; one cannot be found without the other. Subtle objects exist, but are not perceived by ignorant persons. Ignorance accounts for the non-perception of Real Existence.

As wherever there is appearance, Existence is inevitable, so wherever there is Existence, Awareness is inevitable. Consciousness is present in every appearance and existence; thus, appearance, Existence, and Awareness cannot be separated from one another; they are identical. The appearance of an external object is possible only through an awareness of it. When we perceive gold in a ring, our "gold" Consciousness forms into "ring" Consciousness. An imaginary object is just the idea of the object; therefore, it is an illusory object. Consciousness or Awareness pervades all forms of phenomenal Existence.

According to the philosophical existential approach, as the intrinsic Nature of the sun is light, so the intrinsic Nature of *Ātman* is Absolute Existence, Absolute Consciousness, Absolute Reality, and Bliss. The world orignates from it by apparent change. *Brahman* manifests itself in diverse apparent entities without undergoing any modification in its essential Nature.

Constant changes occur in the process of being and becoming, but they cannot transcend Existence. *Brahman* is present as the central nucleus in all mental and material, internal and external, subjective and objective phenomena, although these phenomena vary in their forms.

In the realm of relativity, every higher experience reduces lower experience to the point of unreality. For example, dream experiences are contradicted by waking experiences. In the realm of Absolute Reality, regardless of contradictions among the different forms, Ultimate Existence, *Brahman*, remains uncontradicted, but it contradicts all forms of relativity. In denying illusory dreams, we do not deny the existing reality behind them, which is the cause of dream phenomena; likewise, when *Yogins* deny the world of multiplicity passing through cause and effect, space and time, they do so on the basis of the perception of Ultimate Existence, *Brahman*; hence Existence is inconceivable to the mind passing through cause and effect, space and time, for it is beyond the mechanism of causality. The Cosmic Existence, Consciousness, is the only Reality changing in us, and what is that which is never changing. From Existence, *pāramārthika Sattva.*

Let us examine practically what is that which is constantly changing in us, and what is that which is never changing. From morning awakening until evening, the body, sensations, and mentations are constantly changing; but consciousness exists behind them without change. At night we sleep; sleep may be shallow, and with dreaming or deep without perception of subject or object worlds. The three modes of the world in time are past, present, and future; and the three modes of the world in person are the waking person, the dreamer, and the deep sleeper. Every process of being and becoming in the three modes of the world is supplanted by a higher contradictory experience. No definite and particular form of existence of the three modes of the world will remain permanently; none can transcend the possibility of contradiction. Ultimate Reality alone is that which persists Eternally, beyond the process of being and becoming.

It is real, simple existence that includes all conditional existences and transcends all. Steadfast continuance and pervasion are the criteria of existence.

Contradiction is 1) experiential and 2) logical. When the perception of a snake in a rope is contradicted by a higher perception of it as a rope, it is experiential contradiction. The substance of a jar and a house exclude, falsify, and contradict each other. According to the criterion of reality, logically, both a jar and a house are inconsistent with the nature of reality, although the perception of a jar is not experientially contradicted by the perception of the house. It is only simple Existence, *Ātman* which is uncontradicted experientially and logically.

There are three types of differences: 1) *Sajātīya bheda*, the difference of one entity from others in the same class, as a cow is differentiated from other cows; 2) *Vijātīya bheda*, when an entity is differentiated from others in a different class, such as a cow is distinguished from a horse; and 3) *Svāgata bheda* difference in the same entity, such as a head is different from the legs in the same cow.

Simple existence is beyond these differences. Pure Existence is non-partite, indivisible, unique, One-without-a-second.

Phenomenal existence precedes the essence, and it is experienceable in different forms in different conditions. The change in perception, and the consequent contradiction by a higher perception, makes every relative existence representative of real Existence. We can never be ultimately certain in relativity that what exists as a jar or a house will not exist otherwise later on. A man cannot be said, therefore, to exist permanently as a man. He will positively exist but, due to changing conditions of his existence, he may exist as God in the Absolute sense. He who perceives all existence in one existence, and one existence in all existences is happy eternally.

Physical existentialism has the character of applied science rather than pure science. It is fundamentally a basic unit and medium of Self-analysis. The quest starts from this point. We are doomed to failure if we search for Absolute answers in conditional existence. Every branch of science or philosophy has to go beyond its own limits for Absolute answers to its problems.

Psychological existentialism has the character of pure science. From the viewpoint of experimentation, first we perceive physical existence, then psychological existence, and ultimately metaphysical Existence.

Our present analysis will be limited to the fundamental structure of man and the human mind. Systematic Self-analysis presents a relationship between and a union of, multiplicity in all levels of Existence, just as we see a relationship between the practical and theoretical aspects of science in all fields. This yields penetrating understanding and far-reaching consequences in the progress of Self-knowledge.

In spite of innumerable incarnations, the mind has lost nothing.

On the contrary, its powers are everlasting. We have to focus our attention and concentrate our Consciousness only on the Existence, the understanding, and the underlying substance of individual structure; hence we have to analyze man as an entity, not in fragmentary aspects. The analysis of man will be incomplete if his past and future incarnations are disregarded, just as the treatment of a mentally ill patient will be ineffective if his past history and future plans are kept out of medical discussion. By logical and philosophical inference, the past, the present, and future incarnations become known to the Self-analyst, although they are hidden and unknown to the beginner. The knowledge of past life, and the consequences of actions of the present life on a future life become beacon lights in Self-analysis to obtain Self-knowledge, *Nirvāṇam*.

The existential approach springs up spontaneously in higher meditation, and it leads instantaneously to final liberation.

Man is something more than a collection of cells, tissues, organs, and systems, and he is in the process of emerging from envelopment in matter. Man is one thing one moment, and will become something else in the next moment. This process of being and becoming presents a dynamic approach in Self-analysis, in the study of individual existence and its extension. It cannot be understood without the profound knowledge of cause and effect, space and time. The mechanism of causality is the mother of being and becoming. Closer observation shows that the separation of subjective man from objective nature is an illusion because the objective natural product, when assimilated by man, becomes identical with the subject. A man eats food, for example; the man is the subject—and the food is the object, but is not this man the product of food eaten in the past?

To see a man as purely subject or purely object is an extreme view. The middle path, being and becoming, should be accepted in Self-analysis in relativity. A student is aware of his own existence, which distinguishes his being from other beings.

In the analysis of being and becoming from the existential viewpoint, man and human mind will be considered. No one has seen the mind as an objective entity, but it is logically and philosophically inferred from man's behavior as the central organ of thinking. Man is accepted as being although there is no pure being in relativity. Philosophically, the conditional world is pure becoming, but every process of becoming is accepted as being. Ultimate Reality is pure being, while relativity is pure becoming.

The analysis of being and becoming cannot be accomplished without knowledge of ontology, the science of being. A student has to accept his own existence, his being and becoming. His Ultimate Existence is unknown to him, but his phenomenal existence on critical examination splits into two parts. He should investigate the whole of Existence as an impartial judge, a pure witness. His phenomenal existence, mind and body including the sensory and motor organs, is present with him. He is like a physician who will cure the body and mind of physical and mental diseases.

This being is present in time, space, and person, Cause and effect will operate on his being to produce becoming. A self-conscious body is a particular point in time and space, and it is responsbile for receiving and transmitting his existence, his presence.

The term: "being" is a gerund, a verbal noun from the infinitive: "to be," ending in "-ing," implying always that the person, the individual, is in the process of becoming something. A being is neither a static substance, nor a permanent entity, nor an unchanging unit, but it should be understood in Self-analysis to mean *potentia*, the source of potentiality. Being is the potentiality by which a seed becomes a tree, and an infant becomes a man or woman. Being is a dynamic process.

To study human mind, we have to study the motion and actions of human beings and human bodies. Mind is only a bundle of thoughts.

*Karma*, action, and motion are physical movement. Physical movement belongs to substance. Motion, or *karma*, is that which resides in substance, and is the direct and immediate cause of the dynamism of being and becoming, of conjunction and disjunction. A substance is the support of both quality and actions. Quality is the static character of things, and action is the dynamic.

Quality is a passive property that does not take us beyond the thing to which it belongs. Action is a transitive process by which one thing reaches another, by which one thing becomes something else.

Actions and motions are innumerable, but all may be classified into five groups: 1) *Utkṣepaṇam*, moving upward; 2) *Avakṣepaṇam*, moving downward; 3) *Ākuñcanam*, centripetal and contractive motions; 4) *Prasāraṇam*, centrifugal and expansive motions; and 5) *Gamanam*, movement in general locomotion.

A student can understand the motion of his mind, and the mind of others, by observing the motion and action of the body in space, by seeing what he is moving toward, and what he is becoming. He can understand himself only as he projects his potentialities in motion and action.

Another distinctive aspect of a higher living-being, especially a human being, is that in addition to automatic unfolding, as a tree from a seed, it has a conscious mechanism of unfolding and discovering, which is called Self-Consciousness. A student must become aware of himself as a particular being, if he is to become a higher being.

This brings the multiplicity of Self-consciousness; by understanding it, further progress is possible. Self-analysis is not the process of adding something to the body and mind, like adding clothing to the body to protect it from cold and rain. It is a process of becoming, unfolding, discovering. It implies a necessary change in being to become something else. Many students fail in Self-analysis because they want to obtain Self-knowledge as a foreign addition to Self-consciousness without changing their fundamental behavior and character. A tree will not come out of a seed if the seed remains unchanged and unsprouted; likewise, the attainment of Self-knowledge will be impossible unless necessary change, action and motion are produced in the pre-existing being. In short, no being is Absolute in its present form.

Lack of the knowledge of the process of being and becoming brings fear of non-being and non-becoming, that is, the fear of dying. One is in process of constant birth and death. Old phenomena are passing, and new phenomena are arriving; the fear of annihilation, or nothingness, indicates ignorance, yet everyone sometimes feels this fear. Two distinct feelings are running parallel, the feeling of mortality and the feeling of immortality. The logical and ontological explanation is that the fear of death and nothingness comes because of one's identification with material being and becoming in which one ignorantly lives. The feeling of immortality comes as a result of identification with Spiritual being and becoming, which one knowingly is.

At any moment an individual may cease to exist because death may inescapably arrive for him. This is the fundamental experience of material being and becoming. Without this experience, no one would go into a deeper state of Self-analysis. Man is personalized, and he has to reach the impersonal state to overcome the fear of nothingness. With the Consciousness of his being in the future, he has a vital interest in investigation of his Real Existence, and in experiencing the heightened Consciousness of enlightenment. Even a skeptic, a doubter, who believes nothing, has his being and becoming as a pre-existing fact. Everyone feels, "I am." No one feels "I am not."

Anxiety, fear, guilt, frustration, depression, feelings of hopeless-

ness and helplessness, and others are ontological characteristics of the material being and becoming of man, rooted in his material existence, and they cannot be checked without turning the wheel of being and becoming from materiality to Spirituality. Anxiety, fear, and these other feelings are not foreign attributes to man; they are inherent in his material existence. They are always a threat to the foundation, the center of his existence. They are his experiencing of the threat of non-being; anxiety, fear, guilt are not something we have, but something we mentally are. They are the subjective experience of a being facing the impending threat of non-being, the feeling of annihilation of our very existence.
subjective experience of a being facing the impending threat of non-being, the feeling of annihilation of our very existence.

As are anxiety, guilt, fear, and other feelings inherent in the material being and becoming, so are enlightenment, immortality, awakening, and fearlessness inherent in Spiritual being and becoming.

These feelings of anxiety, fear, guilt, frustration, depression, hopelessness and helplessness, ontologically are the state of one's becoming aware that one's Existence can become lost, that one can lose one's Self and one's World, that one can become nothing. A person cannot stand outside anxiety and other feelings, which are a threat to a person's very existence.

Man can transcend material being and becoming, and by so doing, he can transcend the immediate impending situations and suffering. *Yogins* have tremendous capacity to bring the past of many incarnations into the present, and similarly to bring the long-term future into the present, as a guide to enlighten the present existence.

Owing to the ignorance of his real Nature, the beginning of which cannot be specified, the individual erroneously identifies with the material being and becoming. In this state he forgets that his essential Existence is *Brahman*. He behaves like a finite, limited, miserable being, pursuing worldly objects, feeling pleased to obtain them, and regretting to lose them.

Identifying himself with being and becoming, he feels, "I am happy, I am unhappy, I have done this, and I shall do that, I am ignorant, I am intelligent, I have conquered this enemy, and I shall conquer others in the future." Thus the Self is confused with what is generally termed the function of the ego. The ego is part of nature; it is limited and opposes itself to the rest of existence. The whole concept of ego, indeed, is rooted directly in the subject-object dichotomy, while the Real Existence, *Brahman*, is beyond subjective-objective phenomena. The ego is not, therefore, the Real Self, but is only an apparent limitation of it. *Ahaṁkāra*, ego, is not *Aham*, I, but it is the instrument of *Aham*.

If essential and Real Existence is beyond the subject-object dichotomy of our times, then how is the subject set over against the objective world? How does one say, "I know"? If Real Existence is prior to the dichotomy of subject and object, then how does it split into the subject-object dichotomy, while yet remaining beyond them?

## SUTRA NO. 24

आत्मनः सच्चिदंशश्च बुद्धेर्वृत्तिरिति द्वयम्।
संयोज्य चाविवेकेन जानामीति प्रवर्तते ॥२४॥

ĀTMANAḤ SACCIDANŚAŚ CA BUDDHER VṚTTIR ITI DVAYAM.
SAMYOJYA CĀVIVEKENA JĀNĀMĪTI PRAVARTATE.

| | | |
|---|---|---|
| आत्मनः | Ātmanaḥ | Of the Self |
| सत्-चित्-अंशः | Sat-cit-anśaḥ | The existence-knowledge aspect |
| च | Ca | And |
| बुद्धेः | Buddheḥ | Of the intellect |
| वृत्तिः | Vṛttiḥ | Movement |
| इति | Iti | Thus |
| द्वयम् | Dvayam | The two |
| संयोज्य | Samyojya | Blending, having united |
| च | Ca | And |
| अविवेकेन | Avivekena | Due to indiscrimination |
| जानामि | Jānāmi | "I know" |
| इति | Iti | Thus |
| प्रवर्तते | Pravartate | Operates |

In the relative world, the thought, "I know," is produced by the union of modifications of the mindstuff with two aspects of the Self, Existence and Consciousness. This union is the product of non-discrimination between the Self and not-self.

When the Existence and Consciousness of *Ātman* are united with the dynamics of perceptual mechanisms, such an idea of subject-object dichotomy as "I know it," is produced in the relative plane due to ignorance of the real Nature of *Brahman*.

Consciousness-Existence of *Ātman* is reflected in the perceptual mechanism, *Buddhi*, and thus becomes limited by conditions of the body and *cittam*. The senses and *cittam*, mind-ego-intellect, become instruments through which Consciousness splits into the dichotomy of subject and object.

Consciousness becomes limited by subject-object phenomena. Such empirical, finite knowledge is of two types:

1. Immediate or direct (without intervening medium), and

2. Mediate or indirect (involving an intermediate agency.)

Immediate knowledge of external objects arises when *cittam*, mindstuff goes into contact with objects through the sensory organs, and *cittam* is modified into the form of the object, and the light of *puruṣa* is reflected in it. This reflection of the Consciousness of *Ātman* with modification of *cittam* produces the subject-object dichotomy such as "I know." Examples of mediate are inference, testimony, comparison, and image formation.

Real Existence, *Ātman*, remains forever unattached to the dichotomy of subject and object. This union is phenomenal only, and is a case of non-discrimination and illusory superimposition. Union of *Ātman* and *cittam* is as impossible as union of light and darkness.

Individual consciousness, subjective-objective knowledge, can be imagined metaphorically as a reflection of Infinite Consciousness on the finite mirror of *cittam*. As reflections depend on the condition of the reflecting substance such as a mirror or water—that is, reflections vary according to the media—so the reflection of Infinite Consciousness varies according to the condition of *cittam*. Purification of *cittam* through meditation is the means of obtaining Realization of and Union of *Brahman* with *cittam*.

## SUTRA NO. 25

आत्मनो विक्रिया नास्ति बुद्धेर्बोधो न जात्विति।
जीवः सर्वमलं ज्ञात्वा ज्ञाता द्रष्टेति मुह्यति ॥२५॥

ĀTMANO VIKRIYĀ NĀSTI BUDDHER BODHO NA JĀTVITI.
JĪVAḤ SARVAṀ ALAM JÑĀTVĀ JÑĀTĀ DRAṢṬETI MUHYATI.

| | | |
|---|---|---|
| आत्मनः | Ātmanaḥ | Of the Self |
| विक्रिया | Vikriyā | Action, change |
| न | Na | Not |
| अस्ति | Asti | Is |
| बुद्धेः | Buddheḥ | Of the intellect (mind-stuff) |
| बोधः | Bodhaḥ | Knowledge, understanding |
| न | Na | Not |
| जातु | Jātu | At all |
| इति | Iti | Thus |
| जीवः | Jīvaḥ | The individual self |
| सर्वम् | Sarvam | All |
| अलम् | Alam | Enough |
| ज्ञात्वा | Jñātvā | Having known |
| ज्ञाता | Jñātā | The knower |
| द्रष्टा | Draṣṭā | The seer |
| इति | Iti | Thus |
| मुह्यति | Muhyati | Is deluded |

The Self, "I," never undergoes change, but mindstuff never remains changeless. *Ātman* is Consciousness, but mind-stuff is never endowed with Consciousness. The Consciousness in mind-stuff is nothing but a reflection of the Self. The individual self, because of ignorance of this reflection, feels the Self to be identical with the body and mind-stuff, and believes himself to be the seer and the knower.

*Cittam* never becomes pure Consciousness. *Brahman* and pure Consciousness never undergo any change; but human consciousness believes *Ātman* to be identical with *cittam*, and falls under such notions as that the individual is the subject, and the world is the object. Dichotomy of subject and object cannot produce any change in the Nature of real Existence, *Ātman*.

Pure Consciousness, *Ātman*, is reflected through the mechanism of *Buddhi* without undergoing any change, in the same way as the sun is reflected in water or in a mirror without undergoing any change. The perceptual mechanism, *Buddhi*, is like a mirror; it is unconscious principle. It reflects Consciousness without being Consciousness. Due to this juxtaposition and mutual reflection of *Ātman* and *Buddhi*, it is so difficult to discriminate beteen the two that the unenlightned *jīva* is confused, and understands himself to be the agent and performer of activities. This activity is very similar to programs seen on a television screen. The electronic vibration of energy has power to imitate performers or speakers; when we see a performer or speaker on television, we have no doubt about who is acting, although everyone knows that what we see is not really the man, but only the electronic vibration which has assumed the form of the actor; likewise, the mind has power to imitate and to assume the form of *Puruṣa*, Self. Being unaware of this fact, the ignorant person is confused, and he superimposes the activity of wisdom on Consciousness.

Results of false and true identification are described in the following sloka.

## SUTRA NO. 26

रज्जुसर्पवदात्मानं जीवं ज्ञात्वा भयं वहेत्।
नाहं जीवः परात्मेति ज्ञातञ्चेन्निर्भयो भवेत्॥२६॥

RAJJUSARPAVAD ĀTMĀNAṀ JĪVAṀ JÑĀTVĀ BHAYAṀ VAHET.
NĀHAṀ JĪVAḤ PARĀTMETI JÑĀTAÑ CENNIRBHAYO BHAVET.

| | | |
|---|---|---|
| रज्जु-सर्पवत् | Rajju-sarpavat | Like a serpent in a rope |
| आत्मानम् | Ātmānam | The Self |
| जीवम् | Jīvam | Individual self (body, etc.) |
| ज्ञात्वा | Jñātvā | Having understood |
| भयम् | Bhayam | Fear |
| वहेत् | Vahet | Is overcome (by) |
| न | Na | Not |
| अहम् | Aham | I |
| जीवः | Jīvaḥ | Individual self |
| परात्मा | Parātmā | Supreme Self |
| इति | Iti | Thus |
| ज्ञातम् | Jñātam | It is known |
| चेत् | Cet | If |
| निर्भयः | Nirbhayaḥ | Fearless |
| भवेत् | Bhavet | Becomes |

As in semi-darkness a rope may be mistaken for a serpent, so, in the darkness of ignorance, this Self, I, is understood to be the body. As in proper light the true form of the rope is realized, and the fear of a serpent disappears, so in true cognition of the Self, the self of the individual is realized as identical with the Universal Self. On this realization one's fear of birth and death disappears.

Because human consciousness identifies with *cittam*, the perceptual mechanism understands itself to be individual soul, and is therefore suffering from anxiety, fear, guilt, etc. Just so, a man, who mistakes a rope for a snake, experiences fear and anxiety. When human consciousness overcomes the delusion of individuality and identifies itself as Pure Existence, *Brahman*, it regains fearlessness and freedom from bondage.

When human consciousness follows the motion of *cittam* toward its objects through sensory organs, it comes into contact with the objective world. This contact produces a mighty wave of desire in driving forces to have that object. This wave of desire has one of two results: either it may have that object, or it may not have that object. In either case, the result will be anger and anxiety. In having that object, human consciousness will try to possess the object absolutely and permanently. This is an impossibility in the world of relativity. On not having that object, human consciousness will feel lack and this will cause anger and anxiety. Anger and anxiety will cause delusion, folly, and unreasoning emotion, which in turn will cause loss of memory and loss of knowledge. Loss of memory and knowledge will bring impending ruin to *cittam*, which will present the threat of annihilation to human consciousness.

When human consciousness identifies with Pure Existence, *Ātman*, its identification with *cittam* gradually disappears. It identifies with Pure Existence, which includes the entire subject-object dichotomy, and transcends all. It become complete in itself in every respect.

*Jīva*, individual consciousness, is overpowered by fear and anxiety because it understands itself to be the product of causality, and is conscious of the duality of subject and object, and of the Creator, God. As long as man does not overcome this dualism by meditation, and does not identify with Absolute Existence, he will remain in the clutches of fear, anxiety, and death. Even the slightest difference between him and real Existence will be enough to maintain him in the state of fear. He, who understands himself as separate from *Brahman*, does not understand the real Nature of Self-realization and liberation. In the relative sense he is an individual, but in Reality he is indivisible from *Ātman*; hence his fear is groundless, and is due to non-realization of *Brahman*.

When individual consciousness attains identity with Pure Consciousness, dualism disappears, and one attains everlasting peace. The Self-luminous *Ātman* manifests all subjective and objective worlds, but cannot Itself be manifested by them.

## SUTRA NO. 27

आत्मावभासयत्येको बुद्ध्यादीनीन्द्रियाण्यपि।
दीपो घटादिवत्स्वात्मा जडैस्तैर्नावभास्यते ॥२७॥

ĀTMĀVABHĀSAYATYEKO BUDDHYĀDĪNĪNDRIYĀNYAPI.
DĪPO GHAṬĀDIVAT SVĀTMĀ JAḌAIS TAIR NĀVABHĀSYATE.

| | | |
|---|---|---|
| आत्मा | Ātmā | The Self |
| अवभासयति | Avabhāsayati | Illumines |
| एकः | Ekaḥ | Single, alone |
| बुद्ध्यादीनि | Buddhyādīni | Intellect, mind, etc. |
| इन्द्रियाणि | Indriyāṇi | Senses |
| अपि | Api | Also |
| दीपः | Dīpaḥ | A lamp |
| घटादिवत् | Ghaṭādivat | Like pots, etc. |
| स्वात्मा | Svātmā | Own Self |
| जडैः तैः | Jaḍaiḥ Taiḥ | By them, being inert |
| न | Na | Not |
| अवभास्यते | Avabhāsyate | Is illumined |

As the sun alone illumines all the planets, so the Self alone reveals all activities of the body, mind, and senses. As the sun cannot be illumined by the planets, so the Self cannot be revealed by the activities of the inert body, mind, and senses.

Self-luminous *Ātman* alone illumines *cittam*, mind-ego-intellect, the sensory and motor organs of the subjective world, and the phenomena of the objective world, but it cannot be manifested by them. It can be seen by its own light in the same way as the sun illuminates all subjective and objective phenomena of the world, but itself cannot be manifested by any light other than its own.

"By what power, willed and directed, does the mind project its light on objects? By what power commanded does *prāṇa*, primal energy, start the motion of relative life? By what power do people utter speech, and by what power do sensory and motor organs move for sensation and motion?" Every transitory experience depends on permanent Reality, *Ātman*.

"The Ultimate Existence is that which is the mind of minds, the power of speech, the eye of eyes, the ear of ears, the life of lives; by identifying their Ultimate Existence, one becomes Eternal."

This formula solves the problem of self-control. At first, control of the senses seems to be impossible, but, after deep observation one realizes that all suffering, troubles, and problems are self-invited, self produced and created. First we invite problems; then when we begin to suffer, we want to be rid of them. Is there any trouble or suffering that is not self-created and self-invited? Some troubles and suffering are created and invited in this present life, and some in previous incarnations, but they are never uncreated and uninvited.

When we think or do something wrong, our Self-consciousness is engaged to a wrong object through the respective sensory and motor organs. When Consciousness is withdrawn, these organs cannot operate freely because by themselves they are inert, insentient, and material in nature. All senations and motions of the body depend on *Ātman* for their existence. They will disintegrate, as we see in a dead body, if the power of *Ātman* is withdrawn.

There are two great pains in mental life: one is to lack something, and the other is to possess that which we lacked or desired. To rid himself of these two great pains, a seeker must realize his own form. In this way he transcends both the lack and the possession. The self within is shining like a lamp placed in a jar with many holes. The body is like the jar, the sensory and motor organs and the mind are like the holes in this jar with the light of Conscousness radiating through all these holes. The body and senses can operate only as long as they are in juxtaposition with the Self. Consciousness reveals their sensations, but the senses cannot reveal *Ātman*. Upon knowing the Self, the seeker becomes the Self.

Understanding this truth gives one a key to the mechanism of self-control and the mechanism of body and mind. All-pervading Consciousness, *Ātman*, is the only real light and energy. The light and energy of matter and nature are borrowed from *Ātman*.

A true seeker does not need to know the various *tattvas* or elements, or to know what mind or ego is. For him the most important thing is to experience "Who am I?" In this inquiry of the Self, the mind with all its power returns to its original source, and in the state of *Ātman* the seeker finds that there is no such thing as mind existing independently. In such a state, the mind is automatically controlled. Without Self-inquiry, one is as unlikely to control the mind by means of the mind as for a thief appointed detective to expose the perpetrator of the theft. Self-inquiry is the method *par excellence* to discover what mind is as well as to know the real "I."

## SUTRA NO. 28

स्वबोधे नान्यबोधेच्छा बोधरुपतयात्मनः।
न दीपस्यान्यदीपेच्छा यथा स्वात्मप्रकाशने ॥२८॥

SVABODHE NĀNYABODHECCHĀ BODHARŪPATAYĀTMANAḤ.
NA DĪPASYĀNYADĪPECCHĀ YATHĀ SVĀTMAPRAKĀŚANE.

| | | |
|---|---|---|
| स्वबोधे | Sva-bodhe | In the sate of Self-knowledge |
| न | Na | Not |
| अन्य-बोध-इच्छा | Anya-bodha-icchā | Need for other knowledge |
| बोध-रुपतया | Bodha-rūpatayā | Because its form is knowledge |
| आत्मनः | Ātmanaḥ | Of the Self |
| न | Na | Not |
| दीपस्य | Dīpasya | Of a lamp |
| अन्य-दीप-इच्छा | Anya-dīpa-icchā | Need for another lamp |
| यथा | Yathā | As |
| स्व-आत्मा-प्रकाशने | Sva-ātma-prakāśane | In the Self-luminous state |

Consciousness is Self-evident and Self-existent. It does not need another Consciousness to cognize its own Consciousness, just as a lighted lamp reveals itself. There is no need of another light to see the lighted lamp.

*Ātman* is Pure Consciousness, pure knowledge, and is Self-luminous; hence, other consciousness and knowledge are not needed to know *Ātman*, in the same way as in the physical world the sun is self-luminous, and one does not need other light to see it.

We perceive things by means of light; but do we need another light to perceive that light? We perceive things by means of light, and we perceive that light also by means of the same light. As a matter of fact, the Self, Consciousness, is the light of lights because Consciousness reveals everything but nothing else can reveal it; thus we experience the subjective-objective Universe and the phenomena of body, senses, and mind-stuff by means of Consciousness of the Self, and we experience this Self-Consciousness by means of the same Self-Consciousness.

Simple and Pure Conscousness cannot be seen by compound gross consciousness. Logical inference depends on direct perception, but direct perception depends on nothing but itself.

How does one know progress is Self-Realization? How would one know when one became liberated? How do we know that we are in such and such place and in such and such time? We know by direct perception of the place and time; but what is that which is the foundation of this direct perception? That is Consciousness, the light of the Self. In Yoga philosophy perception is called direct if it is directly perceived by Consciousness. Perception is indirect if it is perceived through the medium of senses and mind; thus, ordinary direct perception is designated here as indirect perception.

*Ātman* is transcendental Consciousness. All other Consciousness depends on it. It is not perceived by sense-consciousness and by mind-Consciousness. *Ātman* is experienced directly, without an intervening medium, by the Consciousness of *Ātman* alone. Instrumental consciousness is not needed to know one's Self.

Mediate and indirect perception, dependent on the instrumentality of mind and senses, is never pure and simple; it is always colored by mental-sensory phenomena. Self-Realization is direct perception, without medium, and becomes possible only when mind and senses are self-controlled and self-disciplined. It is individual consciousness devoid of sensory and mental consciousness that experiences identity and union of *Brahman* Consciousness. *Ātman* Consciousness in man is equivalent to *Brahman* Consciousness in the Cosmos.

Consciousness and knowledge are not attributes of *Ātman* they are intrinsic in *Ātman* as luminosity is intrinsic in the sun. The Self is known by Self-knowledge alone. If other kinds of knowledge be admitted to know Self-knowledge, then the question would arise as to this consciousness or that consciousness, and we would continue *ad infinitum*.

No thinking or perception is possible without the Consciousness of "I AM" behind every thinking and every perception. The real "I" behind "I AM" is *Ātman*. Does anyone need proof to know that he exists?

## SUTRA NO. 29

निषिध्य निखिलोपाधीन्नेति नेतीति वाक्यतः ।
विद्यादैक्यं महावाक्यैर्जीवात्मपरमात्मनोः ॥२९॥

NIṢIDHYA NIKHILOPĀDHĪN NETI NETĪTI VĀKYATAḤ.
VIDYĀD AIKYAṀ MAHĀVĀKYAIR JĪVĀTMAPARAMĀTMANOḤ.

| | | |
|---|---|---|
| निषिध्य | Niṣidhya | After negating |
| निखिल-उपाधीन् | Nikhila-upādhīn | All limitations and conditionings |
| न इति | Na iti | "Not this" |
| न इति | Na iti | "Not this" |
| इति | Iti | Thus |
| वाक्यतः | Vākyataḥ | From the scriptural statements |
| विद्यात् | Vidyāt | One should know |
| ऐक्यम् | Aikyam | The oneness |
| महावाक्यैः | Mahāvākyaiḥ | By the great vedic statements |
| जीवात्म-परमात्मनोः | Jīvātma-Paramātmanoḥ | Of the individual Self and the Supreme Self |

I am neither body, senses, mind, ego, super-ego, nor *prakṛti*. By rejecting all limitations and superimpositions of not-self on the Self, know for certain the Oneness of the individual self with the Universal by means of the great vedic statements, "Thou art that," etc.

With the help of the scriptural statement, "It is not this, it is not this," one should overcome the identity of individual consciousness with different bodily and mental states. By means of the *mahāvākyas*, the great statements, realize the Oneness and identity of individual consciousness with Supreme Consciousness.

The body, mind, and senses are inert like a jar and pots, in which there is no sense of "I" or Self. In dreamless sleep, where there is no body-consciousness or mind-consciousness, the Self shines by itself;

thus the principle of "I," Self, is not the body, senses, mind, ego, intellect, nor even *Prakṛti*, Cosmic Energy, which is the cause of manifestation of the physical Universe. The I-principle is *Saccidānanda*, eternal Existence-Consciousness-Bliss.

Ultimate and absolute truth is *Ātman*, which is one although it appears as many different individuals. The world apart from *Ātman* has no reality. All events, mental and physical, are transitory appearances. The only Absolute and unchangeable Truth underlying them all is *Ātman*.

A seeker should reach beneath the surface of appearances and search for the final and Ultimate Truth underlying the microcosm, the individual, and the macrocosm, the Universal, subject and object.

The famous instruction of *Śvetaketu*, the most important *Upaniṣad* text says, "Thou art that, O *Śvetaketu*." Comprehension of the identity of individual soul with Cosmic Soul is the highest knowledge. When this identity is realized, and when the Supreme is recognized as Ultimate Truth and as one's own Self, cognition of all *upādhis*, including subject-object-world-appearance, automatically ceases for the Self-realized One.

Human consciousness cannot comprehend this truth unless it is chastened, purged of all passions and desires. Once a glimpse of this truth is attained, human understanding is eager for freedom and liberation. One becomes able to follow the instruction of the *Mahāvākyas*. The *Sadguru*, the preceptor, instructs him "Thou are that." After deeper Analysis, he recognizes truth and he becomes Truth itself, identical with pure Intelligence and Bliss. The knowledge of multiplicity and diversity disappears.

The external world is reality to the man who is not liberated. Due to faulty knowledge of his Self, he identifies with his bodily and mental states, worldly experiences, joys and events, and performs good and bad works accordingly. The force of accumulated *karma* leads him to experiences of multiplicity. Although reaping the results of past *karmas*, he is ignorant of them as well as of his own Self. He works under the delusion of a false relationship between himself and the world; thus the wheel of world processes continues to revolve. We do not know what the world around us is; nor do we know what we are; thus our ignorance is both subjective and objective.

The process of Self-analysis is described as *adhyāropa* and *apavāda*. *Adhyāropa* is superimposition of one thing upon another, as the perception of a rope as a snake in semi-darkness. *Apavāda* is removal of that superimposition to perceive a thing as it is, as direct perception of the rope as a rope, and refutation of the idea of a snake. The activities of body, mind, and senses are superimposed on *jivatman*. By Meditation and direct perception of the Self, this superimposition is negated.

There is wide divergence of opinion about the meaning and value of Self. Some identify self with the body, some with the senses, some with the mind, some with life, and some with Consciousness. Buddhists and some empiricists regard the Self as identical with the stream of Consciousness. Some logicians regard the Self as an unconscious substance, and regard its conscious property as conditional and accidental. These are actually states in Self-analysis. When the second stage of Self-analysis is realized, the first is negated and the student feels, "It is not this," that is to say, this is not Self; the Self is something more than this. When the nature of the Self is realized, all previous notions, which were superimposed on the Self are negated by the experience of "It is not Self; it is not Self," and the Self is realized finally as Pure Consciousness, Intelligence, Existence, Reality, and Bliss—the only Truth in world and man.

These are the *Mahāvākyas*, the five great statements of the *Upaniṣads*:

1. *Tat tvam asi*, Thou are that.

2. *Aham Brahmāsmi*, "I AM" is *Brahman*.

3. *Ayam ātma Brahma*, This Self is *Brahman*.

4. *Prajñānam Brahma, Brahman* is Consciousness.

5. *Satyam-jñānam-anantam Brahma. Saccidānandam Brahma. Brahman* is Pure Existence, Consciousness, Reality, and Bliss.

These *Mahāvākyas* are the main pillars of Self-realization. They were originally four in number, but the fifth *Mahāvākya*, which really includes two statements with a little change, is regarded as extremely important for further explanation of Reality.

It is not the universe that is negated, but its appearance of multiplicity as other than *Brahman* that is negated; that is, unreality is negated and reality is recognized.

Since cause and effect are theoretically identical, their difference is in the practical viewpoint. As the Universe and its Cause, *Brahman*, essentially are identical, their difference is apparent only from a practical viewpoint.

## SUTRA NO. 30

आविद्यकं शरीरादि दृश्यं बुद्बुदवत्क्षरम्।
एतद्विलक्षणं विद्यादहं ब्रह्मेति निर्मलम् ॥३०॥

AVIDYAKAM ŚARĪRĀDI DṚŚYAM BUDBUDAVAT KṢARAM.
ETAD VILAKṢAṆAM VIDYĀD AHAM BRAHMETI NIRMALAM.

| | | |
|---|---|---|
| आ-अविद्यकम् | Ā-avidyakam | Up to the causal body of ignorance |
| शरीरादि | Sarīrādi | Body, mind, senses, etc. |
| दृश्यम् | Dṛśyam | Perceived objects |
| बुद्बुदवत् | Budbudavat | Like bubbles |
| क्षरम् | Kṣaram | Perishable |
| एतद्- | Etad- | From all these |
| विलक्षणम् | Vilakṣaṇam | Different |
| विद्यात् | Vidyāt | Know |
| अहम् | Aham | I |
| ब्रह्म | Brahma | Brahman |
| इति | Iti | Thus |
| निर्मलम् | Nirmalam | Pure |

The body, mind, and senses and all limitations are the products of ignorance. They are of the Nature of objects and are perishable like bubbles. Know for certain that your Self, "I," is completely different from perishable objects, and is absolutely identical with the Universal Self.

Realize through Self-analysis that your essential Existence is

*Brahman*, which is beyond physical and mental phenomena. One identifies oneself with physical and mental phenomena due to ignorance.

Daily experience shows us that mental and physical phenomena have order and laws, but that they do not represent Ultimate Truth. The moment our real Existence, Self, is realized, all mental and physical phenomena, including world appearances, become unreal and *Brahman*, Pure Being, shines forth as the only Truth.

Our experience of identification of Self with the body and mind is an illusory perception, like seeing silver in a conch shell. At first perception of the silvery appearance, a man may run to take possession of it, but when he sees that it is only a fragment of conch shell, he rejects it and never again is deluded by its deceptive appearance. The illusion of silver in a conch shell is inexplicable. It is true as long as it persists, but it vanishes upon discernment of the real Nature of the object.

Body and mind phenomena also, which are changeable and non-eternal, will perish like bubbles when insight into the Real Existence, *Ātman*, is gained. They exist as they are perceived, but they have no accordance with the perceiver.

*Ātman* is bodiless, behind the phenomena of body, and it is firm and restful behind the restless mind; thus, realizing this great principle of the Self as "I AM THAT I AM," one overcomes death and becomes Eternal and immortal. The Real Self is forever young and Eternal, ever ancient and ever new.

## SUTRA NO. 31

देहान्यत्वान्न मे जन्मजराकार्श्यलयादयः।
शब्दादिविषयैः सङ्गो निरिन्द्रियतया न च ॥३१॥

DEHĀNYATVĀN NA ME JANMAJARĀKĀRŚYALAYĀDAYAḤ.
ŚABDĀDIVIṢAYAIḤ SAṄGO NIRINDRIYATAYĀ NA CA.

| | | |
|---|---|---|
| देह-अन्यत्वात् | Deha-Anyatvāt | Since "I AM" is other than the body |
| न | Na | Not |
| मे | Me | Of me |
| जन्म-जरा- | Janma-jarā | Birth - old age |
| कार्श्य-लयादयः | Kārśya-layādayaḥ | Suffering - death, etc. |
| शब्दादि-विषयैः | Śabdādi - viṣayaiḥ | With sense objects such as sound, etc. |
| सङ्गः | Saṅgaḥ | Association |
| निर्-इन्द्रियतया | Nir-indriyatayā | Because "I Am" is without sense organs |
| न | Na | Not |
| च | Ca | And |

Since the Self is beyond the body, mind, and senses, I am free from birth, old age, emaciation, sickness, suffering, and death, because these belong to the body and are part of the not-self. Since the "I" transcends all senses and sense organs, they cannot involve the Self, "I," nor produce any change in the Self.

Body and mind phenomena are passing through constant changes such as pregnancy, birth, childhood, youth, adolescence, old age, suffering, and death but the Real Existence, *Ātman*, is not affected by these changes. The phenomena of sensation, feeling, and motion cannot touch *Ātman* because *Ātman* is subtler than they, and beyond them.

Feelings, experiences, and perceptions present knowledge to us, either subjective identity or objective knowledge. The most interesting aspect of our Consciousness is emotion, by which we identify Self with body, mind, and sensory phenomena. Through feelings we experience and accept thoughts as part of ourselves. Psychologically, a fine discrimination is made between sensation and perception. Sensation is the act of receiving a stimulus by means of a sense organ. Everything we experience comes to us by means of sense organs, which are receiving stations for stimuli that come from outside and within the body. We have eyes for seeing, ears for hearing, a tongue for tasting. Perception is the act of interpreting a stimulus registered in the brain by sensory mechanism.

It is common psychological experience that we do not notice our own mistakes unless our attention is drawn to them by others, though they be as high as the Himalaya Mountains. On the other hand, we notice others' defects easily, be they ever so slight. The mechanism which leads us to this particular weakness is called our identity. Due to our identification with sensation, perception, and experiences, we regard feelings, character, and behavior as part of ourselves, in contrast to others' feelings, character, and behavior. An emotional, superstitious, religious man faithfully and blindly follows his system of worship, and does not critically examine his own religious practice and beliefs, while he may be antagonistic to others' religious systems and faiths, regardless of their truth or rationale. This is the result of identification.

When a man reaches beyond mind-body identification, he realizes the magnanimity and grandeur of Self, and recognizes the transitory nature of mind-body phenomena.

When we rationally examine our feelings and experiences, we may be astounded by our discoveries. We may find that our professed faith and beliefs are not truly representative of our inmost Self. Objective and subjective phenomena, which precede a conscious act, play an important role in our feelings. These phenomena impress us according to the quality and quantity of our feelings; hence they can be regarded as mere feelings.

In lower living beings, we find automatic reflex actions, which are crude manifestations of feelings. These are not on the level of knowledge. The lower the level in evolution, the lesser is the intensity of feeling in a being. In inorganic entities we find only physical and chemical action and reaction. Then, when matter is consumed as food, the physical and chemical action and reaction again transform it into feelings in higher life. Feelings indicate the earliest mark of Consciousness. Matter-complexes become, at a higher level, feeling-complexes combined with Consciousness, Experience, and knowledge. Feeling-complexes, at a lower level, become matter-complexes with physical and chemical action and reaction. these.

1. *Sattva*, Intelligence-stuff;
2. *Rajas*, energy-stuff;
3. *Tamas*, mass-stuff.

All manifestations of thought and matter are manifestations of feeling substances.

The three classes of feelings are:

1. Pleasurable;
2. Painful;
3. Listless, inert, neither pleasurable nor painful, originating in ignorance, depression, and dullness.

Thus we find corresponding manifestations in the realm of thought and matter. The three manifestations of thought such as pleasure, pain, and dullness are similar to the three manifestations of matter:—*satoguṇa*, protonic nature; *rajoguṇa*, electronic nature; and *tamoguṇa* neutronic nature. Feelings are therefore things in themselves, the Ultimate substance of which thoughts and matter are made up.

When a man realizes feelings in pure form free from the body, mind, and senses, he becomes independent of body-mind identity. When a man overcomes body-mind identity, he realizes the true Nature of *Ātman*.

A sense organ is a specialized part of the body which is selectively sensitive to some types of change in its environment and not to others. For example, the eyes, receptory organs for the sensation of light waves, are impervious to sound stimuli; likewise, to a deaf man, a gently ringing alarm clock and a wailing siren bring no difference in sensation.

Anything causing change in a sense organ is called a stimulus. There are many types of stimuli, such as mechanical, physical, chemical, and emotional. Their important feature is change. By long continued exposure to any stimulus we become accustomed to it. Its effectiveness as a stimulus is diminished and ultimately lost. Through longstanding identification with the body and senses, man has lost the capacity to receive warning from them.

Meditation is a process of total release of energy by which we awaken our Consciousness and sharpen our senses, so that we may detect even the slightest change in environment around and within us. By recognizing signals given by our senses we can use them to transform our Consciousness to a higher level, and we can protect ourselves from dangerous situations by knowing the signficance of danger signals; thus, meditation is the analysis of signals received by our perceptual mechanism from the Eternal source of feeling, guiding the individual soul, just as a radar signal guides mechanisms.

The Self, the real "I," is only manifested through the body, which is like Cosmic television. Birth, growth, decay, and death of the body cannot be happening to the Self.

## SUTRA NO. 32

अमनस्त्वान्न मे दुःखरागद्वेषभयादयः।
अप्राणो ह्यमनाः शुभ्र इत्यादि श्रुतिशासनात ॥३२॥

AMANASTVĀN NA ME DUḤKHARĀGADVEṢABHAYĀDAYAḤ.
APRĀNO HYAMANĀḤ ŚUBHRA ITYĀDI ŚRUTIŚĀSANĀT.

| | | |
|---|---|---|
| अमनस्त्वात् | Amanastvāt | Being other than the mind |
| न | Na | Not |
| मे | Me | Of me |
| दुःख-राग-द्वेष- | Duḥkha-rāga-dveṣa | Sorrow-Like-Dislike |
| भयादयः | Bhayādayaḥ | Fear, etc. |
| अप्राणः | Aprāṇaḥ | Beyond Cosmic Energy |
| हि | Hi | Verily |
| अमनाः | Amanāḥ | Beyond mind |
| शुभ्रः | Śubhraḥ | Pure |
| इत्यादि | Ityādi | Etc. |
| श्रुति-शासनात् | Śruti-śāsanāt | From the instruction of the Veda |

Pain and pleasure, love and hatred, belong to the mind. Since I am beyond the Mind, these cannot produce any change in me. The Vedas declare that the Self transcends Cosmic Energy, transcends mind. It is pure and Self-luminous.

*Ātman* is pure Consciousness. It is most subtle and beyond the characteristics of mind-stuff—such as pleasure, pain, and inertia; beyond attachment, anxiety, malice, and fear. It is beyond physical motions and sensory sensations, such as motion of the respiratory system, cardiac system, and others. It is pure and simple, hence, imperishable.

Analysis of the word "I" shows pure Consciousness to be the real Essence of *Ātman*. The word "I" seems sometimes to indicate the body (e.g. I am thin), sometimes the sensory organs (e.g. I am blind), sometimes the motor organs (e.g. I am lame), sometimes mind-stuff (e.g. I am happy), and sometimes consciousness (e.g. I know).

In analysis of Consciousness, one should always question, "This is I?" or "This is mine?" For example, eye, ear, organ of smell, feet, arms, all systems and organs, body, mind, ego, intellect–all belong to "This is mine." Anything which is expressed by means of the possessive case, such as "my clothes," is the possession or instrument of "I," not "I" itself. Here 'clothes' is modified by the possessive pronoun "my"; therefore clothes exist to serve the purpose of "I," but they cannot be "I."

Every entity should be examined according to this scale; thus we come to the conclusions that "I"-consciousness is beyond all entities. A mixed form of Consciousness is not the real form of "I," because it is used as "my consciousness" in the possessive sense. The word "I" symbolizes master, experiencer, and seer. All other relative consciousness, sensation, and motion are experiences, objects, and servants to execute the requirements of Pure Consciousness. As in "my house, my coat, my car," the real possessor is beyond what is possessed, so in the above analysis "I" is beyond all entities.

When all entities are excluded, the "I" seems either to be annihilated or to be a combination of all these entities. This is not true. In the process of experiencing, every experiencer feels the separate existence of "I-ness," but under ordinary circumstances the psychological "I"-consconsciouness is never identified with pure and simple "I"-consciousness. An ordinary man must practice Self-analysis to identify his Essence as pure "I"-Consciousness. If an ordinary man could already identify with pure "I"-Consciousness, then no one would have to go through the arduous process of Self-analysis to obtain freedom.

When we use the term "my consciousness," this consciousness is not *Ātman*. It is the psychological consciousness which is experienced equally with the other entities, although it is experienced subjectively, while the others are experienced objectively. The real "I" is beyond subjective-objective Consciousness.

The psychological "I"–consciousness will serve the purpose of the meditator subjectively until he attains pure "I"–Consciousness. With the help of physical and psychological "I"–consciousness, the pure, simple, and metaphysical "I"–Consciousness is analyzed because the psychological "I"–consciousness is the direct reflection of pure "I"–Consciousness. Then the linguistic expressions, my body, my senses, and my intellect, show that the self can divert itself from these, and treat them as external objects distinct from itself. These external elements cannot be regarded as the inherent and real Essence of the Self. Their relationship to *Ātman* is that of servants to master, possessed to possessor, seen to seer, object to subject, experienced to experiencer.

The linguistic use of Consciousness of *Ātman* and *Brahman* Consciousness shows the relationship of Consciousness to possessor and possessed, of noun and adjective, but these terms should be understood as figurative and relative. In the phrase, Consciousness of *Ātman* and *Brahman*, the possessive case does not indicate distinction but identity, as "the city of New York." *Ātman* Consciousness and *Brahman* Consciousness are not compound terms, or nouns and adjectives in the sense of experience although the wording may make them appear to be so. Here their use is in the Absolute sense to distinguish them from relative use. When we use the term "my consciousness," we mean psychological consciousness. It is as alien to *Ātman* and *Brahman* as "my mind" and "my intellect" are.

The psychological "I"-consciousness is material in nature; consequently it passes through birth and death, and is subject to other changes of matter. It is felt subjectively because of its proximity to *Ātman* and because it is a direct reflection of *Ātman*. By means of it, *Ātman* Consciousness or *Brahman* Consciousness is realized. As long as pure Consciousness is not realized, this psychological "I"–consciousness guides the individual as subjective consciousness.

By comparing and analyzing the different meanings of the Self, expressed by the word"I," we discern pure Consciousness, Existence, Bliss as the inherent Nature and Essence of *Ātman*, Self, I.

How to establish relationship of *Ātman* with the relative world? *Ātman* manifests itself by itself, from itself by its wondrous power, conscious Energy, as the organic and inorganic world . . .

## SUTRA NO. 33

एतस्माज्जायते प्राणो मनः सर्वेन्द्रियाणि च ।
खं वायुर्ज्योतिरापः पृथिवी विश्वस्य धारिणी ॥३३॥

ETASMĀJJĀYATE PRĀṆO MANAḤ SARVENDRIYĀṆI CA.
KHAM VĀYUR JYOTIR ĀPAḤ PṚTHIVĪ VIŚVASYA DHĀRIṆĪ.

| | | |
|---|---|---|
| एतस्मात् | Etasmāt | From it |
| जायते | Jāyate | Are manifested |
| प्राणः | Prāṇaḥ | Cosmic Energy |
| मनः | Manaḥ | Mind |
| सर्व-इन्द्रियाणि | Sarva-indriyāṇi | All senses |
| च | Ca | And |
| खम् | Kham | Ether |
| वायुः | Vāyuḥ | Gas |
| ज्योतिः | Jyotiḥ | Light |
| आपः | Āpaḥ | Liquid |
| पृथिवी | Pṛthivī | Solid |
| विश्वस्य | Viśvasya | Of the Universe |
| धारिणी | Dhāriṇī | Supporter, maintainer |

From the Self are manifested Cosmic Energy, mind, all senses, solid, liquid, gas, light, and ether, and the various Universes. Self, *Brahman*, maintains and supports all beings.

From *Ātman* is manifested the organic world, including *prāṇa*, *manas*, and all sensory and motor organs, as well as the inorganic world, including *ākāśa*, *vāyu*, *jyotis*, *āpaḥ*, and *pṛthivī*. What is the relationship between the Supreme principle, *Ātman*, and the phenomenal world? In the Ultimate sense there is no creation at all The real cannot be subject to change; for if it were, the immortal would become mortal. A thing cannot be changed into its opposite. All becoming is apparent and unreal.

Subjective and objective creation, organic and inorganic division is *citta-dṛśyam*, a creation of mind; hence, it is apparent. *Ātman* and *Brahman* and subject and object are identical in the Absolute sense, but not in the relative sense. Their evolution is extremely important in recognizing the identity of *Ātman* and *Brahman*.

Evolution of the Universe obeys a mathematical order in the relative plane. Each state of experience and perception shows the character of reality which is its foundation. From the inherent energy of *Brahman*, which is *prakṛti*, arises *ākāśa*, the pervader of space and matter. *Ākāśa* is infinite, omnipotent, omnipresent. It is all-pervasive, an exceedingly subtle form of nature, filling all space and all products of matter.

*Ākāśa*, ether, is the first manifestation of nature in the relative plane. It is called *ākāśa* because it is shining everywhere. All relative conscious and unconscious energy operate through its power. From *ākāśa*, *vāyu*; from *vāyu*, *jyotis*; from *jyotis*, *āpaḥ* and from *āpaḥ*, *pṛthivī*.

The inorganic world, in ascending order of reality, is as follows:

1. *Pṛthivī*, solid state;
2. *Āpaḥ*, liquid state;
3. *Jyotis* or *tejas*, light;
4. *Vāyu*, gaseous state; and
5. *Ākāśa*, ethereal state.

The organic world includes:

1. *Prāṇa*, energy;
2. *Cittam*, mindstuff; and
3. *Indriyāṇı*, senses.

All forms of matter belong to *ākāśa* and all forms of energy belong to *prāṇā*. *Prāṇa* and *ākāśa* are manifestations of the energy of *Brahman*. In the subtle state, *prāṇa* transforms into *ākāśa* and *ākāśa* into *prāṇa* because they derive from *prakṛti*, the energy of *Brahman.*

The order of creation is reversed at the time of dissolution: solid becomes liquid; liquid, fire; fire, gas; gas, *ākāśa*; *ākāśa*, *prāṇa*; and ultimately they re-enter the energy of *Brahman*.

In organic nature a new principle comes before us, the principle of life, *prāṇa*, by which organic beings are able to realize a state of closer approximation to perfection. A stone does not live in the same sense in which a plant lives because it has no inward or outward tendency of growth. Plants have the power of growth—sprouting, bearing leaves, blossoming, and bearing fruit. Animals have a higher state of life than plants because they sense and perceive. Plants move only in time while animals move both in time and space.

Human beings have a much higher form of life than other animals, being endowed with faculties of reflection, understanding, thinking, and willing. In human beings, we find inorganic nature represented in the form of minerals and other elements. We find also the power of growth as in plants, and sensation and perception as in animals; but in man also is the discriminative knowledge of *Ātman* by means of which he differentiates the real from the unreal, the eternal from the noneternal, and can choose good rather than the pleasant. Men who realize the nature of *Ātman* are gods.

Organic nature is in five classes:

1. Microscopic being;
2. Plants;
3. Animals;
4. Men; and
5. Gods.

These five classes of the organic world are arranged according to the evolution of *prāṇa*, *cittam*, and senses. From first to fifth they are in higher and higher evolution. Thus, Self-analysis is the process of evolution of the organic and inorganic principles of human existence from lower to higher, from darkness to light, from death, disease and suffering to immortality, from conditional reality to unconditional reality. In the embodied state, souls exist together with *prāṇa*, vital forces; *cittam*, the perceptual mechanism, subtle bodies; and organic and inorganic elements until their liberation.

We hear, see, smell, breathe, drink and eat by means of the energy of the sun through the ethereal, gaseous, light, liquid, and solid state of nature because we cannot assimilate energy directly from the sun; thus we are using the relative form of solar energy. Only when we are able to assimilate the sun's energy directly, as in the state of liberation, do we no longer need to use the relative form, the gross form of energy. During pregnancy, an embryo lives in the uterus like a *yogin*, without breathing, eating, or drinking. After liberation these activities are again no longer needed.

## SUTRA NO. 34

निर्गुणो निष्क्रियो नित्यो निर्विकल्पो निरञ्जनः ।
निर्विकारो निराकारो नित्यमुक्तोऽस्मि निर्मलः ॥३४॥

NIRGUṆO NIṢKRIYO NITYO NIRVIKALPO NIRAÑJANAḤ.
NIRVIKĀRO NIRĀKĀRO NITYAMUKTO' SMI NIRMALAḤ.

| | | |
|---|---|---|
| निर्-गुणः | Nir-guṇaḥ | Without qualities |
| निः-क्रियः | Niḥ-kriyaḥ | Without actions |
| नित्यः | Nityaḥ | Eternal |
| निर्-विकल्पः | Nir-vikalpaḥ | Without indecision or doubt |
| निर्-अञ्जनः | Nir-añjanaḥ | Without pollution |
| निर्-विकारः | Nir-vikāraḥ | Without change |
| निर्-आकारः | Nir-ākāraḥ | Without form |
| नित्य-मुक्तः | Nitya-muktaḥ | Eternally free |
| अस्मि | Asmi | I am |
| निर्-मलः | Nir-malaḥ | Ever-pure |

I, *Brahman*, am beyond *satoguṇa*, *rajoguṇa*, and *tamoguṇa*, free from all change, Eternal, pure, beyond birth and death, formless and nameless, eternally free and One with the Universal Self.

*Nirvāṇam* has two phases: 1) Freedom and liberation from bondage, and 2) Enlightenment and Realization of *Ātman*.

Without experiencing liberation from the lower nature, one will have no higher attainment. There are two phases of knowledge. Knowledge dealing with freedom and liberation from the material aspect of human existence, coupled with the manifestation of

*Brahman*, is called *aparā vidyā*, lower knowledge. Knowledge dealing with *Ātman* and *Brahman* is called *parā vidyā*, higher knowledge.

*Parā vidyā* is Absolute truth. Its content is the Oneness of *Ātman* and *Brahman*, and their manifestation. From the standpoint of empirical experience and consciousness, the world extended in space and time, cause and effect, is not illusory and deceptive, nor is it final and ultimate. The higher monistic and the lower pluralistic views are true but not in the same sense. A fall from higher knowledge leads Consciousness to lower knowledge, from *Brahman* to the manifestations of *Brahman* and *Ātman*. In the state of bondage, our perception is partial and, according to partial vision, our conclusions and knowledge are finite.

What is positively felt and experienced in the relative and empirical sense is lost in the vastness and infinity of *Ātman*; therefore, from the standpoint of empirical experience, *Ātman* can be described only by means of a negative method, although *Ātman* is highly positive from the viewpoint of the Absolute.

*Ātman* is beyond the characteristics of Cosmic forces. Physical, chemical, atomic, and nuclear actions and reactions cannot cause action and reaction in *Ātman*, which is Eternal, devoid of plurality and multiplicity, pure, changeless, Self-luminous, ever free, nameless and formless. It is immanent and transcendent in relation to the world, yet it is not the pluralistic world.

In Self-analysis we do not question the facts of psychology any more than we do the facts of physical science; however, our main objective is to consider the nature of Ultimate Reality. Metaphysics is a consideration of the final Nature of the Universe. Our aim is not only to observe and tabulate the facts of Consciousness, but also to become aware of the Real Existence and Ultimate Nature of Consciousness. Consciousness leads us not only beyond the objective world, but also beyond subjective identification with mental and bodily phenomena; hence Self-analysis is concerned with the implications of the proof regarding the nature of Reality.

Self-analysis cannot take anything for granted or as postulated. Is there anything in empirical experience which may be postulated as foundational and fundamental for the purpose of our analysis? Certainly not. There is nothing fundamental in finite language. Our senses are limited and our knowledge is finite. Then how can the final Nature of the world be discovered when it is beyond the senses and sensations? What we feel as highly positive may be highly negative in the Ultimate sense. Waking, dreaming, and sound sleep, past, present, and future may be fallacy and illusion.

Scriptural knowledge depends on faith and belief. Matters of faith and belief are open to the challenge of doubt. Some believe that we need to transcend doubt and skepticism to experience our faith.

No one has created his own body and mind. No one moves the systems within his own body. If he had such power, he could stop the motion of his heart. Who does these things in us and for us? Logic and philosophy indicate that an unknown factor within us keeps performing all these acts; hence knowledge of the Self is incomplete until we know the Self totally including our unknown, immanent, and transcendent Existence.

Immediate Self certainly is the basis of truth because it is untouched by doubt and skepticism. We find examples of this Self in our daily existence. Everyone is conscious of the existence of his own Self. Before any dealings he is certain of his own existence. No one thinks, "I am not." If the existence of Self were not real, then everyone would think, "I am not." This notion is contrary to popular experience. One's real existence, *Ātman*, is prior to the stream of psychological consciousness, prior to empirical truth and falsehood, prior to relative reality and unreality, good and bad. All actions and knowledge exist only as dependent on Self-existence; hence Self-existence is Self-evident, Self-luminous, and is its own proof. There is no necessity to prove Self-existence, for every proof is a latecomer to the existence of Self.

The very existence of our psychological understanding and its functions presupposes an existence which is known as *Ātman*, Self. *Ātman* is Self-established; it is served by psychological functions as master. Each subjective and objective phenomenon in us and around us such as hearing, seeing, breathing, smelling, tasting, grasping, eating, thinking, and experiencing appears only on the basis of *Ātman*. All functions and faculties, sensations and motions, perceptions and experiences, serve *Ātman* on their plane, and depend on it for deeper Existence; therefore *Ātman* cannot be doubted, for it is the essential Existence—even of one who doubts or denies it.

We know things positively by our senses, mind, and thoughts, but we cannot know *Ātman* by means of senses and thoughts because these are latter creations, and they have the characteristics of matter. If we attempt to grasp *Ātman* by suppressing and postponing logical proof, critical methods, and philosophical interpretive powers, we remain in ignorance and superstituion. By deeper Self-analysis we come to know that *Ātman* is not contrary to logical proof, but is beyond it. One cannot think away *Ātman* because there is no thinking apart from it. *Ātman* is not apart from our experiences, logical proof, knowledge, and thinking. It transcends them, remaining positively open for our experience.

Even if one were to logically declare the whole world void phenomenon, without Reality, such phenomenon presupposes the logical existence of a knower of itself; thus *Ātman* is prior to any concept of logic. The existence of *Ātman* is not dependent and interdependent as is the existence of material objects. For example, books on a table depend on the table, which in turn depends on the floor and on the house. The house depends on the earth, which depends on the attraction of the sun, and so on. This is called dependent and interdependent existence.

*Ātman* is Self-existent. Metaphysically, Self-existence means that which is Eternal, immutable, complete, and dependent on nothing but itself; thus Self-existence is in itself, from itself, for itself, and complete in itself; hence, to declare the Self-existence of *Ātman* means to affirm the Real Essence of individual existence as Eternal *Brahman*, *ātmā ca Brahma*. *Brahman* is the Reality and fundamental ground of every individual self.

It can be experienced by transcending all thoughts and mind, but it cannot be experienced only by describing it in positive and determinative terminology, for such terminology is material in character and is the product of mind. It is both *saguṇa*, determinate, and *nirguṇa*, indeterminate, known and unknown. The real "I" must be distinguished from the not-"I." The real "I" excludes not only the outer world, but also the body, organs, senses, and the whole apparatus of understanding. In daily life, we regard bodily and mental phenomena as subjects, and physical states as objects, but, from the Self-analytical viewpoint, both orders of phenomenal and material—are equally objective.

## SUTRA NO. 35

अहमाकाशवत् सर्वं बहिरन्तर्गतोऽच्युतः ।
सदा सर्वसमस्सिद्धो निस्सङ्गो निर्मलोऽचलः ॥३५॥

AHAM ĀKĀŚAVAT SARVAṀ BAHIRANTARGATO' CYUTAḤ.
SADĀ SARVASAMASSIDDHO NISSAṄGO NIRMALO' CALAḤ.

| | | |
|---|---|---|
| अहम् | Aham | I |
| आकाशवत् | Ākāśavat | Like the ether |
| सर्वं | Sarvam | All things |
| बहिः | Bahiḥ | Outside |
| अन्तः | Antaḥ | Inside |
| गतः | Gataḥ | Pervading |
| अच्युतः | Acyutaḥ | Changeless |
| सदा | Sadā | Always |
| सर्व-समः | Sarva-samaḥ | Same in all |
| सिद्धः | Siddhaḥ | Perfected, pure |
| निस्-सङ्गः | Nis-saṅgaḥ | Without attachment |
| निर्-मलः | Nir-malaḥ | Without stain |
| अचलः | Acalaḥ | Motionless |

I, *Brahman*, pervade the total Universe, inside and out, like *Ākāśa*, ether. I am changeless and the same in All. I am equal to All, stainless, immutable, and unattached.

*Ātman* is immanent and transcendent. It fills all things inside and out like *ākāśa*, ether. It is beyond the concept of time—

past, present, and future. It is changeless and is the same force in All. It is pure, immutable, Self-shining, unattached, untouched, stainless, ever-present everywhere, and consequently, immovable.

Self should not be confused with the psychological self, which grows and goes on gathering its experiences through memory and inner feelings, accompanying the continuous change of mental attitudes and contents of thoughts developing in time. The real Self is *acyutaḥ*, the undivided present, where temporal categories of empirical past, present, and future are transcended. It is pure duration and Eternity, which has no otherness and divisions. The psychological self is not antecedent to knowledge—for it is itself an object of knowledge. It is true that the psychological self precedes every activity, and presents itself as an agent but, due to its constantly changing nature, the psychological self can never be the same at two different moments of time. Timelessness is inherent in the Consciousness of pure Self.

Salvation belongs to the psychological self, not to the real Self. The real Self is ever free. Bondage and release refer to the conjunction and disjunction, respectively, of the psychological self and *prakṛti* resulting from nondiscrimination and discrimination. *Prakṛti* does not bind *puruṣa*, Self. *Prakṛti* binds itself in various forms and shapes. The Self, *puruṣa*, is entirely free from the snares of natural impulses. When the psychological self is active toward *prakṛti* without the direct light of *puruṣa*, the result is bondage due to nondiscrimination; thus nondiscrimination is the cause of bondage, and discrimination is the cause of liberation.

When the psychological consciousness is active toward *puruṣa* in *samādhi*, it catches the pure reflection of *puruṣa* and, in identification with this reflection, overcomes identification with matter. The change appearing in *puruṣa* is unreal and fictitious, for it is *acyutah*, changeless and the same in All.

In the quest of the Self, "Who am I?" it is the individual "I" which is investigating itself, not the real "I." The real "I" or "I AM" is beyond thoughts and mental operations. By identification of "I am" with "I AM," the individual self obtains freedom from the bondage of matter and material existence. The real "I AM" is like ether, filling the whole Universe, externally and internally; it is omnipresent, omniscient, and omnipotent.

Meditation on *saguṇa Brahman*, Eternal sound current, is the one infallible method by which psychological consciousness is united with *Brahman* by nullifying all *karmas*. Sound current, *nādam*, is a manifestation of *Brahman*, and it comes from beyond the region of mind and *māyā*. If a meditator submits his psychological consciousness to it, he will be able to reach its source and origin, *Brahman*. This supersonic sound current eradicates all obstacles and *karmas*, and frees the Soul from bondage. One should devote oneself to *nādam*. One should practice *śabdābhyāsa*, union of the Soul with *śabda Brahman*.

There are seven planes of sound current and five stages. The seven planes of Consciousness of sound current are:

1. *Bhū*, manifestation of sound current. It is like the union of electricity with the apparatus of radio or television.

2. *Bhuvaḥ*, the state of communication with the Cosmic sound current. It is like having a desired program on radio or television.

3. *Svaḥ*, the plane of sound current in which one begins to experience inner Bliss.

4. *Mahaḥ*, the plane of sound current in which one begins to experience one's own heart as the center of Cosmic sound current.

5. *Janaḥ*, the plane of sound current in which one experiences Cosmic and divine intoxication. By reaching this state and remaining in it, man conquers desire for the intoxication of material things, such as drink, drugs, etc.

6. *Tapaḥ*, the state of sound current in which the meditator reaches beyond the operation of mind and senses.

7. *Satyam*, the state of sound current in which man experiences union of the individual "I am" with the Cosmic "I AM."

The five stages of sound current are:

1. *Oṁkāra*, the state of delightful Cosmic music.

2. *Rāraṁkāra*, the stage of sound current in which specific

divine and Spiritual revelations are experienced by constant meditation on *Brahman*.

3. *Jyoti-nirañjanam*, the stage of sound current through which the seeker experiences the unalloyed light of Consciousness.

4. *So'ham*, the stage of Cosmic vibration of sound current. In this stage the seeker experiences identity of his "I" with the Cosmic "I." The word *saḥ* (so) means "that" and *aham* ('ham) means "I"; thus *so'ham* means "I am that."

5. *Saccidānandam Brahma*. In this stage the Self goes beyond all sound current and experiences Self as Eternal Existence-Consciousness-Bliss.

Innumerable varieties of sound current are within these seven planes and five stages. A seeker should not suppose the sound current to be his Self; he should understand that the real Self is beyond that, and it is his own Self. Sound current is the vehicle by means of which one crosses the ocean of suffering and ignorance, and reaches his destination, I AM.

## SUTRA NO. 36

नित्यशुद्धविमुक्तैकमखण्डानन्दमद्वयम् ।
सत्यं ज्ञानमनन्तं यत्परं ब्रह्माहमेव तत् ॥३६॥

NITYAŚUDDHAVIMUKTAIKAM AKHAṆḌĀNANDAMADVAYAM.
SATYAṀ JÑĀNAṀ ANANTAṀ YAT PARAṀ BRAHMĀHAM EVA TAT.

| | | |
|---|---|---|
| नित्य- | Nitya- | Eternal |
| शुद्ध- | Śuddha- | Pure- |
| विमुक्त- | Vimukta- | Free- |
| एकम् | Ekam | One |
| अखण्ड-आनन्दम् | Akhaṇḍa-Ānandam | Indivisible Reality |
| अद्वयम् | Advayam | Non-dual |
| सत्यम् | Satyam | Truth |
| ज्ञानम् | Jñānam | Knowledge |
| अनन्तम् | Anantam | Infinity |
| यत् | Yat | That which |
| परम् | Param | Supreme- |
| ब्रह्म | Brahma | Brahman |
| अहम् | Aham | I |
| एव | Eva | Alone, even |
| तत् | Tat | That |

There is no difference between my Self, I, and the Universal I, *Brahman*. I am Eternal, pure, free, One-without-a-second, indivisible, non-dual; and of the Nature of *satya*, truth; *jñāna*, knowledge; and *ananta*, infinity.

*Brahman* is truth, knowledge, and infinity. It is Eternal, pure, free, One-without-a-second. It is Absolute Bliss. A meditator should meditate on it as his Real *Ātman*, his Real Existence.

*Brahman* is described from two viewpoints:

1. Determinate, *saguṇa Brahman*. From this viewpoint, *Brahman* is the cause, creator, sustainer, protector, and destroyer of the Universe. It is omniscient, omnipotent, and omnipresent. This view is practical; by understanding this view one's meditation becomes smooth, peaceful, and successful. *Brahman* is *Īśvara*, God.

2. Indeterminate, *nirguṇa Brahman*. From this viewpoint, *Brahman* is *satyam jñānam anantam*, truth, knowledge, infinity. This view is essential and theoretical.

There are two ways to define *Brahman*:

1. *Tatastya lakṣaṇa*, practical view, secondary definition; and

2. *Svarūpa lakṣaṇa*, theoretical view, primary definition.

Suppose that a shepherd appears on a stage in the role of king, that he wages war, conquers a country and rules it. The description of this man as a shepherd is real and essential, while his role of king is accidental, practical and purposive. As long as one does not know one's real Nature and relation with *Brahman*, one feels *Brahman* to be the creator, protector, and sustainer of the Universe and the individual. This is *tatastya lakṣaṇa* of *Brahman*. It is important from a practical viewpoint, but when a meditator reaches into higher and higher states of *samādhi*, and Nature begins to open the secrets of the Universe, the meditator realizes the Oneness of his Existence with the Universe and *Brahman*. Multiplicity and duality of the subjective-objective universe is melted into the Oneness of *Brahman*, which is Eternal Truth, Knowledge, Existence, and Bliss. This is *svarūpa lakṣaṇa*, the essential Nature of *Brahman*.

Meditation begins with the first state and ends in the second state. The world of multiplicity is not transformed into the Absolute, or vice versa. Due to ignorance, Absolute *Brahman* is experienced as multiplicity of the world. When ignorance is removed, one gains insight into Reality and the multiplicity is realized as *Brahman*. They are identical. Transformation of the one into the other is figurative and descriptive.

Comparison of waking, dreaming, and sound sleep shows that the Essence of all Existence is pure Consciousness; for Consciousness is common to all these states. In the waking state there is Consciousness of internal objects. In the state of sound sleep no objects appear; however, there is no cessation of Consciousness. Without the presence of Consciousness, the experience of the sleep state as one of peace and freedom from worries would not be possible; thus the persistent factor is Consciousness. This shows that the Essence of *Ātman* is pure Consciousness.

Pure Consciousness, unlike psychological consciousness, is not a product of Nature; therefore, it is not dependent on objects and natural phenomena. The Consciousness of *Brahman* is Self-existing and Self-revealing. Pure Consciousness is Bliss in its intrinsic nature, and it is independent of psychological Consciousness. In sound sleep and in *samādhi*, the consciousness of sound sleep and *samādhi* is Bliss, *Ānanda*. The fleeting pleasures of waking and dream states are fragmentary manifestations of the Bliss, which forms the Essence of *Brahman*. Man derives pleasure in owning property by identifying it with his self. Self is the Ultimate source of Bliss. The Bliss of the relative world is finite and short-lived, because man limits his self by identifying with finite and fleeting objects.

Sorrow and suffering occur on the loss of something desirable, and on the advent of something undesirable. Joy and bliss occur on the gain of something desirable, and the loss of something undesirable. When a man realizes all Consciousness that belongs to him, and loses all material covering that does not belong to him, he attains fullnesss of Self.

Pure Existence, with no specific limitation, is a factor common to the subjective and objective worlds. Consciousness also is present in both. It is manifested in the subjective world and latent in the objective world. The reality underlying the objective world is therefore identical with that underlying the subjective world. If the subjective and objective worlds did not have a common basis, then knowledge of the objective world would be impossible through the subjective perceptual mechanism because knowledge means identity, and one cannot have identity with something foreign to its own Nature.

One's daily sensations, perceptions, and experiences of eating, breathing, and so on, indicate that the subject and object are identical in Nature, but they have apparent and superficial differences. *Brahman*, *Ātman*, the infinite Existence, Consciousness, Bliss, is the only Reality that constitutes *puruṣa* and *prakṛti*, Self and

Nature, subject and object, the experiencer and the experienced, seer and seen. The finite appearance of psychological consciousness, ego-consciousness, "I"-Consciousness, is fragmentary and identifies with the body, mind, and other finite existences. The psychological self does not know its fullness. When it realizes its fullness, its finiteness is transformed into the Infiniteness of *Brahman*.

## SUTRA NO. 37

एवं निरन्तराभ्यस्ता ब्रह्मैवास्मीति वासना ।
हरत्यविद्याविक्षेपान् रोगानिव रसायनम् ॥३७॥

EVAṀ NIRANTARĀBHYASTĀ BRAHMAIVĀSMĪTI VĀSANĀ.
HARATYAVIDYĀVIKṢEPĀN ROGĀNIVA RASĀYANAM.

| | | |
|---|---|---|
| एवम् | Evam | Thus |
| निरन्तर-अभ्यस्ता | Nirantara-abhyastā | Constantly practiced |
| ब्रह्म-एव-अस्मि | Brahma-eva-asmi | 'I am Brahman' |
| इति | Iti | Thus |
| वासना | Vāsanā | Impression |
| हरति | Harati | Removes |
| अविद्या-विक्षेपान् | Avidyā-vikṣepān | Ignorance and agitations |
| रोगान् | Rogān | Diseases |
| इव | Iva | Like |
| रसायनम् | Rasāyanam | Medicine |

Thus, by constant and continuous investigation of the Self, "Who Am I?" it is experienced that my Self, I, and the Universal Self are eternally united. Experiencing the union and identity of the individual self with the Universal Self destroys ignorance and distractions—as proper medical treatment removes disease.

By constant practice of Self-realization through *samādhi*, one realizes identity of one's Existence, Consciousness, and Reality with that of *Brahman*. Consequently, *Brahman* identification removes one's ignorance, which conceals one's real Nature, and projects subjective and objective phenomena, and causes material identification—just as *rasāyanam*, medicine, cures a patient of disease by removing his identification with the disease.

A seeker of Truth should always meditate on *nādam*, which is the personal manifestation of *Brahman*. This *nādam*, sound current, is *saguṇa Brahman*. The meditator should always realize the pure, shining, ever-radiating and ever-vibrating *Brahman*, and he should give up all identification with ego and ego forces, as these lead Consciousness to the material world. Without practicing on *saguṇa Brahman*, sound current, the Self cannot conquer ego and its forces.

*Nādam* is the wonderful, Eternal, Universe-vibrating music which controls the poisonous snake of ego. It is ego that brings the Self into the world of mind and senses again and again, and causes the Self to become unhappy. The Self forgets to dispose of ego.

The world of mind and senses is incomplete; therefore, it is full of fear and frustration. Ego brings desires, and desires nourish ego. This vicious circle increases psychomotor activities that imprison a man in his body. Freedom from desire is liberation. Knowing one's real Self brings completion and satisfaction of all desires, for the purpose of desire is only to satisfy the self. When self is fulfilled, nothing more remains to be desired. Is there any desire independent of the desirer?

Identification is the nature of mind. Mind cannot stand without identification. When there is identity with lower nature, it projects the world of multiplicity; but when it identifies with *Brahman*, it becomes *Brahman*, and dualism disappears. Mind cannot exist independently. It can exist either in *prakṛti* and the products of *prakṛti*, material existence, or it can exist in *Brahman*, the original source of the mind and the Universe.

The essence of human existence is *Brahman*. "Thou art that" indicates that, in any condition, individual existence and Universal Existence cannot be separated from the Supreme. Individual existence and Universal Existence can be classified briefly in two categories: matter and consciousness. The matter and consciousness of an individual are identical with the matter and Consciousness of the Universe.

Practice and theory, experimentation and interpretation are necessary. Experimentation and interpretation are the means of knowledge to the student who wishes to attain *Yoga*, Self-realization. When he has performed some experimentation, then he needs logical and philosophical interpretation of his experience. Through constant and uninterrupted practice, he comes to feel identity with *Brahman*. In *Brahman* Consciousness, identity with body and limitations of the body are dissolved, just as a patient's identification with disease is ended after successful treatment.

It is common psychological experience that anyone, to a certain extent, interpentrates another's existence. This proves that Consciousness is not limited to one's physical existence, although the body is the instrument to reflect or manifest Consciousness. How could we gain knowledge about others, if Consciousness could not penetrate beyond the body?

This free flow of Consciousness, no doubt, depends on the condition of the body; therefore, with development of the body and mind, there is pervasive manifestation of Consciousness. This progressive manifestation of Consciousness indicates that the Ultimate Nature of Consciousness is omnipresence, omniscience, and omnipotence, although this is not realized in the state of bondage.

## SUTRA NO. 38

विविक्तदेश आसीनो विरागो विजितेन्द्रियः ।
भावयेदेकमात्मानं तमनन्तमनन्यधीः ॥३८॥

VIVIKTADEŚA ĀSĪNO VIRĀGO VIJITENDRIYAḤ.
BHĀVAYED EKAMĀTMĀNAṀ TAM ANANTAM ANANYADHĪḤ.

| | | |
|---|---|---|
| विविक्त-देशे | Vivikta-deśe | In a private place |
| आसीनः | Āsīnaḥ | Seated |
| विरागः | Virāgaḥ | Free from desires and thoughts |
| विजित-इन्द्रियः | Vijita-indriyaḥ | Senses subdued |
| भावयेत् | Bhāvayet | Meditate |
| एकम् | Ekam | One |
| आत्मानम् | Ātmānam | Self |
| तम् | Tam | That |
| अनन्तम् | Anantam | Infinite |
| अनन्य-धीः | Ananya-dhīḥ | With undivided attention |

In the quest of Self, one should conduct his investigation in a solitary place, freeing the mind from all thoughts and withholding the senses from all objects. One should meditate with undivided attention on the Infinite *Ātman*, which is One-without-a-second, as his own Self.

A meditator should select a private and solitary place for meditation. He should empty his mind of all desires, and control all motions and sensations of his motor and sensory organs. He should focus unswerving attention on *nādam, saguṇa Brahman*, infinite *Ātman*. Thus he should overcome physical identification and, by means of inner feelings, should recognize and realize Unity and identification with *Ātman*, *Brahman*. Firm abidance of the Self, I am, in the Cosmic Self, I AM, without wavering, is the key to self analysis.

Man is the epitome of the Universe, and human mind is the real Temple of the Supreme, where it can be realized. The process of contemplation opens the secret of this eternal Temple.

The Soul, in its descent into the physical body, has become associated with the mind. In its present form it is dominated by the mind. Mind and Soul are coupled together, so to speak, and the Soul goes wherever the mind goes. The mind receives and retains impressions of the empirical world. These worldly impressions cause desires, hankerings, and psychosexual activities, not all of which can be fulfilled, or which, in being fulfilled, produce problems whose solution is incompatible with the original circumstances. This unending chain, this round of cravings and events is called *rāga* and *vāsanā*. According to these *rāgas* and *vāsanās*, individual soul goes through the processes of birth and rebirth.

Since Soul and mind are apparently knotted together, the Soul is forced to follow the mind, to lend its support, and to suffer the consequences of *rāgas* and *vāsanās*—the longings of the mind. *Vairāgyam* is a state in which the mind is prevented from pursuing *rāgas* and *vāsanās* and sensual pleasures, and permitted to escape the dire consequences of *karmas*. He who is successful in achieving this state, is called *vitarāgah*, detached, dissociated. *Rāga* and *vāsanā* cause the senses to produce gigantic waves of sensual pleasure. Mind should gradually be withdrawn from *rāgas*, *vāsanās*, and sensual pleasures, and should be specifically focused on its center, the third eye, so that it may unite with *nādam*, sound current, the ultrasonic lifestream, and rise above the world of phenomena.

The human body is compared to a house with ten doors. Nine openings lead the individual to the outer world, where he becomes involved in material life. The tenth door, the third eye, leads a student toward the inner world, *Brahmaloka*, the world of *Ātman*, the true home from which the Soul has descended, and brings the wanderings of the mind to an end.

*Mantras* or *nāmas* are of two kinds: 1) *Varṇātmaka*, articulated and expressed through language; 2) *Dhvānyātmaka*, vibration, echoing. There are many *varṇātmaka mantras*, but the *dhvānyātmaka nāma*, *mantra*, is one and the same through all ages. It is the unwritten word, the unspoken language, the Eternal constitution, and Eternal companion. *Varṇātmaka* is the means, while *dhvānyātmaka nāma* is the goal or end. *Dhvānyātmaka mantra* is Eternal; hence, it transscends cause and effect, time and space. Devotion to *varṇātmaka mantra* leads to purification of the mind; devotion to *dhvānyātmaka mantra* leads to union and identity with *Brahman*.

It is within; it resounds in the entire body, making the center of its manifestation within the head behind the eyes. A meditator should focus his consciousness in unwavering attention to the center behind the eyes. This center is the seat of mind and Soul. When mind waves are concentrated here, one begins to feel identity with the vibrating sound currents. Since *dhvanyātmaka mantra* is Universal and Infinite, the student later feels the entire Universe, every compound, molecule, element, and atom vibrating in this Eternal music. It cannot be described, nor can it be learned from books. Only perfected ones themselves can teach it, and only experienced students can understand their teachings.

The place for meditation must be pure, private, and solitary. Communion between the Supreme and the individual is impossible in full form without fulfilling this condition. "*Brahman* is my only support, my father, mother, treasure, friend, beloved, learning, my all in all." This must be the firm determination in meditation. *Brahman* cannot be realized if any other expectation or hope of enlightenment is present in the mind in contra-distinction with *Brahman*.

The sole essence of realization is Love. A fiance for his fiancee, a miser for his wealth, and a mother for her child all have constant love, however busy they are in ordinary or serious activities of life. These forms of love separately are inadequate for Self-realization. One must unite and multiply them to realize *Brahman*. In short, a student must have unique, extraordinary, and infallible love to be able to realize *Brahman*. When this state of realization is attained, the student is called *ananya dhi*, *Brahman* identified.

The meditation place must be thoroughly clean, a place where worldly conversation is never allowed. The meditation seat should be neither too high nor too low, neither too soft nor too hard. The lotus posture is best; however, one may assume any easy posture, provided that the body is balanced, chest supporting neck and head without strain. Trunk, neck, and head must be erect and still. The entire body should be without voluntary motion, so that one can examine the motion of Cosmic Forces within and around oneself. One should deeply relax, so that every cell and tissue of the body have freedom from tension, and can project *tanmātric*, supraelectronic motion of life. Regularity, simplicity, and moderation in eating, sleeping, and entertainment must be maintained. One must adopt the middle path for practice.

Complete effacement of ego forces is essential for Self-realization. There should be elimination of all individual taints, prejudices, and idiosyncrasies.

As the mighty electromagnetic waves of sunlight are not moved by wind, so the mighty electromagnetic motion of mental waves should not be moved from *nādam* by the influx of desires.

When the disciplined mind is established exclusively in *nādam*, in Self, when it is free from all desires, then one is harmonized in *Yoga*. To gain experience of the essential Self, the seeker should, first of all, empty the Soul of all desires, images, operations and representations of the material mind. This is the negative process, which creates the ability of mind to apprehend pure Self, to achieve the beatific vision of the Supreme. Positive radiation of *nādam*, of Self, cannot be experienced without negating individuality. Self-realization is a lifelong process, and *nirvāṇam* cannot be attained in a few days, months, or years; therefore one should not become excited, nervous, or straining for a vision because, by allowing such disturbances, one may suffer disappointment.

The mind will run away from meditation to various attractive objects. Do not feel disturbed by this. Carefully bring it back to *nādam* by practicing sound current. All *karmas* are consumed by the fire of *Brahman* and, by means of a pure and serene mind, one begins to experience the radiation of *Brahman* everywhere. The mind becomes supremely peaceful, all passions are at rest, and Supreme happiness comes. While listening to *nādam*, or meditating on *nādam*, *śabda-Brahman*, the meditator should reach the state where he feels the emanation of all physical and mental energies from *Brahman*. He should feel that each and every cell of his body is related to the mighty waves of the Infinite ocean of sound current. Phenomenon becomes noumenon, and noumenon becomes phenomenon. The world of phenomenon is transformed into Infinite *Brahman*, and *Brahman*, which was noumenon, or unknown, becomes known upon enlightenment. The seeker achieves vivid contact with Reality.

The Self cannot be realized through mere logical and philosophical discussion. Philosophy may carry a seeker to the gates of a promised heaven, but it cannot admit him. For admission he needs to meditate to obtain insight and direct perception.

By practicing concentration on *nādam* he should reach the point where he experiences the entire Universe vibrating in, *nādam*, and perceives radiant *nādam* in every phenomenon of the Universe. When he sees the entire Universe in the Self, and the Self in the entire Universe, he attains infinite happiness, *nirvāṇam*.

According to the evolution and purity of mind, there are two classes of meditation: 1) Meditation on an object or concept, which is called relative meditation; and 2) Meditation without these is called transcendental meditation. When mind is not absolutely pure, then one is advised to meditate on an object or a concept; that is to meditate on God, on sound current, or on anything else, which is Spiritually attractive to the mind. When mind is pure, then one is advised to meditate without proposition, just to meditate: "Who am I?" Meditation on an object is mental, but meditation without an object, only seeking to know "Who am I?" is Spiritual.

It is common experience that after a certain amount of practice of meditation, beginners feel happy in union with *Brahman*, but their union with *Brahman* is so premature and weak, that it is disturbed easily by any phenomenon or happening; consequently a meditator may become angry or disappointed. One should overcome these manifold phenomena and occurrences to experience Identity and Unity.

## SUTRA NO. 39

आत्मन्येवाखिलं दृश्यं प्रविलाप्य धिया सुधीः ।
भावयेदेकमात्मानं निर्मलाकाशवत्सदा ॥३९॥

ĀTMANYEVĀKHILAM DṚŚYAM PRAVILĀPYA DHIYĀ SUDHĪḤ.
BHĀVAYED EKAM ĀTMĀNAM NIRMALĀKĀŚAVAT SADĀ.

| | | |
|---|---|---|
| आत्मनि | Ātmani | In the Self |
| एव | Eva | Alone |
| अखिलम् | Akhilam | Entire |
| दृश्यम् | Dṛśyam | Sense-perceived Universe |
| प्रविलाप्य | Pravilāpya | Having dissolved |
| धिया | Dhiyā | By Intelligence |
| सुधीः | Sudhīḥ | The wise man |
| भावयेत् | Bhāvayet | Should identify |
| एकम् | Ekam | One |
| आत्मानम् | Ātmānam | Self |
| निर्मल-आकाशवत् | Nirmala-ākāśavat | Like the pure ether |
| सदा | Sadā | Constantly |

The wise seeker who carefully investigates his Self, keeping his mind free from all thoughts, will find that every object of the Universe is melting into Consciousness. Experience *Ātman* present everywhere like ether, the colorless, formless atmosphere.

The wise student, through intelligent discrimination, should dissolve all phenomena in *Ātman* alone, and constantly identify with

*Ātman*, which is shining, radiating, overpowering Energy, and is All-pervasive like pure *ākāśa*, ether.

Anger and disappointment, due to disturbances created by others, are natural in an ordinary man. One must develop insight into such disturbances, and learn to treat all as manifestations of *Ātman* and as one's own manifestations. Whatever fault is seen in others, one should know that same fault is in himself. Otherness is the cause of the disturbance. No one becomes as upset and nervous over his own mistakes and disturbances as he does over others' disturbing behavior. To become angry at others' mistakes may be natural to a layman, but the student of *Yoga* philosophy should not become disturbed or angry, for every occurrence brings some new knowledge; thus one's attitude must be impartial and of non-identity. "Think for others whatever you think for yourself, and do not think anything for others which you do not like for yourself." This must be the primary motto of the meditator.

The Ultimate Reality behind you and the person who disturbs you, or gives you some trouble, is one Reality; therefore, every objective and subjective phenomenon should be dissolved in the Ultimate Reality, *Ātman*.

"The more that people disturb me, the more I shall advance in Self-realization and in my aim of life." Give this suggestion to your mind and practice this suggestion for a certain amount of time, and wait for results. Consequently you will realize that people do like you, and their behavior does not then disturb your serenity. On the other hand, on every phenomenon or situation created by others as a problem, you will get more and more encouragement and insight to solve that problem. You will be happy with every problem presented by others, just as a lawyer and a physician are happy with problems presented by their clients and patients.

This is the attitude a meditator should adopt. The success of meditation is demonstrated by tolerance, fellowship, and friendship. Others' attitudes toward you will change. When others' behavior gives us trouble, it means that our own mind is full of trouble. No one else can so disturb us as our own mind. The Supreme is omnipotent; still we suffer. It is omniscient, yet we are ignorant. The mind is the greatest obstacle and disturbance which screens the Supreme from our view, and does not let us behold its omnipresence, omniscience, and omnipotence.

Mind and Soul go together in the world of phenomenon. Real

practice will be possible when the real obstacle is recognized, and dualism is dissolved in Supreme *Ātman*.

The individual is in contact with the outer world by means of mind and senses, but, strangely enough, the mind itself has been enslaved by the senses, which are fond of pleasure. The mind has acquired a phenomenal and downward tendency. It jumps from one object to another without getting any satisfaction. No objective phenomenon can hold it forever or even for any length of time. When the mind is withdrawn from the phenomenal and sensual world and made to go in, it is dissolved with its phenomenal world into *Brahman*, the Supreme and Eternal melody which is echoing in the entire Universe. This something is new to mind and wonderfully attractive. The mind begins to dance with its supraelectronic waves, *tanmātric* motion, and if once it comes into its contact, the mind does not go out again, and it becomes still and serene.

If one wants to take from a child anything which is dangerous to him, one must give him something more attractive; then one can take from him that which is dangerous. Without substituting something equally or more attractive, one will disturb the child. In the same way, one should present this divine melody of *nādam* to one's mind, and one's mind will thus lose all phenomenal characteristics.

There is no other unfailing method to still the mind, and to make it remain steady. Austere discipline, rituals, penance, hard life, and other such measures have only a temporary effect. The light of the sun is covered by the cloud of ignorance. When by the wind of inspiration the cloud is scattered, then the light of the sun of Self will shine in its own glory.

In contact with *śabda-Brahman*, *nādam*, the mind loses its fickleness—becomes quiet, serene, and transforms into the light of *Brahman*. "Thy will be done," should be the attitude of a meditator. He should resign all his work to *Brahman* by fixing his Consciousness in the Self, being free from desires and egoism. Life is a constant struggle, and in this struggle, individuality should be surrendered to Universality, to *Brahman*, who presides over Cosmic Existence and activities.

Whether it is individual existence or Universal Existence, on both sides work is performed by Nature, *prakṛti*, but man, bewildered by the ego, thinks, "I am the doer." He who knows the true character of the two existences of Nature is not bewildered. *Prakṛti* and its Cosmic Forces present the limits of human freedom, such as forces of heredity and the pressure of environment. The psychological self is the product of *prakṛti* in the same way as the whole Cosmic process and the Cosmos are the result of the operation of *prakṛti*.

It is stated in the commentary on verse 23 in the discussion of the philosophical existential approach that substance is inherently related to quality and action. Qualities and actions cannot stand separately from their substances. It is also stated that all other substances are conditional, that only *Brahman* is Ultimate and Unconditional substance. Conditional qualities and actions with their substances should be dissolved in the Ultimate substance, *Brahman*, and the knower of Supreme Reality should live identified with Supreme Reality.

## SUTRA NO. 40

रूपवर्णादिकं सर्वं विहाय परमार्थवित् ।
परिपूर्णचिदानन्दस्वरूपेणावतिष्ठते ॥४०॥

RŪPAVARṆĀDIKAṀ SARVAṀ VIHĀYA PARAMĀRTHAVIT.
PARIPŪRṆACIDĀNANDASVARŪPEṆĀVATIṢṬHATE.

| | | |
|---|---|---|
| रूप-वर्णादिकम् | Rūpa-varṇādikam | Form, color, etc. |
| सर्वम् | Sarvam | Everything |
| विहाय | Vihāya | Discarding |
| परम-अर्थ-वित् | Parama-artha vit | The knower of the Supreme |
| परिपूर्ण- | Paripūrna- | Full, infinite |
| चित्-आनन्द- | Cit-ānanda- | Consciousness-Bliss |
| स्व-रूपेण | Svarūpeṇa | Embodiment |
| अवतिष्ठते | Avatiṣṭhate | He abides |

Thus investigating the Nature of the Self, the "I," deeper and deeper, the Universe of the senses is experienced as nothing but sensation; and sensation is experienced as nothing but the vibration of matter and energy. Going further into deeper analysis of the Self, the "I," the seeker experiences the entire Universe as the radiation of Pure Consciousness, "I"; and he dwells as the embodiment of infinite Consciousness and Bliss.

All the substance of the conditional world with their qualities and actions are impermanent and are changing into one another;

hence, from the viewpoint of the Absolute, they have no separate existence. Subjective and objective multiplicity of names and forms should be submerged and merged in *Brahman*, and the meditator should recognize his Soul as the embodiment of infinite Consciousness, Existence, and bliss. *Yoga* means union and identification. One does not create this union and identification; it is directly perceived and experienced. In this direct perception and realization, the multiplicity of subjective and objective substances with their qualities and actions comes as an obstacle, but it is only an apparent obstacle. When one goes into a deeper state of Self-realization, one will find that this multiplicity serves as a searchlight, a signpost, or a milestone in one's flight and journey of meditation. Gradually one will find that it is because of this multiplicity that one discovers Unity. This multiplicity is melted into the ocean of the Supreme; melting of this Universe will be according to the quality and quantity of meditation.

Thus this multiplicity serves many purposes in the analysis of Self. It is restless support, it is an indicator of one's progress, it is a detacher of one's mistakes, it is a dispenser of hope and faith because it is a manifestation of Reality. This multiplicity will continue to serve its purposes as long as direct identification with *Brahman* is not realized.

How can one measure success in meditation? What is happening? What does one feel? What does one think? What does one speak? What does one see? What does one understand? What does one perceive, infer, and imagine?

These are samples of an inexhaustible stock of questions. To describe through language what is felt by one's inner Consciousness in experimentation is extremely difficult.

Concentration, whether external or internal, is performed by four main agencies: 1) Subject, psychic energy, individual consciousness; 2) Instrumentation–body, including sensory organs for sensation, motor organs for motion; 3) Medium–internal and external environment; and 4) Object–that upon which this experimentation is performed. The result of action and counteraction, motion and sensation, fission and fusion of these four agencies is called knowledge, and this knowledge indicates union and identification of these forces. A change in any force will necessarily make a change in the other three.

A student should unravel the mystery of his own life. This is important to him for it will lead to union with *Brahman* and the Universe. The more zealous he is in application to the practice of meditation, the farther he will go within, and the greater will be his transcendental knowledge.

The physical structure of men within and without is the same; their mental and Spiritual make-up is also the same, but it is difficult to believe because of seeming multiplicity. *Nādam*, *śabda-Brahman*, the way of union, is already present within man, and it serves all living beings and non-living beings alike.

When we see Reality with our inner eye, only then are we convinced of the correctness of the teachings of liberated Souls.

How did we come to this present state of existence? Whence have we come? Where shall we go? To know the answers to these questions one needs to realize identity with *Brahman*.

There are three main existences: 1) Spiritual; 2) Mental; and 3) Material. In the purest state there is only Spirit, radiating light and penetrating love. Mind is like a fish, and *nādam*, Cosmic music, is like an ocean. Directly below this Spiritual Existence are beautiful regions of the mind in which Spirit in its descent unites with mind, and seemingly puts the coverings of causal and astral bodies to function in these regions. The mind is more powerful in mental existence; the Spirit is veiled there. Finally, the Spirit, together with the mind and other coverings, reaches material existence. Here the Spirit has physical limitations and material coverings to work in material existence.

In the material region, the Soul is untraceable; the mind, confined in physical limitations, is confused, restless, weak, and ignorant. Here the mind is in the darkness of *sansāra*, the course of human existence, with no idea of the true Nature of the Soul, and the mind is inclined to be fearful. The mind creates an illusory individuality, which causes the Spirit to forget its union with the Supreme. Here arises the need for light, which will free the mind from the dominion of passion, and show the realm of Reality to the Soul. Light will expose the illusory nature of the material world in which the soul ignorantly lives.

In lower regions the ruling force is *cittam*, mindstuff; subtle and powerful forces of *cittam* isolate Spirit, hold it captive, and prevent its return to the realm of Reality; consequently Spirit, confined to the regions of mind and matter, forgets its original glory and undergoes suffering.

The positive forces of the Soul are captivated here by the negative forces of the mind. These negative forces of the mind are so subtle in their operation that they cannot be controlled except by concentration on *nādam*.

It is common experience that one descends when one is under the influence of mental forces. This is the way of creation; *cittam* is the cause of creation. When the Soul enters the mental world and forms associations with mind and matter, it is disconnected from *nādam*, *śabda-Brahman*, which is the realm of Reality. Thus the Soul and the mind become progressively more subject to the snares of the senses in order to work in the regions of mind and matter.

Through lower desires, and excitation of instincts, man becomes adulterated. For temporary physical satisfaction he runs after tangible things such as alcohol, tobacco, entertainment, hypnotism, stimulants, sedative drugs, tranquilizers, sleeping pills, and other narcotics and intoxicants. Unfortunately such things poison the atmosphere of *Ātman*, and plunge man deeper into the material world from which he is trying to escape. Thus he progressively surrenders to animal desire, and is compelled to assume animal bodies to satisfy his carnal desires; still descending, he passes into vegetable forms.

A wise man does not live heedlessly. Life is not merely a game. It is a consequential proceeding of Nature. We have to know this truth and adapt to life's requisites. In order to free oneself progressively and to find again the original abode of *Brahman*, one should seek to remain in union with *Brahman*.

How to ascend? The Soul is maladjusted and restless in the regions of mind and matter. Its situation has become worse and worse. Companionship cannot exist in disharmony. In the physical plane, the Soul is obscured and the mind is ignorant. Both are under the influence of matter. They wander from place to place, life to life, subject to subject, object to object, object to subject, in the mighty process of transmigration. Soul and mind find no resting place. All creation is unhappy. Only he who is in rapport with *Brahman* is happy.

Pleasures of the material world cannot satisfy the restless mind, nor can the glowing light of mind remove obscuration of the Spirit. In order to create harmony, the mind must follow the spirit, and the spirit must follow the light of *Brahman*; otherwise the mind will remain discontented, and the Spirit will remain undiscovered.

It is common experience of meditators that they feel Unity and identity with *Brahman* in *samādhi*, but when they leave that state, they experience the multiplicity of the subjective-objective world. What will happen to their duality and multiplicity in liberation?

## SUTRA NO. 41

ज्ञातृज्ञानज्ञेयभेदः परे नात्मनि विद्यते ।
चिदानन्दैकरुपत्वाद्दीप्यते स्वयमेव तत् ॥४१॥

JÑĀTṚJÑĀNAJÑEYABHEDAḤ PARE NĀTMANI VIDYATE.
CIDĀNANDAIKARŪPATVĀD DĪPYATE SVAYAMEVA TAT.

| | | |
|---|---|---|
| ज्ञातृ- | Jñātr- | Knower- |
| ज्ञान- | Jñāna- | Knowledge- |
| ज्ञेय- | Jñeya- | Object to be known |
| भेदः | Bhedaḥ | Difference in |
| परे | Pare | Supreme |
| आत्मनि | Ātmani | In Self |
| न | Na | Not |
| विद्यते | Vidyate | Is |
| चित्-आनन्द- | Cit-ānanda- | Of pure Consciousness and Bliss |
| एक-रुपत्वात् | Eka-rūpatvāt | Because of its true nature |
| दीप्यते | Dīpyate | Shines |
| स्वयम् | Svayam | By itself |
| एव | Eva | Alone |
| तत् | Tat | Indeed |

Knowledge of the relative Universe depends on the trinity of the knower, the means of knowledge, and the knowable; but in the state of pure Consciousness, there is no such distinction. The Supreme Self is pure Bliss and it shines alone.

Supreme Self—being the Nature of Ultimate Consciousness, Existence, and Bliss—is beyond the process of empirical knowledge, which includes distinction between the subject (i.e. the knower), instrumentation, object, and medium. The Self is radiating and Self-luminous.

Empirical knowledge is the result of the union of subject, object, medium and instrumentation. The real Self is free from these distinctions; it is equally immanent and transcendental to all four forces. Empirical knowledge is relational and conditional; therefore, it is imperfect. The real Self excludes all relations; hence, its knowledge is Self-revealing and perfect.

The real Self, which is pure Consciousness, is not an object of knowledge because it is equally the basis of the subject, object, instrumentation, and medium; hence it can be neither the subject nor the object in the knowing process.

The subject, object, instrumentation, and medium cannot be excluded and separated from *Ātman*. In no state of mind is the subject seen before itself as an object. A thing becomes an object only when we think of it as having a place in space and time. Cause and effect, space and time, as well as objects that fall within their range of influence, are there only in relation to the Self that holds them together. *Ātman*, *Brahman*, Universal witness of All knowledge, is unmanifest and imperceptible through the senses.

Whatever is presented as an object is a manifestation, a product of cause and effect, space and time. Every manifestation is phenomenon, which is empirically and conditionally real, but from the viewpoint of the Absolute is unreal; thus, whatever is an object is unreal. All objects are unreal. Only the subject, the Universal and constant witness, Self, is real. *Ātman* cannot be grasped as an object of knowledge, because it is beyond causality; hence, it cannot be the object of empirical knowledge. As the sun cannot be seen except by the light of the sun, so *Ātman*, Self, cannot be realized by any self-qualified internal organ, but can be realized by the light of the Self alone.

Processes of empirical knowledge are alike in men and in animals. In animals these processes are going on instinctively without insight or judgment, without consideration of far-reaching consequences, but men use their wisdom; however, this use of wisdom is only a difference of degree in empirical knowledge. Wisdom is not the exclusive property of man; it is manifested in animals too, especially when they have been trained. Even among men, different persons have varying degrees of wisdom.

In all empirical experiences we see that the selective nature of mental activity, practical interest, previous experiences, and predeterminations influence the whole thought procedure. The empirical process of knowledge consists of a narrow range of perception. Internal organs help a man to concentrate his consciousness on a particular limited perception by excluding other perceptions. Empirical perceptions, experiences, and interpretations are never self-explanatory; they are assumed to have a significance for practical purposes. Our logical laws, natural laws, and scientific principles are established according to practical laws and purposes.

Ultimate Reality could not be realized by the empirical process of knowledge even though a man were endowed with thousands of organs of sense perception. It is difficult to separate objective knowledge from subjective experience. The more we examine objective phenomena, the more we see it expanding. Ultimately we feel that our empirical knowledge regarding objective phenomena is incomplete. A man with normal vision can see, but a blind man cannot see. A man having *Brahmanubhava*, sense of *Brahman*—the last and largest sense—sees, knows, and experiences Ultimate Reality. Others, like a blind man, cannot see it. Empirical knowledge is not wrong; it is valid in its premises, but it is not complete in itself.

The instrumentation, i.e., the psychological finite consciousness, is limited to a certain kind and order of experience in which bodily states play an important part; therefore the body, mind, and senses should be purified, so that the body can become the Temple of Reality. To an awakened Soul, the true Temple is mindstuff, through which *citti*, Ultimate Reality, is manifested. The body is the epitome of the entire Universe. Man is the microcosm, and the Universe is the macrocosm. This macrocosm is searched, studied, and identified through the microcosm. When this threshold of the Temple is expanded by contemplation, the Soul finds itself in the realm of Reality.

The objective world of cause and effect, space and time, exists for the knowing subject. The two depend on each other, the empirical subject, Self, and the empirical object. Thinking and logic belong to finite consciousness, while *nādam*, *śabda-Brahman*, transcends the entire empirical process of knowledge. It is Self-revealing, Self-shining, Self-radiating, Self-existing, and complete in Itself. By concentrating your consciousness on it, you will be identified with *Brahman* and you will be beyond the world of birth, death, and suffering, the world of causality. Knowledge of *Ātman* is all-inclusive.

The subject and *Ātman* mean immanent and transcendental Reality. Empirical existence, including one's body and mind, is the object and non-*Ātman*. The empirical subject is as unreal as the object. The object includes the individual subject, body, and the phenonmenal, as well as the material world.

The real subject is Ultimate Consciousness, *Ātman, Brahman*, on which the whole objective world depends. Due to imperfections of the mind, *Brahman* appears as an objective world. It is characteristic of all objects of Consciousness that they cannot reveal themselves apart from being manifested as objects of consciousness through modifications of the mind. The true Nature of *Ātman*, *Brahman* can be realized only through meditation, Self-realization through *samādhi*, not merely by reading scriptural texts; however much one may believe in them. Due to ignorance of the real Nature of *Ātman*, the one Absolute Consciousness seems to be broken into empirical subject, object, instrumentation, and medium. This ignorance is the very constitution of the human mind, and it cannot be removed except by identification with *Brahman*.

Perceptions continue to operate in whatever stage we are, and they are true in their operation in their respective planes. In the waking state we have perceptions of the waking world; in the dream state we have perceptions of the dream world; and in deep sleep we have the perceptions of the world of deep sleep. Perceptions and visions are constantly changeful in their nature. When one is in a moving train, one sees the changing scenery, but the perceiver is without change. Likewise, all perceptions are constantly changeful, but the Self is without change. Self-analysis is not only the procedure of perceiving things exactly and accurately as they are, but, in addition to this, its main aim is to discover the perceiver. When the perceiver is discovered, then perception of the total Universe is discovered in its exactness. Self-analysis is not the discovery of one thing or another; it is the discovery of the discoverer. By this discovery the total Universe of past, present and future will be revealed.

## SUTRA NO. 42

एवमात्मारणौ ध्यानमथने सततं कृते ।
उदितावगतिर्ज्वाला सर्वाज्ञानेन्धनं दहेत् ॥४२॥

EVAM ĀTMĀRAṆAU DHYĀNAMATHANE SATATAṀ KṚTE.
UDITĀVAGATIR JVĀLĀ SARVĀJÑĀNENDHANAṀ DAHET.

| | | |
|---|---|---|
| एवम् | Evam | Thus |
| आत्म-अरणौ | Ātma-araṇau | With the Self as the fire producing stick |
| ध्यान-मथने | Dhyāna-mathane | In the churning of meditation |
| सततम् | Satatam | Constantly |
| कृते | Kṛte | Practiced |
| उदित-अवगतिः | Udita-avagatiḥ | Knowledge which is produced |
| ज्वाला | Jvālā | Flame |
| सर्व-अज्ञान- | Sarva-ajñāna- | Of all ignorance |
| इन्धनम् | Indhanam | The fuel |
| दहेत् | Dahet | Burns |

By constant and continuous investigation of the Self, cognition of the real "I" is kindled; and this fire of the Self reduces all *karma* and ignorance to ashes. Self-investigation, meditation, is like rubbing two sticks of wood together to kindle fire. By the friction of individual self against the Universal Self, the fire of knowledge is kindled.

By constant devotion and practice of meditation one kindles the fire of knowledge, which completely burns up ignorance and *karmas*.

Consciously or unconsciously all persons are in search of Ultimate Truth and Reality, because there is no other way of deliverance from ignorance, sorrow, and suffering. Each person according to his intellect has some imagination, interpretation, understanding, and feeling regarding himself and the Universe. Persons search for Reality in various places and by various methods. The practice of meditation with utmost love is the highest way of Self-realization. Experience obtained in the process of meditation must be properly understood. The process of meditation should be controlled by knowledge.

"Taking as the bow the great weapon of the *Upaniṣads*, knowledge of *Brahman*, one should place in it the arrow sharpened by meditation. Drawing it with a mind engaged in concentration upon that *Brahman*, O beloved, know that imperishable *Brahman* as the target."

The body is the bow; one's Consciousness is the arrow; *nādam*, *saguṇa Brahman*, is the target. Identify your Consciousness with *nādam*, *Brahman*, by completely forgetting your physical consciousness. Developing a one-pointed mind, one becomes united with *Brahman* as the arrow becomes one with the target.

One should persevere until one has achieved one of two things; either one should discover for oneself the Truth about the Universe, or one should learn from someone else. If this is impossible, one should take the best and most practical way of life to cross the ocean of ignorance and to obtain knowledge.

By practice of meditation, the sense of separation is overcome, and actions do not bind because one does nothing for selfish motives. Having attained wisdom, one becomes free from attachment. One will not fall again into confusion, for one sees all Existence as manifestation of *Brahman*. Even though a man be most sinful, he shall cross over all seas of life by the boat of wisdom.

As fire turns fuel to ashes, so the fire of knowledge turns to ashes all work. There is nothing on earth equal in purity to wisdom, but this type of wisdom is not obtained by the reading of books or listening to lectures. Wisdom is obtained by the practice of *yoga*. He who unites his Consciousness with *nādam, saguṇa Brahman*, and becomes perfected by *yoga* finds Eternal wisdom in his Self in due course of time. It needs only constant practice. He who is absorbed in *nādam* and has disciplined his senses, gains wisdom and attains Supreme Peace.

Here is the suggested technique for meditation:

1. Sit in an easy posture and hold the body steady in a relaxed position. Keep chest, neck, and head erect.

2. Withdraw consciousness from all organs and focus your attention on *ājñā cakram*, the third eye, or on *sahasrāram*, the cerebrum, to identify Consciousness with *saguṇa Brahman*, vibrating *nādam*.

3. Have regular and natural flow of breathing. Hold your breath to check the wandering of your mind.

4. Progressively overcome your ignorance by good associations and good reading.

5. Transform your individuality into Universal Existence.

6. Experience and feel the motion of the electricity of *prāṇa* from each and every cell of your body to the Cosmos, and from the Cosmos to the entire body.

7. Feel gradually the melting of the phenomenal world into the ocean of *ākāśa*, ether, and then the ocean of *ākāśa* melting into the ocean of Supreme Consciousness.

8. Feel the entire ocean of Consciousness vibrating in *nādam*, and use mental pressure to stop the wandering of your mind, as air pressure checks and controls a mechanism.

9. Go into deeper state of meditation and feel the entire ocean of Consciousness filled with the dazzling light of *Brahman*.

10. Feel the merging of empirical subject, object, instrument, and medium in the free flow of *Brahma*-consciousness.

Certain *yoga mudras* and *yoganidrā* will begin to manifest. These remarkable signals are given by Nature in meditation as preliminary forms, which produce the manifestation of *Brahman* in *yoga*. Some are fog, snake, sun, wind, fire, fireflies, lightning, crystal, moon, transformation of individual phenomena into Cosmic phenomena; manifestation of mental and astral bodies in the penetrating, simple state of Nature.

When by means of the practice of *Yoga*, as indicated above, the mind becomes tranquil, then the individual "I" becomes blissful. In this state, think wholeheartedly, devotedly, "Who am I?" for without knowing one's Self, one can attain neither relative bliss nor Absolute tranquility. The Eternity of the Self cannot be created by religious practice, or by any system of philosophy, or by *Yoga* methods. All these practices are intended to purify and cleanse the mind. They do not aim to make the Self Eternal, for Eternity cannot be created. The Self is eternally Eternal. When mindstuff is purified, then one's Self is realized; "I am" is experienced as "I AM."

## SUTRA NO. 43

अरुणेनेव बोधेन पूर्वं सन्तमसे हृते ।
तत आविर्भवेदात्मा स्वयमेवांशुमानिव ॥४३॥

ARUṆENEVA BODHENA PŪRVAṀ SANTAMASE HṚTE.
TATA ĀVIRBHAVEDĀTMĀ SVAYAMEVĀNŚUMĀNIVA.

| | | |
|---|---|---|
| अरुणेन | Aruṇena | By morning twilight, dawn |
| इव | Iva | Like |
| बोधेन | Bodhena | By knowledge |
| पूर्वम् | Pūrvam | Before |
| सम्-तमसे | Sam-Tamase | Complete darkness |
| हृते | Hṛte | When removed |
| ततः | Tataḥ | Then |
| आविर्भवेत् | Āvirbhavet | Rises, appears |
| आत्मा | Ātmā | The Self |
| स्वयम् एव | Svayam eva | Of its own accord |
| अंशुमान् | Anśumān | The sun |
| इव | Iva | Like |

As the sun appears following extinction of darkness by dawn, so the cognition of the Self is experienced after the destruction of ignorance by knowledge.

By the light of dawn, first the darkness of night is destroyed; then the sun appears and shines in its own glory. So ignorance of the mind is destroyed by wisdom obtained in meditation, then *Ātman* is revealed to the seeker, and it shines in its own glory.

Self-analysis has twofold dynamics: 1) Recognition of ignorance, which consists of all phenomena including subject and object, mind and body, and 2) Realization of Self, which is immanent and transcendent.

Knowledge produced by the practice of *nāda-yoga*, *śabda-Brahman*, destroys ignorance; this destruction is simultaneous with the revelation of *Ātman*. Enlightenment without destruction of ignorance is insanity. For those in whom ignorance is destroyed by wisdom obtained through *samādhi*, *yoga*, meditation, concentration and contemplation, intuitive wisdom reveals the Supreme Self shining like the sun.

When the unity of *Brahman* is realized by the individual, he is free from sorrow, suffering, birth and death, and he is enlightened with the light of the Self. When the Self of the perceiver includes all existence, there can be no source of sorrow and suffering because sorrow and suffering are indicative of loss.

Direct perception of all existence in Self, and Self in all existence, is the attainment which is the foundation of freedom and joy. The Supreme Self is immanent and transcendent, and all Existence is its conditional and phenomenal manifestation. There is no opposition between Unity, *Brahman*, and multiplicity, the phenomenal world. All manifestations are from the Supreme; therefore they have fundamental Oneness.

## SUTRA NO. 44

आत्मा तु सततं प्राप्तोऽप्यप्राप्तवदविद्यया ।
तन्नाशे प्राप्तवद्भाति स्वकण्ठाभरणं यथा ॥४४॥

ĀTMĀ TU SATATAṀ PRĀPTO' PYAPRĀPTAVAD AVIDYAYĀ.
TANNĀŚE PRĀPTAVAD BHĀTI SVAKAṆṬHĀBHARAṆAṀ YATHĀ.

| | | |
|---|---|---|
| आत्मा | Ātmā | The Self |
| तु | Tu | Indeed |
| सततम् | Satatam | Always |
| प्राप्तः | Prāptaḥ | Obtained, ever-present reality |
| अपि | Api | Yet |
| अप्राप्तवत् | Aprāptavat | Is not realized |
| अविद्यया | Avidyayā | Because of ignorance |
| तत्-नाशे | Tat-nāśe | That being destroyed |
| प्राप्तवत् | Prāptavat | Realized as though newly obtained |
| भाति | Bhāti | Shines |
| स्व-कण्ठ- | Sva-kaṇṭḥa- | On one's own neck |
| आभरणम् | Ābharaṇam | The ornament |
| यथा | Yathā | As |

The Self is an ever-present reality, and everyone expresses himself by means of his Self alone. Everyone knows his Self as "I," yet because of ignorance of the Nature of the Self, it is not cognized. When ignorance is destroyed, this "I" is realized as ever united with the Cosmic "I." The discovery of the ever-present *Ātman* is like the discovery of a necklace hanging about a woman's neck, while she is searching everywhere else for it.

Although *Ātman*, Reality, which is perceived directly and intuitively, is ever present, man has lost the power of direct and intuitive perception. On the practice of concentration, contemplation, and meditation ("Who am I?"), one attains the state of *samādhi*, in which ignorance is destroyed, and *Ātman* is realized.

The Soul, in the course of its descent to a physical body in the material plane, associates with mind and senses, loses its direct and intuitive perception. In its present condition it sees the phenomenal world according to the mind and senses, accentuates the downward and outward tendency to such an extent that the Soul has forgotten its real Nature. It is caught in the net of desires and hankerings after the phenomena of the senses and mind.

To work out its *karma*, it is entangled with the mind. By this entanglement, it is born again and again. It acquires fresh *karmas* and fresh associations. The bond thus becomes tighter and tighter, and the load of *karmas* becomes heavier and heavier with each rebirth. The Soul has lost its way, and does not know how to come out of this miserable plight.

By the practice of *samādhi*, ignorance is destroyed, and *Ātman* as Conscousness, Existence, and Bliss is recognized. All-pervading *Ātman* is Self-luminous, free, and pure, although it is not recognized by one whose ignorance is not removed by *samādhi*. All Spiritual disciplines—such as study of the scriptures, the practice of austerity, morality, charity, and philanthropic services—are meant to remove ignorance and to purify the mind, so that the mind can perceive and experience the ever-present, ever-shining *Ātman*.

Man need not go afar to search for *Ātman*. It is within him. The head from the eyes upward is the center of manifestation of *Brahman*. There are nine openings in the body from the eyes downward. By means of these nine gates, the mind enjoys the phenomenal world. He who practices meditation and Self-analysis should withdraw his mind from the world and the nine openings, and should focus it on the *ājñā cakram*, the third eye, and on *sahasrāram*, cerebrum, which is the seat of the mind and Soul.

From here he has to go upward. The mind will be connected with *śabda Brahman, nādam*, in the third eye, and he will be able to hear the sweet, melodius, Eternal music. This *nādam* exists in all beings, good and bad, rich and poor, saints and sinners. Although many persons are not aware of its presence and influence, anyone can connect his Consciousness with *saguṇa Brahman, nādam*.

What is the source of *nādam*? It comes from nowhere, for it is omnipresent. It is derived from nothing, for it is Eternal. It is the personal manifestation of the Supreme. It is called *saguṇa Brahman*, for it presides over the *guṇas*, Cosmic Forces and Nature. It is *nirguṇa Brahman*, for it is beyond all. It is manifested in *satya khandam*, *Brahma lokam*, by stages. Upon reaching that higher state, the Soul will be liberated forever from the cycle of births and deaths. Mind attached to the Eternal stream of Consciousness, *nādam*, will no longer crave sensual pleasures. By no other means can attachment of the mind to sensual pleasures be totally rooted out. Everyone should develop intellect and understanding to overcome his ignorance, and thus hear *Ātman* vibrating all Nature as the center of all Existence. It should be experienced.

The mind has gone into the phenomenal world by thinking of worldly things, and its process of withdrawal will be the reverse of this process. One has to undo what one has already done in order to reach the Supreme. The pleasures of the phenomenal world are illusory and reactionary, and their result is suffering. A man is happy having children, wealth, and friends, but if they are contrary to his plans, or they are taken from him, he feels sad. Worldly pleasure is sweet in the beginning, but bitter in reaction in the end. How heartbroken a man feels when his wealth, accumulated by untiring effort, is lost. It is the Bliss of *Ātman* alone, that involves no reaction, and makes a man eternally happy, but this is difficult to learn, and may taste bitter in the beginning.

Self-analysis is the process of research. Every Self-analyst should have knowledge of the methods which have been discovered by great *yogins* and masters. Humanity would not have progressed as it has, if each person had to start from the very beginning, and make every experiment himself. The process of Self-analysis will not be one of discovery but of rediscovery because such experience has already been explored by competent teachers. Everyone can learn from the experience of those who have preceded him. In this way alone will there be progress for humanity.

Rich or poor, high or low, everyone without exception lives in the fetters of *karma*, and everyone will be compelled to clear his account and pay the debt of his *karma*. It is *karma* which keeps a man in the prison of flesh. If one does good deeds, one may be born as a rich man or a nobleman in a good environment; however, such birth will not bring him liberation from the wheel of birth and death. Instead of being a class-C prisoner, he may become a class-A or class-B prisoner, but he is still in prison. This prison cannot be overcome without the knowledge of *Ātman*.

Practice on *nādam* is the way to nullify all *karmas*. This *nā-*

*dam* is beyond the region of mind and *māyā*. When a student submits himself to it, he will be able to reach its source, *Ātman*, *Brahman*.

Many religious persons claim and hanker to discover God, the omnipresent, omniscient, and omnipotent. Is God missing? Is God absent? No, the Self, God, is eternally present in all beings as "I AM." God, Self, is not missing, only misunderstood. Due to misunderstanding, people take as a fact, "I am Mr. So-and-so." When by practice of meditation, this "I am" is detached from identity with the body, then it experiences itself as "I AM." Thus one already is the center of one's being, and cannot be found outside oneself. It can be cognized within, first in the heart, then in the Universe. The Self is as it was countless incarnations before, and it will remain as it is now countless incarnations in the future; therefore, the wise man will seek and find his Self, I AM, eternally abiding at the center of his Existence.

## SUTRA NO. 45

स्थाणौ पुरुषवद्भ्रान्त्या कृता ब्रह्मणि जीवता ।
जीवस्य तात्त्विके रूपे तस्मिन्दृष्टे निवर्तते ॥४५॥

STHĀṆAU PURUṢAVAD BHRĀNTYĀ KṚTĀ BRAHMAṆI JĪVATĀ.
JĪVASYATĀTTVIKE RŪPE TASMIN DṚṢṬE NIVARTATE.

| | | |
|---|---|---|
| स्थाणौ | Sthāṇau | In a stump, post |
| पुरुषवत् | Puruṣavat | Like a man |
| भ्रान्त्या | Bhrāntyā | By mistake |
| कृता | Kṛtā | Is done |
| ब्रह्मणि | Brahmaṇi | In Brahman |
| जीवता | Jīvatā | Individuality |
| जीवस्य | Jīvasya | Of the individual self |
| तात्त्विके रूपे | Tāttvike Rūpe | In its true Nature |
| तस्मिन् | Tasmin | In the Self |
| दृष्टे | Dṛṣṭe | When seen |
| निवर्तते | Nivartate | Is destroyed |

The Universal Self appears to be individual self only because of ignorance, just as in darkness and ignorance one might mistake the stump of a tree for a man. When the Real Nature of the "I" is cognized, the false concept of separateness of the individual soul disappears along with the name and form.

Due to ignorance of the Real Nature of *Brahman*, to a man in bondage, *Brahman*, appears to be an individual soul, *jīva*. This is an illusion, just as in darkness one may mistake a tree stump for a man. When the Real Nature of *Brahman* is realized, this *jīvahood*, individuality, is destroyed.

What is this *jīva*, individual soul? It is I, me and mine. It is the self. Expressions of *jīva* are as follows: "It is I, this is my wife, this is my family, this is my son, this is my property, or my achievement, my position, my religion, my country, my race, and my nation." All that exists belongs to the Supreme, but man thinks himself to be separate from the Supreme. He desires to possess objects, although objects never really become the property of anyone. Having become attached to worldly objects, men exist only for them; thus they continue to be born and to die here. It is not family, relatives, wealth, and possessions which are obstacles and the main cause of *jīvahood*; it is men's mental attitude of attachement and possessiveness.

Individual soul is within everyone and is the Supreme Self. How strange it is that those who live together never meet each other. This separation, or non-meeting, is apparently keeping *jīva*, individual soul, separate from *Brahman*.

The veil of ego is between *jīva* and *Brahman*. This veil cannot be lifted as long as one is fast asleep in the hypnotic trance of attachment. Man has assumed this phenomenal world to be real, and has become part of it, ceasing to even think of *Brahman* and *Ātman*.

People are wasting their valuable days and nights in pursuit of sensual pleasures. As long as people do not long for Self-realization, they cannot come out of this hypnotic trance. Men do not really know love, devotion, knowledge, and unselfish service. No doubt they sometimes think of God, but their prayers and worship are selfish, bargaining for their own comfort and pleasure. If their selfish desires are not satisfied, either they change religions, or they seek another God to make them happy in their own world, or they become atheists. *Nirvāṇam* is not to be created; it is to be realized. Men wish to create their own *nirvāṇam*, to find everlasting satisfaction of their desires. As long as men do not love *Ātman* for the sake of love, they cannot have true love. True longing, true reverence, true devotion, and true knowledge are prerequisites to meditation and Self-realization.

*Saguṇa*, *Brahman*, *nādam*, is the link between man and *Brahman*. Not realizing that One Reality, men are pursued by five enemies, and they suffer various kinds of aches, pains, and sorrows at the hands of these enemies. Who are these five enemies? These are the phenomenal attractions of the five sensory organs. By means of these five sensual attractors, men are caught in the snares of lust, anger, greed, attachment, and egoism. Psychosexual activity is the leader of all these enemies. What is that One Reality? It is the practice of *nāma*, *nādam*, *śabda-Brahman*. Men are entrapped by these five enemies, because they do not practice *OM*. Thieves take whatever they like from a house where the owner is asleep, but they take nothing from a house where the owner is awake! When men practice *nādam*, they awake from the hypnotic trance by which they have been lulled through innumerable incarnations.

When the true Nature of *Brahman* is realized, the notion of individuality and the sensation of dualism disappear. *Jīvahood* is transformed into *Brahmahood*, and it is then realized as the Universal Consciousness, *Brahman*.

About the existence of the Self, no one has any doubt because every activity of life depends on the Self, "I am, I was, I shall be." Only the activity is changing, not the real "I"-principle. In all three times—present, past, and future—the Self remains unchanged. Thus the Self is not in doubt, but it is misunderstood as "I am the body." The body is alive and conscious only because it is in contact with the Self. Without Self, the body is inert as a stone. The moment its contact with Self is broken, the body becomes inert and dead. In investigation of the Self, when the actual and real form of "I" is realized, instead of "I am the body," one experiences "I-am-Consciousness." This "I-am-Consciousness" is indivisible, All-pervasive, and omnipresent. There are not two selves in this Universe. The "I," through which we express our physical and mental manifestations, is not the real "I"; it is the ego, *cittam*. The real "I," free from identity with the body and mind, is God himself.

Knowledge of *Ātman*, obtained through *samādhi* destroys at once such mistaken ideas as "I, mine, thou, thine, he, his," which are the result of ignorance. Practical experience is needed.

# SUTRA NO. 46

तत्त्वस्वरूपानुभवादुत्पन्नं ज्ञानमञ्जसा ।
अहं ममेति चाज्ञानं बाधते दिग्भ्रमादिवत् ॥४६॥

TATVASVARŪPĀNUBHAVĀD UTPANNAṀ JÑĀNAM AÑJASĀ.
AHAṀ MAMETI CĀJÑĀNAṀ BĀDHATE DIGBHRAMĀDIVAT.

| | | |
|---|---|---|
| तत्त्व-स्वरूप- | Tattvasvarūpān | The true Nature of the Self |
| अनुभवात् | Anubhavāt | Due to experiencing |
| उत्पन्नम् | Utpannam | Produced |
| ज्ञानम् | Jñānam | Knowledge |
| अञ्जसा | Añjasā | Instantly |
| अहम् | Aham | I |
| मम | Mama | Mine |
| इति | Iti | Thus |
| च | Ca | And |
| अज्ञानम् | Ajñānam | Ignorance |
| बाधते | Bādhate | Destroys |
| दिक्-भ्रमादिवत् | Dik-bhramādivat | Like confusion about directions |

In the presence of knowledge arising from the realization of the true Nature of Self, ignorance and the products of ignorance, such as "me" and "mine,"' are immediately destroyed, just as disorientation disappears in the face of the sun.

Wisdom regarding the true Nature of Reality, manifested by Self-realization through *samādhi*, immediately destroys ignorance which creates the phenomenal world, and conceals the Nature of *Brahman*, just as the sun destroys confusion regarding directions.

Where can men find reality? In religious books and in holy scriptures, one may find praise of God, and even a description of the method to see him. There are descriptions of temples, mosques, synagogues, and churches, etc., but one should not forget that God cannot be seen by mere description and prescription. One will find the answer regarding the real Nature of the Universe within oneself. Just as diseases cannot be cured by reading and reciting prescriptions, so Reality cannot be realized merely by reading holy books. However a person may repeat the names of delicious foods in his mind, he is not able to taste them, nor can he satisfy his hunger. On the other hand, when a person prepares delicious food and eats it, he will enjoy it and be satisfied. Likewise, holy books and scriptures contain only the description and prescription of Reality, not Reality itself.

One is not advised to abandon reading scriptures and hearing instructions but, in addition to these things, one is advised to do Self-analysis. One must know one's own ultimate Nature, and the ultimate Nature of the Universe.

There are two main types of seekers: introverts, whose natural tendency is to explore the inner life of Existence; and extroverts, whose natural inclination is toward work in the outer world. The *yoga* knowledge is more suitable for the introvert, and the *yoga* of action is more suitable for the extrovert. This distinction is relative only, for all men are, in varying degrees, both introvert and extrovert. On the other hand, in the Absolute sense, there are no inner and outer worlds. The real Nature of human mind is beyond introvert and extrovert, although it includes both.

Obstacles to Self-analysis cannot be removed, nor can insight be gained, merely by reading books. One must practice Self-analysis. Reality is within everyone, just as the possiblity of fire is within wood, but not every individual can realize it, nor can it be of use to him in his present ignorant state. As fire can be produced by rubbing two sticks of wood together, so knowledge to englighten the mind and senses is produced when *cittam*, Consciousness, is influenced by *nādam*.

The body may be regarded as being of two parts, that above the eyes and that below the eyes. Below the eyes are nine apertures usually open to sensual pleasures. When the nine apertures are closed, and Consciousness is focused on *sahasrāram*, the vital energy is directed upwards to the cerebrum, the seat of *Brahman*, the center of thinking. It may be noticed that whenever a man thinks deeply, his Consciousness is focused in his head, and he may place his hands or fingers on his forehead to aid concentration. Daily when one awakens, this energy of Consciousness dawns on *cittam*, descends from the head to the nine apertures, and through them becomes scattered in the outside world. At the time of going to sleep, this energy of Consciousness goes back to its original home, and remains there until the next morning. This process of the mind is compared to sunrise and sunset. In meditation, Consciousness goes higher and higher to realize the unity of the Universe where "I" and "mine," and all relations created by ignorance are destroyed. It is as in the physical world where in higher regions the sun always shines, and the processes of day and night do not exist.

To obtain such a higher state, one should prevent his attention from going outward and downward below the plane of the eyes. One should take one's attention higher and higher by merging it into *nāda*-Consciousness. One cannot return to one's real home without the practice of *OM*. When one's attention has been focused behind the eyes, one finds the sweetest and most melodious sound resounding, attracting, and calling one toward it. In this state, subjective and objective phenomena are submerged and merged in *nādam*. There is no distinction of nationality, race, class, creed, color, sex, wealth, authority, or possessions.

Withdrawing one's attention from the world of the nine openings, and concentrating it on *nādam*, step by step, one reaches higher and higher regions, and eventually one reaches the door of liberation. When one has reached the first rung of the ladder, one has hope of reaching the top as well. The secret of the withdrawal of attention from the nine apertures, and the technique of connecting it with sound current, must be learned from an expert teacher.

Good associations and company, where students know the secret of *nādam*, are important because these associations remove various doubts and difficulties. Consciousness comes to know its origin, its home, and then a mighty electrical current is generated in *cittam* for union with the Supreme. That the mind is conditioned by its associations is an Eternal law; therefore one should occupy one's mind with Spiritual law. In due course of time, one's practice is completed, and one's Consciousness is united with supreme Consciousness. There is no distance or difference between Oneself and that One which is without a second.

This is the method by which one can obtain *tattva-svarūpānubhava*, Experience of Oneself and the Universe. One attains deliverance from all delusions by *sahaja samādhi*, *śabda-Brahman*. Thus *jīvātman*, individual soul, overcoming all subjective and objective differences, merges in *paramātman*, Supreme Soul, and becomes One with it.

The "I"-thought is the foremost of all thoughts. Upon arising of the "I"-thought, other personal pronouns arise, such as he, you, and we; and on disappearance of the "I"-thought, all personal pronouns disappear as in dreamless sleep; thus this "I"-thought is the creator of relations indicated by all grammatical pronouns. Truly realizing the Reality behind this "I"-thought is the only way to deliverance from suffering. The real I is not limited by time or space. It is limitless Consciousness, but the "I"-thought is limited by time and space, cause and effect, and it creates a distinction of thought such as I, you, and he. On experiencing the center of one's individual I, one feels that the Real I is not this individual I, but that it is Cosmic and transcendent.

One should feel one's existence. Scriptures and books give only words and meaning; they cannot give feeling. Once the seeker has the feeling of Self, he can understand words and meaning of the scriptures correctly. On the contrary, one who is expert in the words and meaning of the scriptures, but who has not felt his real I, cannot have exact knowledge of the meaning of the scriptures. Hence one should experience constantly and feel, "Who am I?" and "Where am I?"

## SUTRA NO. 47

सम्यग्विज्ञानवान्योगी स्वात्मन्येवाखिलं जगत् ।
एकं च सर्वमात्मानमीक्षते ज्ञानचक्षुषा ॥४७॥

SAMYAK VIJÑĀNAVĀN YOGĪ SVĀTMANYEVĀKHILAṀ JAGAT.
EKAṀ CA SARVAMĀTMĀNAM ĪKṢATE JÑĀNACAKṢUṢA.

| | | |
|---|---|---|
| सम्यक् | Samyak | Correctly |
| विज्ञानवान् | Vijñānavān | The realized man |
| योगी | Yogī | The Yogi |
| स्वात्मनि एव | Sva-ātmani-eva | In his own Self |
| अखिलम् | Akhilam | Entire |
| जगत् | Jagat | Universe |
| एकम् | Ekam | One |
| च | Ca | And |
| सर्वम् | Sarvam | Everything |
| आत्मानम् | Ātmānam | The Self |
| ईक्षते | Īkṣate | Perceives |
| ज्ञान-चक्षुषा | Jñāna-cakṣuṣā | Through eye-of-wisdom |

The *Yogi* endowed with realization of the true Nature of the Self, experiences, through the eye of wisdom, the entire Universe in his own Self. He regards everything as pervaded and manifested by the Self, which is One-without-a-second.

When a *Yogi* reaches the state of Absolute englightenment, he attains penetrating intuitive knowledge by which he experiences

Unity in the multiplicity of the entire Universe as his own Self in the same way that an ignorant person feels his body to be his own Self.

"All that the Constitution guarantees is the pursuit of happiness. You have to catch up with it yourself." This is a point to ponder. Self-analysis means discovery of the guarantee of the right to pursue eternal happiness. By practice of *sahaja-yoga samādhi*, identity with *nādam*, one may overtake happiness.

Enlightenment is progressive, which is relative and indicates progress in meditation, and it is Absolute, which is *nirvāṇam*.

When the brilliant sun of Self's majesty arises in the firmament of *cittam*, mindstuff, the three spheres of waking, dreaming, and sound sleep, the earth, interspace, and all the luminous starry worlds, are filled with radiance. The night of ignorance is dispelled. The mists of sin disappear; lust and passion wither. All *karmas*, the elements of Nature, cause and effect, space and time, and individualism, envy, pride, folly, conceit, and artfulnesss have no room in the state of enlightenment. These are negative signs.

These are the positive signs and indications of enlightenment. On the pools of righteousness blossom the various lotuses of wisdom and mystic intuition. Happiness, contentment, continence, and discretion appear in the mind. When the mind is enlightened with the light of the sun of the Self, the positive qualities increase in oneself and negative qualities fade away.

People have forgotten the real Nature of the Self and are rushing to their destruction through addiction to sense enjoyment. Some persons even say, "There is no Self and Ultimate Reality in this world, so let us have a great time here. Who knows whether there is anything after death? Why should we deprive ourselves of enjoyment in this world for the uncertain hope of happiness in the next world?"

Men have become so blind to Truth that they have forgotten their own inevitable death. An individual does not think that he will die. Men see misery and death all around them, but they fancy themselves immune to it. They see friends and relatives die, and their bodies carried to the cemetery or crematory, but they never think of their own end. Everyone must die sometime; this body, the fundamental cause of egoism, will be consumed by fire or interred in earth. Afterwards, everyone has to take a new birth according to past acts and *karmas*.

Individual self is a reflection of the Supreme, but, owing to its association with the mind, it has forgotten the Supreme. *Brahman*, Soul, and mind are tied together in a knot, as it were. The Soul has forgotten its enlightened Nature, and in its present form is enslaved by the longings and hankerings of the mind. Under the influence of natural elements, time, *karmas*, and mind, the Soul must incarnate in various forms of life. For ages it has been doing just this, and thus enduring the resultant suffering. Forgetfulness of the enlightened Nature of the Self, and ingratitude for the activities of the Self, are the cause of misery. Real happiness is forgotten and worldly happiness, which is only an illusion, has become the aim of life.

Animals are slaughtered mercilessly to satisfy our appetites. How would we feel were we to change places with them and suffer similar tortures? One should never forget that the law of *karma* is inexorable, and that one shall reap whatever one has sown. Those beings whom we slaughter now will one day slaughter us.

Poverty, disease, want, and barrenness fall to the lot of man, and fill him with sorrow and anxiety. Unemployment, widowhood, murders, riots, revolts, and wars are playing havoc with men's lives. National life, international life, social life, and political life are fraught with conspiracy and hypocrisy. There is no happiness except in Self-realization, and in showing great love and compassion to all beings. Without Self-realization, there will be no attainment of enlightenment and Eternal salvation, however virtuous and meritorious a man may be. Good *karmas* present a happier, higher, ethical and moral life, and thus they purify the mind, but one should not forget that without meditation these good *karmas* will not grant liberation. One may attain a higher life by virtue of good *karmas*, but as long as one is not liberated, one's body is like a prison, and a prisoner is a prisoner, whether he is Class-A or Class-C. Under the influence of *karmas* one must be born again to reap the fruits of one's meritorious and demeritorious actions as rich or poor, high or low, and then to do good and bad *karmas* again, and so on *ad infinitum*.

One should come out of the cycle of *karmas*, birth and death. The only way to attain freedom from this cycle is to surrender oneself to Self-realization by becoming absorbed in *śabda Brahman*. All of us, rich and poor, happy and unhappy, healthy and unhealthy, man and woman, adult and child, are bound by the vicious cycle of *karmas* and its consequences. Self-realization is not possible until all *karmas*, good and bad, are destroyed.

One should accept with equanimity the consequences of *karmas*, whether good or bad, for they are one's own creation. One should be neither elated, nor depressed, nor resentful in the operation of the consequences of *karmas*. One should bear them without attachment; and thus they will not contaminate one. Bad actions should not be repeated because they inevitably bring sorrow and suffering. Every good action should be performed as a duty and without any selfish motive. Action must be impersonal and rational, and must be performed without desire to secure and enjoy the fruits thereof. Actions performed in this way will not bind the doer. If one performs good and meritorious actions with desire for their fruits, one's rebirth to reap the result of such *karmas* is inevitable.

The cycle of birth and death can be ended when all *karmas* are destroyed by divine fire in meditation, just as a forest can be reduced to ashes when kindled by a spark of fire.

Good karmas purify the mind; thus indirectly they improve meditation, but one should understand clearly that meditation and Self-realization cannot be superseded by good *karmas*. If in this precious human life, one fails to devote oneself to meditation and Self-realization, and goes on performing good and bad *karmas*, one will remain caught in the cycle of birth, suffering, and death. One should practice union with *Brahman*. Union with *Brahman* is the only way to escape the prison of relative existence. First things must be considered first, and second things second; otherwise one may be paying all attenton to good *karmas*, and none to Self-realization.

Due to the desire for pleasure and sense enjoyment, people repeat their mistakes in the round of births and deaths, and they miss the highest opportunity in human life; therefore they will go again and again in the cycle of birth and death. Do not procrastinate, and do not postpone Self-analysis until tomorrow. In all earnestness, ponder these facts, and begin your practice here and now.

Men think, "We shall meditate on God when we are old. This age is not good for meditation. Let us enjoy life now, attend to our wives and children, and make proper provision for them. There will be enough time in old age for devotion to God." This is fallacious reasoning. Old age is a state of involution, when all physical, chemical, biochemical, endocrine, and endopsychic forces turn toward death, and the aging body becomes a moving-mental-institution. In this state, persons become deeply attached to the world. A man cannot begin his meditation in old age because of the set of his habits, attitudes, and his dying physical condition. Furthermore, no one knows when death will overtake him and suddenly end his drama of imagination and planning.

The body consists of three parts—physical, mind or mental, and Spirit; therefore, its activities should be equally apportioned in time—eight hours in each twenty-four for each phase of life. Man has misappropriated the time for Spiritual life—eight hours daily, and therefore he suffers. One would be wise to begin practice now when mind and body are in good health. Do not be anxious for *samādhi* and higher meditation at once. Be content to start and do the best you can. Experiences of meditation will enhance your practice. If concentration is not one-pointed, mind wanders. If you have little time, still do not be discouraged. Nature counts your effort and love. *Yogins* do not ask you to renounce your family, or to become a burden to society. You are expected to earn your bread, to fulfill your duties, and to apportion your time properly, keeping your attention on *Brahman*.

Attachment should be for *Brahman*-identification; love must be expressed in devotion to *nādam*, and the goal must be Self-realization. Other things should be done as a matter of duty, and only to the extent necessary to support oneself and one's family, and to the extent that they do not hinder one's Self-analysis program. With this attitude toward friends, family, society, and nation, all effort should be directed to research of *Ātman*, which is one's Real Existence. All things will be left here after death; only *Ātman* will be there; hence one should not neglect research of *Ātman*.

It is great good fortune to be born a human being, a blessing scarcely to be won by the Gods, as all holy books declare. The human body is an instrument for virtuous and meritorious *karmas*, and the gateway to liberation. Those who have been born as man or woman, and still have not realized *Ātman*, suffer here, and are uncertain about the next world. They are full of mistakes; they beat their heads in vain remorse, and foolishly and falsely assign the blame and cause of their unfortunate condition to fate, destiny, or God. They do not know that fate is nothing but their own past *karmas*, that destiny is nothing but their own driving forces, and that God is not supposed to give reward or punishment to them except on their good or bad *karmas*. Whatever they are, such ideas they project regarding the Universe and God.

The Ultimate object of human life is not enjoyment of material things; even the joys of heaven are short-lived and end in pain. Those born as men, and devoting themselves to sensual pleasures, are foolish indeed. By such devotion, they drink poison instead of the nectar of immortality. Is it not only the foolish or stupid person, who neglects the philosopher's stone, and picks up a worthless rock? Such a man wanders endlessly and aimlessly from one birth to another, under the influence of *māyā*, ignorance, causality, individualism, and the elements and impulses of Nature.

Sometimes the Supreme, who is kind even to the undeserving,

out of compassion and love, gives him a human body, a ship to carry him across the ocean of birth, death, and suffering. In a human body he has an opportunity to win favor and grace of learned men and good teachers, and thus he can overcome suffering and attain liberation—if he uses all possible effort. He who does not practice Self-analysis, and attain *nirvāṇam*, liberation, does not cross the ocean of birth and death. He, who does not recognize and utilize these means to liberation—human mind, body and senses, is ungrateful and careless. This carelessness is real suicide (*sui*, Soul + *cidal* killing). When a man destroys his physical life, he is not really committing suicide; he might more properly be described as committing bodycide.

Mind is the obstruction between individual soul and the Supreme Self. The individual and the Supreme become identical when the mind is purified. Until then the individual self, which is chained to the mind, is dragged along by the mind, which is passionate for worldly pleasures. Thus the individual self suffers the consequences of the wandering of the mind. The individual soul attains freedom when the mind is controlled by the practice of meditation.

The methods to control the mind include: the counting of beads, doing penance, worshiping, praying, and reading scriptures. These methods are temporary, inadequate, and halfway measures. The mind cannot be controlled in this way. A serpent, secured in a basket, will strike again as soon as the basket is opened. When its bag of venom is removed, it becomes completely harmless. Similarly, by adopting various methods, one may make the mind serene and quiet for the time being, but it will attack again, when it sees an opportunity. The practice of firm abidance in the Self as "I AM" removes its venom of doubt, skepticism, and ignorance, and the mind becomes inherently peaceful, serene, and calm.

The mind is naturally fond of pleasure, but only Spiritual joy can satisfy all conditions of the mind; no material enjoyment in the world can hold it permanently. It jumps from object to object for pleasure and, in a short time, becomes tired of every object. It becomes steady when it finds enjoyment which is greater than that found in worldly pleasures. Greatness is happiness and lowness is suffering. This is an Eternal psychological formula. Such greatness, happiness, and Bliss can be attained only in the practice of meditation. To discard the desire for sensual pleasure, the mind must get a taste of Self-analysis.

Individual self, freed from the control of the mind, is able to rise to the state of the Supreme *Ātman*. It is united with it, and experiences everything as the manifestation of *Ātman*.

## SUTRA NO. 48

आत्मैवेदं जगत्सर्वमात्मनोऽन्यन्न विद्यते।
मृदो यद्वद् घटादीनि स्वात्मानं सर्वमीक्षते ॥४८॥

ĀTMAIVEDAṀ JAGAT SARVAM ĀTMANO' NYAN NA VIDYATE.
MṚDO YADVAD GHAṬĀDĪNI SVĀTMĀNAM SARVAṀ ĪKṢATE.

| | | |
|---|---|---|
| आत्मा | Ātmā | The Self |
| एव | Eva | Verily |
| इदम् | Idam | This |
| जगत् | Jagat | Universe |
| सर्वम् | Sarvam | All |
| आत्मनः | Ātmanaḥ | Than the Self |
| अन्यत् | Anyat | Other |
| न | Na | Not |
| विद्यते | Vidyate | Is |
| मृदः | Mṛdaḥ | From clay |
| यद्वत् | Yadvat | In the same way |
| घट-आदीनि | Ghaṭādīni | Pots, etc. |
| स्व-आत्मानम् | Sva-Ātmānam | His own Self |
| सर्वम् | Sarvam | Everything |
| ईक्षते | Īkṣate | Perceives |

This entire Universe is nothing but *Ātman*. Whatever is perceived and sensed is not other than *Ātman*. As pots and jars of clay are verily clay, and cannot be anything other than clay, so to the Enlightened, All that is perceived is nothing but *Ātman*, which is the Ultimate Cause of the Universe.

As pots and jars made of clay are verily clay, and cannot be anything other than clay, so to the Enlightened One All that is perceived is the manifestation of *Ātman*. The Universe of the senses is verily *Ātman*; nothing whatsoever exists other than *Ātman*.

The cause of the appearance of multiplicity is mindstuff. The Universe is *Brahman*, but its appearance as other than *Brahman* is the result of mindstuff; thus, mind, *cittam*, comes between the individual and the Universal Soul. It is the cause of the subjective-objective dichotomy. *Cittam*, in its present condition, stands as a huge, impenetrable barrier between the real subject and the object. *Cittam* is a mighty force with which one has to deal when seeking Self-realization, although it is a product of Nature, and depends on the Soul for its power and sustenance.

Living beings perform their actions through the union of *cittam* and Soul, and wherever mind goes, Soul must go with it. Mind is the instrument by means of which the individual makes his contacts with the exterior and interior worlds, and gathers experience. As the outward tendency of the mind is predominant, the practice of meditation is necessary to turn the mind inward, thus enabling the contact of the individual Soul and the Supreme Soul. When the individual reorientates his mind on its inward course, and brings it back to the third eye, which is its headquarters in the physical body, then it becomes the means of attaining freedom and *nirvāṇam*, instead of being the cause of bondage.

Union of the mind with *Ātman* through the third eye and *sahasrāram* is not easy. The mind goes out continually and does not stay even for a moment at the third eye; thus the mind presents a challenge to the individual, and involves him in a chain of action and reaction. The mind must come back to the third eye, the thinking center, in order to unite with *Ātman*. The mind is naturally fond of pleasure, and cannot be prevented from going outward unless it is offered something greater and more pleasant than it can find in the phenomenal world. Once the mind is led inward by inner Spiritual sound and begins to enjoy the Bliss of the radiating Energy of *Brahman*, it becomes so Blissful that it automatically ceases its wandering. People look for happiness, Bliss, and Eternity outside—but it is within. The nectar which transforms mortal mind into immortal Soul can be drunk only when the mind goes inward.

This nectar is being showered on everyone's *cittam*, but the vessel of mind in which the nectar is to be received, is turned upside down; attention is without instead of within. If you put a cup outdoors during rainfall, upside down, it will not be filled no matter how long the rain continues; but if you turn the cup right side up, it will be soon filled. So it is with the mind. Consciousness, with full attention, must be focused on *nādam*, so that the rain of nectar from *nādam* may fill the mind and transform it into Soul.

One's inner home is full of inestimable treasure, but the mind roams outside. Without entering the inner home, the mind cannot obtain the inner gems. People look for happiness everywhere except within themselves, just like the musk deer, which keeps running in all directions for the perfume of its own musk, never thinking that the fragrance is in itself. People are like a beggar who has a treasure hidden in his house, but not knowing it, he goes about begging alms from place to place. The practice of meditation makes our own treasure within ourselves available to us.

In what sense is the world appearance false? The world is merely a product of *māyā*. This world appearance has been explained as indefinable and indefinite, neither *sat* (is) nor *asat* (is not). Here the opposition of *sat* and *asat* is solved by the category of time. The world appearance is *asat*, is not true, for it does not continue to manifest itself in all times. It has its manifestation until right knowledge dawns. It is not *asat*, false, in the same sense in which we have castles in the air, for these are called *asat*, absolutely nonexistent. The world appearance is *sat*, true, since it appears to be so as long as the state of ignorance persists in the individual. Since it exists for a time, it is *sat*, true, but since it does not exist for all time, it is *asat*, false. This is the appearance and disappearance of world phenomena. It is true in the relative sense and false in the Absolute sense.

As long as right knowledge of *Brahman* as the only reality does not dawn, the world appearance continues in an orderly mathematical manner, uncontradicted by the accumulated experience of all men; and as such, it must be held to be true. It is only because a state comes in *samādhi* in which this world appearance ceases to manifest itself that from the Ultimate and Absolute viewpoint the world appearance is false and unreal.

A cause, in essence, is non-different from its effect, just as clay is non-different from clay pots and other articles made of clay, or as gold ornaments are non-different from gold. What differentiates the cause from the effect is just a name and a form. A man, whether walking, running, sitting, or sleeping, is the same person. The change is only in conditions. Omnipresent, omniscient, and omnipotent God is the cause of the Universe; therefore, this Universe cannot be, in essence, other than its cause. This fact of Oneness of the Universe with *Ātman*, *Brahman* can only be realized when the pure and real Consciousness is felt and experienced without the admixture of mindstuff.

In relative consciousness we do not experience this Truth of Oneness because we have no knowledge of the cause of the Universe. Suppose that a man came to our earth from another planet by a flying saucer. If different articles and ornaments of gold were presented to him, he would not realize their oneness in essence because he had never seen gold on his planet. He would, however, become aware of their oneness if he were shown how ornaments were made from gold. Likewise, he who has felt and experienced his own Self, and has perceived the evolution, growth, and involution of the mind from the Self, will not have difficulty understanding that this entire Universe of past, present, and future is nothing but Self.

## SUTRA NO. 49

जीवन्मुक्तस्तु तद्विद्वान्पूर्वोपाधिगुणांस्त्यजेत्।
सच्चिदानन्दरूपत्वात् भवेद्भ्रमरकीटवत् ॥४९॥

JĪVANMUKTAS TU TADVIDVĀN PŪRVOPĀDHIGUṆĀNS TYAJET.
SACCIDĀNANDARŪPATVĀT BHAVED BHRAMARAKĪṬAVAT.

| | | |
|---|---|---|
| जीवन्मुक्तः | Jīvanmuktaḥ | The liberated one |
| तु | Tu | Indeed |
| तत्-विद्वान् | Tat-Vidvān | Endowed with Self-knowledge |
| पूर्व-उपाधि-गुणान् | Pūrva-upādhi-guṇān | Previous limiting traits |
| त्यजेत् | Tyajet | Should abandon |
| सत्-चित्-आनन्द- | Sat-cit-ānanda- | Existence-Consciousness-Blis |
| रूपत्वात् | Rūpatvāt | Because of his Nature |
| भवेत् | Bhavet | Becomes |
| भ्रमर-कीट-वत् | Bhramara-kīṭa-vat | Like a certain insect that is said to be transformed into a bee |

A *jīvanmukta* endowed with the knowledge of *Ātman* becomes free from the limitations of the body, mind, and senses; hence, he forsakes their attachment. He is identified with Pure Consciousness, whose Nature is Existence-Knowledge-Bliss. He verily becomes *Brahman*, as a certain small insect is said to be transformed into a bee when in contact with the bee.

The knower of *Brahman* becomes *Brahman*. When a man is endowed with Self-knowledge, his mind is enlightened, and he is called *jīvanmukta* because he has attained freedom from all previous *upādhis* and their consequences. *Jīvanmukta* is identified with *Brahman*; hence, he is of the Nature of Absolute Existence, Knowledge, and Bliss. In identification with *Brahman*, the individual soul is transformed into *Brahman* in the same way as an iron ball is transformed into fire in the union with fire.

In the state of ignorance it seems incredible that Consciousness can be directly experienced. It seems to be the product of body and mind because it is influenced by the states of body and mind qualitatively and quantitatively. However, after long practice of meditation, this incredible parable becomes the life of the meditator. He feels that he is related to every object of the Universe in the same way as he is united with his body and mind. This experience leads him to direct identity with the Supreme, and his mind-body becomes a receiving and transmitting set in *Brahman*. In this state his identification with the mind-body unit ends.

This does not mean that the *jīvanmukta*, liberated Soul, has no Consciousness of body and mind. He knows the real Nature of the body and mind, and only his "I"-consciousness for his body is eliminated. His relationship to the body-mind unit becomes natural. Man in the state of ignorance is related to his body-mind unit unnaturally.

This relationship of *jīvanmukta* is changed not only with his body and mind, but also with the rest of the Cosmos, because subjective-objective relationships stand and fall together. It is impossible that *jīvanmukta* be liberated from his body and mind, and not be liberated from the Cosmos simultaneously. In this case he would not be *jīvanmukta*. There is no subject-object division in Ultimate Reality. There is no division of macrocosm and microcosm in the Absolute. These divisions are figurative and descriptive, not prescriptive. A knower of *Brahman*, verily, becomes *Brahman*.

## SUTRA NO. 50

तीर्त्वा मोहार्णवं हत्वा रागद्वेषादिराक्षसान् ।
योगी शान्तिसमायुक्त आत्मारामो विराजते ॥५०॥

TĪRTVĀ MOHĀRṆAVAṀ HATVĀ RĀGADVEṢĀDIRĀKṢASĀN.
YOGĪ ŚĀNTISAMĀYUKTA ĀTMĀRĀMO VIRĀJATE.

| | | |
|---|---|---|
| तीर्त्वा | Tīrtvā | Having crossed over |
| मोह-अर्णवम् | Moha-arṇavam | The ocean of delusion |
| हत्वा | Hatvā | Having killed |
| राग-द्वेष-आदि- | Rāga-dveṣā-ādi | Of personal like, dislike, etc. |
| राक्षसान् | Rākṣasān | The monsters |
| योगी | Yogī | The Yogi |
| शान्ति-समायुक्तः | Śānti-samāyuktaḥ | Completely united and integrated with peace |
| आत्म-आरामः | Ātma-ārāmaḥ | One rejoicing in the Self |
| विराजते | Virājate | Shines |

A self-realized *Yogi*, after crossing the ocean of ignorance and killing the demons of material love and hatred, pain and pleasure, obtains tranquillity and is established permanently in the Absolute Self.

A *Yogi*, who wants to attain the state of *jīvanmukta* (liberated soul), should cross the ocean of ignorance, *māyā*, *avidyā*, conquer the demons and monsters of passion and aversion, material love and hate, ego and its consequences, should have serenity and tranquility in mind, and should dwell in the Existence-Consciousness-Bliss of *Brahman* derived from Self-realization.

These four are the basic qualifications of *jīvanmukta*. Ignorance and enlightenment cannot stand together any more than day and night. These qualifications include many others, both positive and negative. A negative sign is the freedom from selfish desires. A positive sign is the state of identity with the Supreme. These are merely examples.

*Jivanmukta* state or *nirvāṇam* is the state where there is a constant, continuous, and flawless flow of Supreme Consciousness. Health is the greatest gain, contentment is the greatest wealth, self-confidence is the best friend, and *jīvanmukta* is the highest happiness.

Tranquillity, serenity, Consciousness of Spiritual strength, of liberation, courage, and energy, and identity with *Ātman* are the characteristics of *jīvanmuktas*. They represent the growing point of the evolution of Consciousness. By their very existence, character, and Consciousness, they show that human consciousness can rise above its assumed limitations; they proclaim that the ebb and tide of evolution is pushing forward to a new high level. They present an example to stimulate us to rise above our present selfishness and miserliness.

Wisdom is the supreme means of liberation; but this wisdom is not obtained without the evolution of the inner Self. Individual soul takes its departure in the state of purity, carrying with it clinging impurities with which it was unwillingly snared during the unenlightened life. *Ātman* gathers itself into itself, and transforms all objective and subjective pheonmena in the radiating energy of *Ātman*.

Ego is the ten-headed demon because it manipulates the five sensory and five motor organs in relativity. This demon utilizes divine wisdom for its own design. The residence of the ego is surrounded by the ocean of life and death. This story reminds us of the epic of *Rāmāyana*. *Rāma*, the hero of the epic, represents the Self. The ocean represents the misery and suffering of life, and *Sītā*, the consort of *Rāma*, represents wisdom. *Rāma* crossed the ocean, conquered the ten-headed demon and his monster army, brought *Sītā* back, and established *Rāmarājya*, the kingdom of God on earth. Likewise, a seeker must cross the ocean of his personal ignorance, misery and suffering, must kill his own ten-headed demon, the ego, in order to release wisdom from its snares, and thus establish the kindgom of God in his own life. The same story is indicated in other scriptures in such passages as "Thy will be done on earth as it is in Heaven." It is possible for "thy will" to direct one's life only when "my will" is absolutely surrendered to the Supreme. When this is done, naturally the operation of the Supreme is experienced as ruling one's life eternally. The kingdom of heaven is eternally established; it is in Eternal readiness for all. One can only experience it.

## SUTRA NO. 51

बाह्यानित्यसुखासक्तिं हित्वात्मसुखनिर्वृतः ।
घटस्थदीपवत्स्वस्थः स्वान्तरेव प्रकाशते ॥५१॥

BĀHYĀNITYASUKHĀSAKTIṀ HITVĀTMASUKHANIRVṚTAḤ.
GHAṬASTHADĪPAVAT SVASTHAḤ SVĀNTAREVA PRAKĀŚATE.

| | | |
|---|---|---|
| बाह्य- | Bāhya | External |
| अनित्य- | Anitya | Changing, transient |
| सुख-आसक्तिम् | Sukha-āsaktim | Attachment to happiness |
| हित्वा | Hitvā | Having abandoned |
| आत्म- सुख- | Ātma-sukhah | Bliss of the inner Self |
| निर्वृतः | Nirvṛtaḥ | Satisfied (with) |
| घट-स्थ-दीपवत् | Ghaṭa-stha-dīpavat | Like a lamp placed in a jar |
| स्वस्थः | Svasthaḥ | Well-placed |
| स्व-अन्तः | Sva-antaḥ | Within himself |
| एव | Eva | Alone |
| प्रकाशते | Prakāśate | Shines |

The enlightened One relinquishes attachment to material happiness, which is transient and illusory. He experiences the Eternal Peace and Bliss of *Ātman*, that shines inside and outside this body through the senses and mind, as a lamp, placed in a jar with many holes, shines.

The sun shines in its own glory in the firmament of the sky; it is detached from the rest of the solar system, yet it attracts the entire solar system by its magnetism. It is the light and life of the entire solar system and its inhabitants. Similarly an enlightened one shines in his own glory, *Ātman*. He is detached from the entire phenomenal world, yet he is the help, hope, and life for the entire Cosmos.

There are two distinct powers; material and Spiritual. Material power brings external happiness; it is elusive, and is derived from the contact of sense organs with external objects. The entire world hankers after material power, but there are few men who aspire to Spiritual power. The results of material attractions are disease, suffering, death, rebirth, jealousy, hate and war. The results of Spiritual attraction are unity, love, health, and Eternity. Material power is dependent upon the Spirit. Spiritual power is Self-dependent or independent.

How can the reality of the sense-perceived material world be denied? Reality cannot be discerned through the senses. Ultimate Reality cannot be defined as that which is the content and object of right knowledge, for no one can have any concept of right knowledge without a concept of Reality, or a concept of right knowledge. The concept of Reality comprehends within it the ideas and characteristics of unalterability, Absoluteness, and independence. These qualities cannot be apprehended from sense experience because sense experiences are empirical, dependent, relative, and conditional. Sense experiences give Truth, which is only apparent and temporary, never Ultimate and Absolute. Judged from this viewpoint, Ultimate Reality, *Ātman* in all experiences: waking, dreaming, and sound sleep—is the one Self-luminous light of Consciousness, which is identical with itself in all its manifestations of appearance. There is no guarantee that one's present sense experience regarding the world will not be contradicted later. What really exists in all experiences is *sat* and *cit*, pure Existence and Consciousness, not its manifestations.
Consciousness, not its manifestations.

This *sat* and *cit*, associated with all experiences, is not a Universal genus, nor merely the individual appearance of the moment; it is the Existence, Consciousness, True Being, *Sat-cit-ānanda*, the Truth, which forms the substratum of all subjective and objective events and appearances. Things are existent not because they possess the genus of Being, but because they are the appearance of multiplicity imposed on one identical Existence, which is the ground and basis of all experience.

This Absolute Existence, Consciousness, is not the subject matter of the senses. The Supreme, which is the source of all light, the Master light of all revelation, cannot be known by any earthly light or empirical experience. "The sun does not shine there, nor the moon, nor the stars. Then where is this fire, how to speak of this earthly light? Everything shines only with the effulgence of that shining light. Its shining alone illumines all this world."

We can describe what we can perceive, but we cannot guarantee whether it is reality or illusion. We all perceive with our senses that the sun is small; however, our sense perception is contradicted by scientific investigation. Hence, sense perception is not Ultimate, because it is erroneous. In the relative world, though we depend on sense perception, it is not proved valid. In the state of *samādhi*, the world appearance is transformed into *Ātman*; it is not perceived in its present form. In the unenlightened state, through the sense organs, the mind illumines external objects, and one perceives them according to the presentation and coloration of one's own mind and senses; the *jīvanmukta*, the enlightened one, withdraws the mind and sense organs from the outside world and turns them inward. His mind is enlightened with the light of the Self, and the subjective-objective world becomes his *Ātman*. His knowledge and Spiritual radiation constantly issue forth through the organs of sense, like the glow of a powerful lamp placed in a pot with many openings or holes.

When one is liberated, one's mind projects constant Spiritual radiation through the body in the same way as an electric filament projects constant radiation of electric light through its covering globe.

Among the greatest discoveries of our times is the discovery of the tube of light. When air is removed from the tube, the electric filament radiates glowing light. This tube has made possible many other inventions and discoveries such as radio, X-ray, and television. In the same way, when the force of wishes and desires is removed from the tube of the heart, then mind radiates glowing Spiritual light, which is the light of light. It is possible only when the hope of happiness from external objects is completely renounced, and one has determined by experience that eternal happiness and Bliss are the Self alone. When this is determined, the chamber of the heart becomes free from external wishes and desire; and within this empty tube of the heart, the mind begins to reflect the full light of the Self, as the moon reflects the light of the sun, when it is not shadowed by the earth.

The pursuit of happiness is natural for all living beings. No one is trained to pursue happiness, but everyone is born with intent to remain in happiness. This drive to gain happiness, and to avoid unhappiness, indicates that the real Nature of Self is nothing but happiness; hence happiness can be achieved only when this individual self, I am, renouncing all attachment to the external world for the sake of Eternal Happiness, establishes itself in *Brahman*, I AM, for his own Self. Then, and only then, this Self can experience the glowing light of Bliss and tranquillity.

It is not easy to change the direction of the physical, chemical, biological, and electrical flow of the body and mind toward the most desirable destination. Naturally this flow of body and mind is attached to the sensation of objects through the sense organs, and the illumination of the external world and its objects. By means of Self-investigation, "Who am I?" this current of the psychophysiological organism returns to its original source, and illumines the inner heart. The current flowing toward sense objects is called *dhāra*. When the mind is established in *Ātman*, then this current is reversed, becoming *rādhā*; hence the mythical name of Consciousness is *rādhākrishṇa*, which means the pure Consciousness, which can attract the flow of body, mind, and senses from the world to its original source. This is possible only when the mind is established in the self.

*Brahman*, pure Consciousness, though unperceived, gives an appearance of Reality to the names and forms of the relative world, which are superimposed on it. When it is cognized, names and forms have no lasting meaning. Cognition of pure Consciousness gives recognition of every manifestation as the radiation of Consciousness; however, one should not understand this phenomenal world to be unreal during the state of ignorance. As long as one experiences this world as other than *Brahman*, he must continue practice of *Yoga*.

## SUTRA NO. 52

उपाधिस्थोऽपि तद्धर्मैरलिप्तो व्योमवन्मुनिः ।
सर्वविन्मूढवत्तिष्ठेदसक्तो वायुवच्चरेत् ॥५२॥

UPĀDHISTHO' PI TADḌHARMAIR ALIPTO VYOMAVAN MUNIḤ.
SARVAVIN MŪḌHAVAT TIṢṬHED ASAKTO VÁYUVACCARET.

| | | |
|---|---|---|
| उपाधि-स्थः | Upādhi-sthaḥ | Associated with limitations of body, mind, senses, etc. |
| अपि | Api | Though |
| तत्-धर्मैः | Tat-dharmaiḥ | By their attributes |
| अलिप्तः | Aliptaḥ | Unstained |
| व्योमवत् | Vyomavat | Like the space |
| मुनिः | Muniḥ | The Self-realized man |
| सर्व-वित् | Sarva-vit | All-knowing |
| मूढवत् | Mūḍhavat | Like a fool |
| तिष्ठेत् | Tiṣṭhet | Remains |
| असक्तः | Asaktaḥ | Unattached |
| वायुवत् | Vāyuvat | Like the wind |
| चरेत् | Caret | Moves |

The enlightened One, identified with his real "I," remains free from the changes of body, mind, and senses, although he operates through them. A Self-realized man has the Nature of contemplation. He is uncorrupted by the defects of the body, mind, and senses, just as the sky is not flawed by the defects of objects. A Self-realized *Yogi* remains unaltered under all conditions. He moves freely like air, and he remains unattached like space. He examines everything as a witness.

The enlightened One inhabits his body and lives in the relative world; still he is not limited by his body and the relative world. By the power of his Spiritual life, he is untouched by all *upādhis*, ignorance and *māyā*, even as space is untouched by manifestations. Though the mighty air, moving everywhere, abides in etheric space, still etheric space is not touched by it. In the same way, a liberated Soul, residing in his body in the relative world, is untouched by manifestations. He is so calm and serene that at first glance he may seem to an unenlightened person to be ignorant, but he is recognized by the wise. He has the Nature of omnipresence, omniscience, and omnipotence, although he still maintains his body. His mind is All-pervasive and penetrative. It moves about unattached like electricity.

Space is the true, Universal, All-pervading, infinite background on which phenomena of the atmosphere appear. Its Nature is permanent and immutable. The liberated Self, too, is immutable although various manifestations of the body are present in him. Atmosphere exists in space, but it does not consist of space, and has nothing essentially in common with space. Likewise, bodily phenomena exist for the liberated Soul, but they do not comprise the Soul. A liberated Soul attains the Nature of transcendence and immanence. The Self causes the body and other things to exist, but the Self does not depend on them for Existence. All phenomena exist on account of the wondrous power of the Self. The Self so completely transcends the Universe that it is separated from all worldly beings, and is opposed to the world as the-wholly-other.

It is the identity of Consciousness with the body which causes one to be attached to the body and to relatives, which are the product of the body. When one's Consciousness is realized as Pure Consciousness, then one becomes detached, not only from one's body, but also from the sense-perceived Universe.

## SUTRA NO. 53

उपाधिविलयाद्विष्णौ निर्विशेषं विशेन्मुनिः ।
जले जलं वियद्व्योम्नि तेजस्तेजसि वा यथा ॥५३॥

UPĀDHIVILAYĀD VIṢṆAU NIRVIŚEṢAṀ VIŚENMUNIḤ.
JALE JALAṀ VIYADVYOMNI TEJAS TEJASI VĀ YATHĀ.

| | | |
|---|---|---|
| अपाधि-विलयात् | Upādhi-vilayāt | Due to destruction of identity with upadhis |
| विष्णौ | Viṣṇau | In the all-pervading Spirit |
| निर्विशेषम् | Nirviśeṣam | Totally |
| विशेत् | Viśet | Is absorbed |
| मुनिः | Muniḥ | The Self-realized man |
| जले | Jale | In water |
| जलम् | Jalam | Water |
| वियत् | Viyat | Space |
| व्योम्नि | Vyomni | In space |
| तेजः | Tejaḥ | Light |
| तेजसि | Tejasi | In light |
| वा | Vā | Or |
| यथा | Yathā | As |

On the destruction of identity of the Self as the body, the *Yogi* becomes free from the limitations of the body, mind, and senses; and the association with this body is established with the matter of the Universe. As the water of a river becomes one with the water of the ocean, as limited space becomes one with Cosmic space on the destruction of limitations, and as light of low intensity becomes one with the light of greater intensity, so the matter and energy of his body become One with the matter and energy of the Universe, and his Self, Pure Consciousness, I, becomes One with the Universal Self.

At the time of dissolution of the identity of One's Self with the body, mind, and senses, they return to Cosmic matter, and one's Consciousness returns to Cosmic Consciousness. As a matter of fact, returning of One's matter into Cosmic matter and One's Self into Cosmic Self is merely figurative. The Truth is that One experiences that One's body, mind, and senses already are the product of Cosmic matter, and that they belong to that, and that One's "I" is the reflection of the Cosmic "I." This solves the question of why a person does not die upon enlightenment. Birth and death, growth and decay, belong to the body; when the body is not identified as the Self, the body is disconnected from the Self; thus one experiences One's Self as unborn; and that which is unborn will never die. Just as water returns to water, light into light, space into space, air into air, so the material elements of One's body return to Cosmic matter. That is to say, One experiences the identity of the matter of the body with Cosmic matter.

Construction and composition of the body, mind, and senses are the work of Cosmic matter and Cosmic energy in every being. We know positively that we cannot make, and have not made, a single tissue of our body in its real form. By surgical procedure we can only transplant living organs of one body to another body; we cannot make a living organ. No doubt we can make certain organs artificially, but they cannot imitate living organs chemically, biochemically, and biologically. Only physically can the real organs be imitated. In short, body, mind, and senses are Cosmic in Nature even now. We understand them to be individual existence due to our ignorance. As electricity and water cannot flow without completing a cycle, so the body cannot work without completing its cycle with Cosmic matter. One example of cycles in the work of the body is the inhalation and exhalation of air. The inhaled air comes from the Cosmic ocean of air, and the exhaled air goes back to the Cosmos.

A Self-realized man experiences this cycle every moment; hence he is called *jīvanmukta* or liberated *Brahman*. *Jīvanmukti* and *videhamukti* have different meanings to different writers, but here the words are used synonymously with a difference in viewpoint. *Jīvanmukti* means liberation of One's Self from the attachment to the body while One is Alive. *Videhamukti* means that One experiences that One is not the body. Some authors describe *jīvanmukti* as liberation while one is alive, and *videhamukti* as liberation at the death of the body. *Jīvanmukta* and *videhamukta* are agential nouns, naming the person, the agent that experiences; *jīvanmukti* and *videhamukti* are abstract nouns, naming the state or process.

*Videhamukti* cannot be obtained without first obtaining *jīvanmukti*. If a man is not liberated before his death, he will not be liberated after death. He must return in another incarnation to progress to *jīvanmukti*; hence, *jīvanmukti* is the supreme liberation. Knowledge of *Atman* while one is alive is a prerequisite of liberation. *Jīvanmukta* is called incarnation of the Supreme. Although he is in the relative world, he is always in *Brahma*-Consciousness.

The process of meditation in *Yoga* is described as the process of gradual and progressive incarnation of the Supreme, *Brahman*, in the Consciousness of the individual. When this process becomes complete, the meditator becomes *jīvanmukta*. He who knows the secret of meditation attains full incarnation of the Supreme in due course of time.

The very fact that the *jīvanmukta* lives in his body after liberation shows his great compassion and love for all living beings. The purpose of keeping his body is to awaken and enlighten those who are in need, and who seek guidance in this world. He is man in God and God in man. The process of meditation completes its circle from man to God, and then from God to man. The liberated One, *jīvanmukta*, comes down into the world to show the light of the Self.

As flowing rivers are transformed after entering the ocean, losing their names and forms in the oneness of the ocean,so the enlightened One, freed from name and form, is transformed into *Brahman* that is greater than the great, and subtler than the subtle.

In short, to an enlightened One, there is no real difference in the two kinds of liberation. The knower of *Brahman*, both prior to death and afterward, enjoys Supreme Existence, Consciousness, Bliss, freedom, and peace. It is a great loss to the world when such a One leaves, for He is to the world as swans are to a lake. Wherever swans live, they enhance the beauty of the place.

The death of a liberated person is not like the death of an enlightened One. An enlightened One has the power to manifest himself any time. Eternally he continues to enlighten and to awaken those who deserve such help.

Prison authorities live in a prison to educate and reform the moral character of the prisoners, yet the prison authorities are not prisoners. Physicians live in hospitals or sanitariums among patients to cure them, to improve the physical and mental condition of the patients, yet physicians are not patients. Similarly, enlightened persons live in the world among the unenlightened, to enlighten and awaken them physically, ethically, morally, mentally, and Spiritually; yet enlightened Ones are not part of the world, nor are they under the influence of *karmas*.

## SUTRA NO. 54

यल्लाभान्नापरो लाभो यत्सुखान्नापरं सुखम्।
यज्ज्ञानान्नापरं ज्ञानं तद्ब्रह्मेत्यवधारयेत् ॥५४॥

YALLĀBHĀN NĀPARO LĀBHO YATSUKHĀN NĀPARAṀ SUKHAM.
YAJJÑĀNĀN NĀPARAṀ JÑĀNAM TADBRAHMETYAVADHĀRAYET.

| | | |
|---|---|---|
| यत्-लाभात् | Yat-lābhāt | Than the attainment of which |
| न | Na | No |
| अपरः | Aparaḥ | Other |
| लाभः | Lābhaḥ | Attainment |
| यत्-सुखात् | Yat-sukhāt | Than the Bliss of which |
| न | Na | No |
| अपरम् | Aparam | Other |
| सुखम् | Sukham | Bliss |
| यत्-ज्ञानात् | Yat-jñānāt | Than the knowledge of which |
| न | Na | No |
| अपरम् | Aparam | Other |
| ज्ञानम् | Jñānam | Knowledge |
| तत्-ब्रह्म | Tat-brahma | That-Brahman |
| इति | Iti | Thus |
| अवधारयेत् | Avadhārayet | One should realize |

*Brahman* is that by attainment of which nothing is left to be attained. *Brahman* is that Bliss by experiencing which no Bliss is left to be experienced. *Brahman* is that knowledge by knowing which nothing is left to be known.

*Brahman* is the highest attainment, happiness, peace, tranquillity, Consciousness, and knowledge. It is All-inclusive, leaving nothing more to be attained. No other Bliss is to be desired and no more knowledge remains to be known. One should realize this Truth through Self-analysis and meditation.

To an awakened Soul, *Brahman* is the highest goal, success, world, and Bliss. All other creatures, the unenlightened, live on a small fraction of that Bliss. By knowing *Brahman*, one knows everything and becomes *Brahman*.

Human life consists of *lābha*, possessions and gain; *sukham*, peace, Bliss and tranquillity; and *jñānam*, knowledge. All these are absolutely accomplished in identity with *Brahman*.

Death cancels all gains and possessions, all forms of happiness, and every type of knowledge; hence, when one realizes that One is Eternal, naturally one gains everything, and one becomes happy Eternally. Now in the Eternity of Self, one can know everything. We have proof from history that many persons whose names are written in golden letters—famous rulers, scientists, scholars, and thinkers—died without satisfaction because the positions and kingdoms they had achieved could not be taken with them. But the man of Self-realization becomes united with the Cosmic Self; he feels his Self to be Eternal, and knows the total Universe as his possession. He feels content because he experiences his immortal Self.

## SUTRA NO. 55

यद्दृष्ट्वा नापरं दृश्यं यद्भूत्वा न पुनर्भवः ।
यज्ज्ञात्वा नापरं ज्ञेयं तद्ब्रह्मेत्यवधारयेत् ॥५५॥

YADDṚṢṬVĀ NĀPARAṀ DṚŚYAṀ YADBHŪTVĀ NA PUNARBHAVAḤ.
YAJJÑĀTVA NĀPARAṀ JÑEYAṀ TADBRAHMETYAVADHĀRAYET.

| | | |
|---|---|---|
| यत्-दृष्ट्वा | Yat-dṛṣṭvā | That which, having seen |
| न | Na | Not |
| अपरम् | Aparam | Anything else |
| दृश्यम् | Dṛśyam | To be seen |
| यत्-भूत्वा | Yat bhūtvā | That which, having become |
| न | Na | Not |
| पुनर्भवः | Punarbhavaḥ | Wish to become other again |
| यत्-ज्ञात्वा | Yat-jñātvā | That which, having known |
| न | Na | Not |
| अपरम् | Aparam | Anything else |
| ज्ञेयम् | Jñeyam | To be known |
| तत्-ब्रह्म | Tat-Brahma | That Brahman |
| इति | Iti | Thus |
| अव-धारयेत् | Avadhārayet | One should realize |

Know certainly that to be *Brahman* by experiencing which nothing is left to be experienced; that which having seen, nothing more is left to be seen. When identity of this individual self once is born in *Brahman*-Consciousness, it does not need to be born again in the world of relativity. *Brahman* is that knowable Reality, by realizing which no object of the Universe is left to be known.

Realize *Brahman* to be that which excels and transcends the beauty of all worldly phenomena; that which having become, one does not wish to become something else; and that which, when known, leaves nothing else to be known.

It is common psychological experience that everyone, knowingly or unknowingly, consciously, or unconsciously, willingly or unwillingly, directly or indirectly, in one form or another runs after:

1. Beauty and beautiful, from the lower to the higher;

2. Being one thing in one moment, and in the next moment wishing to become something else, from lower existence to higher existence; and

3. Knowing something more, from lower knowledge to higher wisdom.

This is the common wandering of the mind. If a man's mind does not run after these, then either he is idiotic, impotent, incapacitated, or he has become enlightened.

Wandering of the mind after these things is not wrong but, from the viewpoint of Self-analysis, such wanderings should be analyzed. The mind seeks beauty. When you have one beautiful object, your mind begins to pursue other objects, which are more beautiful. The moment you become something, you want to become something else, which is more beautiful and higher in existence. The moment you know something, your mind seeks to know something else, which is more beautiful, higher, and better that you now have.

The wandering of the mind in the relative world is never satisfied. The racecourse of beauty, being and becoming, and knowing something higher and higher, never ends. On the other hand, one's participation on this racecourse is increased according to the evolution of intelligence and knowledge. In every walk of life you will find this racecourse. Even higher academic fields are no exception to this rule. Consequently, man dies in dissatisfaction, disappointment, and frustration because he could not have a more beautiful partner, could not obtain a higher position and existence, and could not know higher wisdom; thus intelligent persons die in agony in their last moments.

This attraction of beauty in the opposite sex, for being and becoming in position and existence, and for knowing more is ever increasing proportionally according to the qualitative and quantitative evolution of intelligence. The more intelligent you are, the more you want and appreciate beauty, position, knowledge. On the other hand, the want of these things stimulates the evolution of your intelligence in technique and methods for their acquisition and application. For instance, when you see a beautiful person of the opposite sex, a wave of desire to have him or her is aroused. Desire for that beautiful person increases fascinating ideas and images to deal with that friend according to your ever-increasing intelligence to obtain gratification.

There is some psychological truth in these desires and attractions. Attraction to a beautiful person, a desire to be something more, and a curiosity to know more are not wrong, but the usual way to satisfaction is wrong because the whole approach is material and external.

All beauty, all being and becoming, and all knowledge are expressions and manifestations of *Brahman*. Howsoever you may run after them, they will be ahead of you. You cannot grasp them because they are your own shadow. *Brahman* is Ultimate Reality, which is manifest in beauty, being and becoming, and knowledge. By knowing that, you will have Absolute beauty, being, and knowledge. To realize *Brahman* which is inclusive of all these, one needs a disciplined and pure mind.

A common conflict is noted in a religious person's life. Every theistic and religious man has a keen desire to see God, and he wishes omnipotent, omniscient, and omnipresent One to make his heart the seat of his throne; but where would this Almighty sit when man's heart is full of worldly desires and impure cravings so that practically no room is left for Deity? Unless the mind and heart, the place He wishes him to grace with His Presence, is absolutely cleansed of all dirt and filth, how can He care to occupy it? God's light penetrates only a pure and holy heart.

It is common experience that the image of one we deeply love occupies our thoughts, mind, and heart even when we are engaged in other pursuits. The forms and figures which have become the center of our love and attractions during our lifetime, like cinema film on a screen, begin to move before our eyes, and thus they constitute a greater part of our personality. Even after death they do not leave us. We assume the form, and take birth in that family and place to which our mind was attracted in the previous lifetime. There is a mighty and pervasive attraction due to long and deep association, and it draws one like a magnet. Attachment to the beauty of worldly phenomena; attraction to face and form, family, and relatives; love of wealth, worldly pleasures, countries, religions, and nations bring one back again and again unless the right expression and symbolic meaning of attachment, attraction, love, and beauty are properly resolved.

If a man goes to visit a friend and is interested only in his friend's property, wealth, house, or status, such a man will not be regarded as a real friend. Wealth and status constitute the external life only. The reality behind them is the friend. Similarly, phenomenal love, beauty, attainment, happiness, knowledge, and phenomenal being and becoming are the external life of *Brahman*; Reality is still to be realized.

After realizing this truth, one should sublimate one's love and intensive longing to the Realization of the Supreme. If one sees the phenomenal world, which is the expression of the Supreme, as a world separate from the Supreme, one has created dualism and a dilemma. One cannot have both: "Ye cannot serve both God and mammon."

This artificial division apparently splits Ultimate Reality into two aspects, God and mammon. The only way to avoid this dilemma is to understand properly *Brahman*, and its expression, the phenomenal world of beauty, love, and attraction. *Brahman* is the Real and fundamental substance, Eternal source of love, beauty, Bliss, knowledge, and attraction; the world is its expression, reflection, and shadow. Any artificial division of Reality will turn the outer world into mammon; the result will be endless unhappiness and suffering. To be involved in this dilemma means that a man is afraid of his own shadow. How will he be happy when he understands his own body, mind, and shadow as a devil? It is true that God and mammon cannot be served together, but it is also true that God cannot be served without resolving the nature of mammon.

At the death of relatives and on separation from a dear friend, how piteously and how bitterly do persons weep and cry! What a restless night of grief men pass upon departure of dear ones from this world, and how terribly they miss them! But do they ever think of their long, long separation from *Ātman*, *Brahman*, the most beloved of all relatives? Have they ever passed a single night restlessly and sleeplessly on not finding *Ātman*? Without intensive love for Self-analysis, the rays of *Ātman* cannot enter the dark chamber of the mind.

Those are truly happy who reach their Eternal home. One's Eternal home cannot be found in temples made of brick, wood, or stone. Mind is the Real Temple; Enlightenment is the Real Heaven; therefore, men should search for the Supreme within their own

Temple of the mind. By attaching Oneself to a man-made temple, one may neglect the Eternal Truth, "The kingdom of heaven is within you."

When focusing your attention on the center of your head, you will hear a sweet melody of *nādam*, which flows from the highest heaven. This celestial music is resounding in the body of every being. The voice of the Supreme constantly invites each one toward itself. He who pays attention to this sweet music, reaches the place where it issues forth. This *nādam, saguṇa Brahman* comes from *satya-lokam, Brahma lokam*, the region of Eternal Truth and Reality, the everlasting abode of *Brahman*, which is Absolute beauty, being, and knowledge. By realizing *Brahman*, one becomes *Brahman*.

If one is not fulfilled in attainment, beauty, happiness, and knowledge, one must be born again to obtain that fulfillment; therefore, one should meditate on *Brahman*, so that one may be fulfilled here and now and may enjoy perfection and Bliss.

The student approached the teacher and asked, "Sir, what is that by knowing which everything past, present, and future becomes known?"

The teacher replied, "O beloved, you tell me first, how do you know your past, present, and future? There is something in you by means of which you think about your past experience, you deal with your present world, and you plan to build your future. What is that in you?"

The student replied, "That, sir, is Consciousness, because as long as I am conscious, I can think and understand the phenomena of the world."

The teacher instructed further, "That, O beloved, when you know that Consciousness in its purity, then and only then will you know everything about the Universe as well as about your Self."

## SUTRA NO. 56

तिर्यगूर्ध्वमधः पूर्णं सच्चिदानन्दमद्वयम् ।
अनन्तं नित्यमेकं यत्तद्ब्रह्मेत्यवधारयेत् ॥५६॥

TIRYAGŪRDHVAMADHAḤ PŪRṆAṀ SACCIDĀNANDAM ADVAYAM.
ANANTAM NITYAM EKAṀ YAT TADBRAHMETYAVADHĀRAYET.

| | | |
|---|---|---|
| तिर्यक् | Tiryak | All quarters, all dimensions |
| ऊर्ध्वम् | Ūrdhvam | Above |
| अधः | Adhaḥ | Below |
| पूर्णम् | Pūrnam | Fills |
| सत्-चित्-आनन्दम् | Sat-cit-ānandam | Existence-Consciousness-Bliss |
| अद्वयम् | Advayam | Non-dual |
| अनन्तम् | Anantam | Infinite |
| नित्यम् | Nityam | Eternal |
| एकम् | Ekam | One |
| यत् | Yat | Which |
| तत्-ब्रह्म | Tat-Brahma | That Brahman |
| इति | Iti | Thus |
| अवधारयेत् | Advadhāravet | One should realize |

*Brahman*, the I, is that which fills the total Universe in every dimension, which is Existence-Consciousness-Bliss, which is One-without-a-second, and which is the Self of every being in the form of I.

Realize to be *Brahman* that which by its radiation transcends all dimensions and directions, which fills all quarters—all that is above, below, and around—which is Existence, Knowledge, Bliss, and which is non-dual, Infinite, Eternal, and One.

Every seeker is eager to realize Truth; it is the ideal of every earnest seeker. In pursuit of Truth, people travel far and wide, even in most difficult places, and to distant corners of the earth. Yet this Ultimate Reality is around, above, and below us everywhere all the time. It transcends all dimensions of time and space, but its center of manifestation is within the seeker.

Supreme Reality remains a puzzling mirage to those who seek it by eternal means, not because it cannot be realized, but because they are seeking in the wrong place and manner. A man is called a fool if he searches on the road for something which he lost in his house. Yet modern seekers are making the same mistake by searching for Ultimate Reality in certain places and persons, when they have really lost it from their own minds.

Omnipresent Reality should be sought within Oneself, by concentrating on *OM, nādam*, which is resounding in all, and which is imparting electrical, chemical, biochemical, and biological impulses in the deepest part of every cell of the body.

The head, in which is *sahasrāram*, the key of success, has been compared to Infinite space in which *cittam*, mindstuff, like a solar system with planets and satellites of sensory, motor, and other organs, moves constantly. Here *cittam* itself is like the sun in being the source of light, life, radiation, and energy. The light of this sun, the mind, is radiating all around throughout life, although it is unknown and unperceived by unenlightened persons. This Eternal light is in All, has always been there, and will remain there, although it can be seen only by him who has surrendered to Reality.

That Supreme light is manifesting a heavenly sound, *nādam*, which can be heard only by One who has completely withdrawn One's Consciousness from the nine doors of one's body, and has gone above the eye center. External light, sound, and forms of the Universe are merely imitations. The purpose of the external world is only to remind the seeker of the internal Reality. Unfortunately people have forgotten the Real, and have become lost in the imitation. The entire external world is only representative of the true Reality. The intended result behind all this is to arouse in the seeker a wave of Self-confidence to realize the Original.

## SUTRA NO. 57

अतद्व्यावृत्तिरूपेण वेदान्तैर्लक्ष्यतेऽद्वयम् ।
अखण्डानन्दमेकं यत्तद्ब्रह्मेत्यवधारयेत् ॥५७॥

ATADVYĀVṚTTIRŪPEṆA VEDĀNTAIR LAKṢYATE' DVAYAM.
AKHAṆḌĀNANDAM EKAṀ YAT TADBRAHMETYAVADHĀRAYET.

| | | |
|---|---|---|
| अतत् | Atat | "Not this" |
| व्यावृत्ति-रुपेण | Vyāvṛtti-rūpeṇa | By the process of negation |
| वेदान्तैः | Vedāntaiḥ | By vedanta philosophy |
| लक्ष्यते | Lakṣyate | Is indicated |
| अद्वयम् | Advayam | Non-dual |
| अखण्ड-आनन्दम् | Akhaṇḍa-ānandam | Indivisible Bliss |
| एकम् | Ekam | Oneness |
| यत् | Yat | Which |
| तत्-ब्रह्म | Tat-Brahma | That-Brahman |
| इति | Iti | Thus |
| अवधारयेत् | Avadhārayet | One should realize |

Know to be *Brahman* that which is indicated by the *Vedas* and *Vedānta* Philosophy as 'not this, not this.' Know to be *Brahman* that which is non-dual, Indivisible, One and Blissful, and the substratum of the entire Universe.

Realize to be *Brahman* that which is *advayam*, non-dual, *akhandānandam*, Indivisible Bliss, One-without-a-second, and which is indicated by *Vedānta* Philosophy, as the irreducible Ultimate substance after the negation of all relative, tangible substances. All philosophical thinking ends in the realization of *Brahman*.

Mind and Soul are coupled together and tied in a knot; therefore, the Soul cannot go up unless the mind accompanies it. One can never find success in Self-realization if the mind and Soul tend to run in opposite directions. In descending and joining the senses and objects of the senses, the mind goes out and wanders seeking pleasure, satisfaction, and perfection in the world of senses. The whole of meditation is to attain ascendance of the mind. The mind will find everlasting peace and perfection if it goes inward. When mind and Soul combined ascend to *sahasrāram*, cerebrum, the mind merges in the Energy from which it descended; and the Soul, freed from its limitations, rises and merges in *Brahman*.

This body in the state of bondage is compared to a prison. The body is designed and controlled by thinking. If the thinking is wrong, the thoughts work in the body as a force of death to detain the Soul in the world of senses. Forces which lead to wrong thinking are bad *karmas*, the result of one's past actions. The real body is not this body, but the body of Energy. Lame persons feel legs, and toothless feel teeth; the man with polio cannot walk, but moves on his legs in his dream. So the *karmas* reside in the body of vibration, and manifest through the gross body. These *karmas* can be repaid by the ascendance of the mind—the gross body is merged into the body of vibrations, then it is merged into the body of life, and it is merged in turn into the body of Consciousness. That is the journey, and *Yogins* advise that one should use the golden opportunity of being born in a human body by putting one's attention on Absolute *Brahman*, so that the limited time, which is granted to one, may be utilized to the fullest extent for Self-realization.

This world is like a big hotel where all sorts of people come and live together for a period of time, and then depart their different ways. Also it may be compared to a river with logs floating upon it. One current of the river brings them together, then another current separates them. In the same way, people come to this world, meet, form family groups and nations, then make friends and enemies, and later depart. When the Soul leaves the body, no one can prevent its departure; therefore, one should be concerned for Self-realization, which is the only way to save oneself from death.

A man should do his duty toward everyone without any selfish attachment, whether to wife, husband, friends, or enemies. This world is like a stage, where everyone has his role in the drama. An audience sees actors and actresses on stage behaving as though they were intimately connected, and actually living the parts they are playing, but the actors and actresses know that they are only playing roles. When the play ends, they leave the stage and their stage relationships. Similarly, people play the various roles alloted to them by their *karmas* on the stage of the world. The Soul is like the spectator, the psychological self is the actor or actress, and related persons are various partners in this play of life, according to their choice and preference. When the Self is realized, they all return to the state of *Brahman*. If the Self is not realized, they have to return and play again.

One should not misconstrue this as meaning renunciation of the world; one should rightly understand the world, and one's duty toward it. In this hum-drum life one should do first things first, and the rest in due order; one should never forget one's first and Ultimate goal in life, Self-realization. Persons should be dutiful in their roles as husband, wife, and citizen; but they should not ever forget their impending death. They should know the Reality supporting all. In an abbattoir, animals are being slaughtered, but even so, the animals reserved for the next day's slaughtering do not consider their own end. Similarly, when we know of a person dying, or we accompany a corpse to the cemetery, we do not think of our own death. Each behaves as though, in his present body, his time and opportunity were limitless. People think as though they are immortal in this body. If persons anticipated their own death, they could take steps to overcome their death. The world and relatives should be served rightly, but one should know that, without Self-realization, death cannot be postponed or overcome.

Fix your consciousness with full attention on vibrating *OM*, and investigate the mystery of *nādam*. Merge your Consciousness in *nādam* so that you may soar to *Brahman*, and realize that which is non-dual, Indivisible, Eternal Bliss. *Brahman* can only be realized; it cannot be described through language and tongue. The entire manifested Universe is the holy book of *Brahman*. Other books are artificial, written by men.

When this I, through which man expresses himself, is investigated in its completeness, one will find that it is nothing but pure Consciousness. The moment one concentrates, "Where am I?" one will feel that one is not located anywhere in the body. "I am then when 'when' is not, and I am there where 'where' is not." It means that pure Consciousness cannot be localized in space and time. It cannot be divided by the limitations of body. Throughout the changes of body, mind, and senses, it is Consciousness which exists without any change; it remains Consciousness. Realizing this Consciousness, one transcends birth, suffering, and death; hence, Consciousness, is called *saccidānanda*, Existence-Consciousness-Bliss. In this life or death, man or woman, God or human, in heaven or on earth, in whatever form a being is born, he can express himself only by means of Self, which is the "I"-principle. This "I" in its pure form is *Brahman*.

## SUTRA NO. 58

अखण्डानन्दरूपस्य तस्यानन्दलवाश्रिताः ।
ब्रह्माद्यास्तारतम्येन भवन्त्यानन्दिनो लवाः ॥५८॥

AKHAṆḌĀNANDARŪPASYA TASYĀNANDALAVĀŚRITĀḤ.
BRAHMĀDYĀSTĀRATAMYENA BHAVANTYĀNANDINO LAVĀḤ.

| | | |
|---|---|---|
| अखण्ड - आनन्द - | Akhaṇḍa - Ananda | Of unbroken Bliss |
| रूपस्य | Rūpasya | The Nature |
| तस्य | Tasya | Of that |
| आनन्द - लव - | Ānanda - lava | A particle of Bliss |
| आश्रिताः | Āśritāḥ | Depending on |
| ब्रह्माद्याः | Brahmādyāḥ | The Creator and other gods |
| तारतम्येन | Tāratamyena | In proportion |
| भवन्ति | Bhavanti | Are |
| आनन्दिनः | Ānandinaḥ | Of Bliss |
| लवाः | Lavāḥ | Particles |

Know to be *Brahman* that by experiencing which Bliss in integrity is experienced. Deities such as *Brahmā*, the Creator God, taste only a particle of that unlimited Bliss of *Brahman*.

Mythical deities such as *Brahmā*, *Viṣṇu*, and *Śiva* have obtained only a particle of the Supreme Bliss of *Brahman*, and they enjoy in proportion their shares of that particle.

The Soul is in *Brahman*, and *Brahman* is in the Soul, but their Unity and identity are discovered only through Self-realization. A large banyan tree is potential in its tiny seed, but the sprouting and development of that tree are possible only when one sows the seed in suitable soil, waters it, and gives it proper care. Then the sapling in due course develops into a banyan tree of such enormous size that it can shelter thousands of people beneath it. In the same way, when individual soul is fully manifested, it takes the huge form of the Universe, and overcomes the fear of birth and death.

Intrinsically the Soul is sinless and pure, but its association with the mind, which is full of desire and psycho-sexual activity, causes the Soul to sink into the material world. The material mind is ruled by the senses which alienate from *Brahman* the Soul associated with mind. This association is like that of pure rain water which falls to the ground, and becomes muddy and dirty when it combines with dust and dirt; however, under the influence of the mighty nuclear action and reaction of the sun's electromagnetic rays and heat, water rises again as vapor, is condensed and forms clouds, and thus is purged of impurities as it returns to its origin. The Soul, too, is cleansed as it rises gradually in Self-realization.

*Ātman* is the foundation and source of all pleasures, the only Absolute and everlasting Bliss. Bliss in other objects is fragmentary, temporary, and evanescent. Beauty, the attraction of love, the luster of light, the complexion of skin—all are borrowed from *Brahman*, and exist only to indicate the real origin of pleasure. By reaching *satyalokam* through *sahasrāram*, the cerebral cortex, and finding union with *Ātman*, one will come to know Absolute Bliss.

Absolute Bliss, Reality, is within everyone, but it is not experienced by all. A man is prevented from seeing his own Soul by: 1) obstacles; 2) lack of practice; 3) lack of knowledge regarding *Ātman*; and 4) attachment to the senses. The main obstacle to the vision of the Supreme within oneself is one's own ego, "I"-consciousness, the unit of individuality, which creates the separation from Universal love, beauty, Truth, and Bliss. To overcome this obstacle, one should submerge and merge oneself in *OM* by practice of *samādhi*; thus, intimate knowledge of *Ātman* will give One power to detach oneself from matter and the material world.

This *OM*, *nādam*, cannot be uttered, written, or heard with the physical senses. It is the echo of Spiritual vibration, and reverberates within All. All desires are born of the mind, and when one prays for fulfillment of one's desires, one is placing one's material mind above the Supreme. By meditation this material mind is transformed into a devotee through surrender to *Brahman*. One should be careful to know the currents of the material mind and the currents of the Soul, for they are different in Nature. The current of the material mind is senses and the world of the senses; the current of the Soul is *nādam*; therefore, in meditation, one should not allow one's mind to go to the senses, but one should turn it toward *Ātman*. Do everything to keep the mind in *Ātman*; do not let it overcome and rule the Self.

One should concentrate and fix one's attention on the eye center, the state of *Brahman*, *Brahmasthiti*, remaining there and functioning from there. This takes time and practice, withdrawal of attention from the outer world, and one-pointed fixation on this center with love and devotion.

One should meditate upon Absolute Truth, whose Existence bestows Reality upon all created things; who is the Source of creation, preservation, and dissolution of the Universe; who is omniscient and All-powerful; who reveals in the mind of a meditator the *Vedas*, the knowledge of the Spirit; and whose Self-effulgence dispels the darkness of ignorance.

*Brahman* is Absolute Bliss; all bliss of the relative universe is fragmentary. Even the bliss of *Brahmā*, *Viṣṇu*, and *Śiva*, the trinity, is relative and fragmentary. According to Hindu mythology, *Brahmā* is the creator, *Viṣṇu* is the protector, and *Śiva* is the destroyer of the Universe. In mythical language, *satoguṇa* is called *Viṣṇu*, *rajoguṇa* is called *Brahmā*, and *tamoguṇa* is called *Śiva*. *Rajoguṇa* is electronic force; hence, it is creative energy. *Satoguṇa* is protonic force; hence, it is protective. *Tamoguṇa* is inertia; it destroys everything so that new creation can take place. These three forces are personified The same forces can be seen at work in our word God. "G" stands for the generative energy of *rajoguṇa*, or *Brahmā*; "O" stands for the organizing and supporting energy of *satoguṇa*, *Viṣṇu*; and "D" stands for the dissolving or destructive energy of *tamoguṇa*, *Śiva*. The conscious energy in these trinities, whether they be the Cosmic forces, the Hindu trinity, or the English word G-O-D, is derived from the Self, I AM.

All creation up to *satyalokam* is perishable, although some regions may last for eons. The vast Universe below *satyalokam* is controlled and managed by *kāla puruṣa*, the process of death. Those who want to go beyond death should go beyond *trikuti*, *ājñā cakram*, the place behind the eyes which is the control center of individual consciousness.

*Kāla puruṣa* is the negative force, *māyā*, of the Universe. Those who worship *kāla puruṣa*, or the gods, are born and die again and again. If they have led a good life, they are regarded with long periods of enjoyment and happiness, but in the long run everything comes to an end, and again they must be born into this world. On the other hand, those who cross the region of *māyā, kāla puruṣa*, by means of *śabda Brahman*, sound current, become Eternally united with the Supreme. Such Souls dwell in the everlasting Bliss of *Brahman*.

The mind is restless because of its indisposition. It has lost its proper place in the world of senses. When the mind reaches beyond *trikuti*, it becomes happy and serene, for it then obtains Absolute Bliss. Those who merge in *nādam* automatically cut the bonds of *māyā*, and never return to the lower existence.

In beauty, existence, and being and becoming, the vegetable kingdom exceeds the mineral kingdom; living beings surpass the vegetable kingdom; human beings excel all other living beings; *Brahman* transcends All. It is Absolute. One desirous of perfection must realize *Brahman*. At the end of life, persons repent for neglecting to do what they ought to have done; they regret that they could not enjoy the beauty and beautiful person they wanted to enjoy; they lament that they did not know what they ought to have learned. These souls pass the end of life in anguish. *Brahman* is the only substance by knowing which everything is obtained and One is fulfilled.

In the language of personification the senses, mind, ego, and superego are called subjective gods; the sun, moon, planets, stars, and other elements are called objective gods. Consciousness in its pure form is called God. All gods in the subjective world are conscious and alive because they derive life and Consciousness from the "I"-principle; thus physical happiness, sensory happiness, and the happiness of mind, ego, and superego are respectively reaching higher and higher in relativity because they approach nearer and nearer to the "I"-principle. Their respective happiness and Bliss are partial and transient.

How does one obtain indivisible and everlasting Bliss? It is possible only through knowing one's Self, I. Each thought occurs only after the rise of the "I"-thought. Since the mind is nothing but a bundle of thoughts, it is only through the inquiry, "Who am I?" that this "I"-thought or "I am" can attain its original for, I AM. The process of investigation of "Who am I?" is also a thought, but this "I"-thought is next to the "I"-principle. After destroying all other thoughts, it also is destroyed and only pure "I" remains. This pure "I" is Absolute Bliss. From this Absolute Bliss, the subjective and objective gods derive their bliss respectively, as they are near or nearer to the Absolute.

The real "I"-principle and Absolute God are identical. This

"I"-principle is called *Ātman, Brahman*, Self. *Ātman* alone exists and is real. The world, individual self, and mental gods are like the illusory appearance of silver in a conch shell. As a matter of fact, all three are the products of mind. The real God, or Absolute God, is Eternally beyond mental phenomena. Mental phenomena appear and disappear. In dreamless sleep, the mind does not operate for manifestation of thoughts, so we do not have the experience of the individual self, nor do we perceive the subjective-objective world, nor are the mental gods present there. But, even in dreamless sleep, the real "I" still is awake. After sleeping everyone says, "I had no dream," and this indicates that the real "I" was not asleep. This "I"-principle alone is Reality. All that exists is nothing but the manifestation of the Supreme "I."

## SUTRA NO. 59

तद्युक्तमखिलं वस्तु व्यवहारस्तदन्वितः ।
तस्मात् सर्वगतं ब्रह्म क्षीरे सर्पिरिवाखिले ॥५९॥

TADYUKTAM AKHILAṀ VASTU VYAVAHĀRAS TADANVITAḤ.
TASMĀT SARVAGATAṀ BRAHMA KṢĪRE SARPIRIVĀKHILE.

| | | |
|---|---|---|
| तत्- | Tat | By that |
| युक्तम् | Yuktam | Pervaded |
| अखिलम् | Akhilam | Entire |
| वस्तु | Vastu | World of objects |
| व्यवहारः | Vyavahāraḥ | Actions |
| तत्-अन्वितः | Tat-anvitaḥ | Following that |
| तस्मात् | Tasmāt | Therefore |
| सर्वगतम् | Sarva-gatam | All-pervading |
| ब्रह्म | Brahma | Brahman |
| क्षीरे | Kṣīre | In milk |
| सर्पिः | Sarpiḥ | Butter |
| इव | Iva | Like |
| अखिले | Akhile | In everything |

Every object of the Universe is pervaded by *Brahman*. All transactions of the body, mind, and senses are possible because of *Brahman*; therefore, *Brahman* permeates everything as butter permeates milk.

*Brahman*, by its Absolute beauty, love, Existence, and Bliss, pervades all Existence of the Universe, and is the basic foundation of all manifestations of names and forms, although it is hidden from sight of the ignorant. All manifestations of the Universe, subjective and objective phenomena, are pervaded by *Brahman*. All actions and reactions, physical and metaphysical, are because of *Ātman*.

*Brahman* permeates the entire Universe somewhat as cream permeates whole milk. Actions and perceptions are possible through the motor and sensory organs only when the self, subjective consciousness, is joined with them. Hence, in all sensations such as hearing, seeing, smelling, touching, and tasting; and in all actions, *Brahman* and *Ātman* dwell as the central force. All experiences indicate the presence of Consciousness, for in the absence of Consciousness we cannot have any experience. When the Self, Consciousness, is realized, all sensations and actions are transformed into *Brahma*-Consciousness. *Brahman* is the cause from which proceeds the origin, subsistence, and dissolution of this world extended in names and forms; which includes all subjective and objective phenomena; which contains the mechanism of cause and effect, space and time, for every happening. *Brahman* is the immediate Consciousness which shines as the Self, and shines as the cognition of objects. This cognition is nothing but the light of the Self. It is the essence of All. It remains undenied even when one tries to deny it, for even in denial it shows forth. It is the Self of All, ever present. As Ralph Waldo Emerson expressed:

> "They reckon ill who leave Me out,
>
> When Me they fly I AM their wings,
>
> I AM the doubter and the doubt."

*Brahman* is pure Intelligence, being, and blessedness. As long as we are in the ordinary waking state or dream state, we identify the Self with thousands of illusory things, all that we call I or mind. When we are in dreamless sleep, without any touch of these phenomenal notions, the Nature of our true state as pure blessedness is partially realized. Then, in the state of *samādhi*, the individual self is discovered to be appearance only. Truth is the true Self, One for All, pure Intelligence, beauty, being, and blessedness.

The Universe exists in the mind, like the image of a city reflected in a mirror, but like a dream which is really within the mind of the dreamer, appears to be outside. As a dreamer realizes the oneness and innerness of his dream when he is awakened, so the enlightened One realizes identity and Unity of *Brahman* and the world, when he is Spiritually awakened.

Like a magician, this mighty *Yogi*, *Brahman*, projects the infinite Universe, like a sprout from a seed. Before creation, this Universe remains potential in *Brahman* and at the end of a creative process, it is submerged in *Brahman*.

Radiation of the Self is issuing forth through the sense organs, like the glow of a powerful lamp placed in a jar with many holes. The light of *Brahman* is illumining and manifesting the entire Universe, and the vibration of this Supreme light on individual existence shines forth as "I"-consciousness.

By its own Infinite power, *Brahman* appears in all forms of Cosmic energy, physical and metaphysical, material and mental, and in multiple names and forms. The ignorant are deluded, and they erroneously identify man, woman, body, *prāṇa*, senses, and "I"-consciousness as *Ātman*; in Reality all these are external manifestations of *Brahman*; hence, they are void and empty. Ultimate Reality, *Brahman*, is beyond them.

The Self of man exists in sound sleep in its pure light freed from the knowledge of multiplicity and duality, although covered by the veiling power of *māyā*, ignorance, and when he is awakened, his "I"-Consciousness feels subjective-objective phenomena again as before. But in the state of *samādhi* this Self shines in its pure light, entirely freed from *māyā*.

*Ātman* is present equally in all four states—waking, dreaming, sound sleep, and *samādhi*—although it is not felt equally in every state, due to changing conditions of the perceptual mechanism, mind. *Ātman, Brahman*, pure Consciousness, is the unconcerned witness of the experiences of the senses and mindstuff during waking, dreaming, and meditation; and observes the absence of experiences during sound sleep and *samādhi. Ātman, Brahman*, the inexhaustible flow of consciousness, persists equally through childhood, youth, maturity, and old age. The psychological self, "I" Consciousness, is the revelation of *Ātman* in the individual heart.

*Brahman* is the center of Consciousness, which is passing through the mechanism of cause and effect, space and time. It is passing through various relationships in multiplicity, such as parents and children, owner and owned, master and disciple, subject and object. Still *Brahman* is untouched by these phenomena and diversities.

*Brahman* is manifested through all phenomena—through nuclei, atoms, molecules, compounds, minerals, vegetables, living beings, and all human minds. It is radiating in everything, and it is shining everywhere. The shining, innumerable stars, the solar systems with their planets and moons, are like beautiful flowers of the tree of Nature in the majestic and mighty garden of *Brahman*. All are manifestations of *Brahman* although, due to its immanence and transcendence, it is beyond All. As the sun is radiating in everything and illumining every part of the solar system, so *Brahman* is radiating in every state of evolution, and illumining every state of Nature.

*Brahman* is *Ātman* Soul of All Souls. Concentration on *nādam* clearly reveals this Ultimate Truth. A student should use these methods to realize *Brahman*:

1. *Śravanam*, hearing it;

2. *Mananam*, thinking about it;

3. *Nididhyāsanam* uniting on it by constant musing; and

4. *Sākṣātkāra*, direct perception and identity with it.

By these four methods, the student attains lordship, acquiring the glory of being the inmost Self of All, and effortlessly he receives the supernatural and majestic powers of the Supreme.

The body is like a tree, but with the roots–the brain, mind, and head–above, and the branches, the extremities, below. Different kinds of knowledge are its leaves. *Nādam, Brahman*, is the central nucleus of evolution of this tree. This *nādam* should be meditated upon as a teacher. It bestows on the meditator direct knowledge of Ultimate Truth. It is the teacher of All. Behold the Supreme teacher in the inner chamber of your Consciousness. It is forever young, Eternal; the students are older than this teacher. It is strange indeed that this teacher instructs all, and only through silence. If one listens to its teachings, all one's doubts are removed, and one attains identity with one's teacher.

This teacher is *nādam*; externally it is called *OM*. Its Nature is pure Consciousness. One's fatigue and frustration are removed by being immersed in it. It brings Eternal newness and freshness; hence, it is called *praṇava* (*pra*, altogether, absolutely + *nava*, new, fresh).

It is the Eternal ocean of wisdom, and the healer of all mental and physical diseases. It removes the necessity of proceeding through birth and death. Realize your young teacher, who through silent instructions, reveals the truth of the Supreme, *Brahman*. It is surrounded by mighty sages and aged disciples devoted to *Brahman*, the Supreme teacher, the Essence of Reality and Bliss. It is revealed by its own light. It is a wonderful teacher, ever a friend and comrade, ever ready to uplift a student and grant him freedom and *nirvāṇam*.

As butter is obtained from milk by churning, so this omnipresent, omniscient, omnipotent, and silent teacher is obtained from Consciousness by intensive churning in *samādhi*, meditation.

## SUTRA NO. 60

अनण्वस्थूलमह्रस्वमदीर्घमजमव्ययम् ।
अरूपगुणवर्णाख्यं तद्ब्रह्मेत्यवधारयेत् ॥६०॥

ANAṆVASTHŪLAMAHRASVAM ADĪRGHAM AJAM AVYAYAM.
ARŪPAGUṆAVARṆĀKHYAṀ TAD BRAHMETYAVADHĀRAYET.

| | | |
|---|---|---|
| अनणु | Anaṇu | Neither subtle- |
| अस्थूलम् | Asthūlam- | Nor gross- |
| अह्रस्वम् | Ahrasvam- | Neither short- |
| अदीर्घम् | Adīrgham- | Nor long |
| अजम् | Ajam | Without birth |
| अव्ययम् | Avyayam | Changeless |
| अरूप-गुण-वर्ण- | Arūpa-guṇa-varṇa | Without form, quality, color, - |
| आख्यम् | Akhyam | And name |
| तत्-ब्रह्म | Tat-Brahma | That Brahman |
| इति | Iti | Thus |
| अवधारयेत् | Avadhārayet | One should realize |

Know for certain to be *Brahman* that which is neither subtle nor gross, neither long nor short, without birth and death, without change, without form, qualities or color.

Realize that shining and radiating Supreme Energy to be *Brahman* which is neither subtle nor gross, neither short nor long, which is subtler than the subtle and grosser than the gross, without birth and without change, and which is beyond all material characteristics such as name, form, color, quality, cause, effect, space, and time. It is Self-abiding, beyond all manifestations. By discerning that, one is freed from death.

*Ātman* is not an object of any sort; it is the Eternal subject. We hear, touch, see, feel, and think by the power of *Ātman*. By withdrawing from all outward things, by retreating into the foundation of our own Soul, in the remotest depths of the Soul, we find *Brahman*. There the Self is realized above all empirical concepts of sense and sensations.

The aim of intellect is to discover the Unity which comprehends both the subject and the object. The aim of logic and life is to tell us that there is such Unity, and the goal of philosophic endeavor is to describe the contents and Nature of that Unity. Due to the inherent incapacity of the intellect, one cannot comprehend the whole. The intellect is inadequate to grasp the whole for it operates through symbols, creeds, and conventionalities. Ultimate Reality cannot be made into an objective representation which the intellect can grasp. Objective knowledge of the subject is impossible. Sense and sensation are inadequate to comprehend it; still they have no existence apart from it. That which one cannot think with the mind, but that by which the mind is made to think, realize that to be *Brahman*. *Ātman* is unseen but seeing, unheard but hearing, unperceived but perceiving, unknown but knowing.

Nothing is so positively experienced as one's own Self, "I." We cannot express or communicate without using the world "I." Our senses are needed only to communicate with the external world, not with Self, I. Language is the way of communication with others, but in experiencing one's own inner condition, such as hunger or thirst, one does not need to use language. We see things with our eyes, but can anyone see the Self with his eyes? We hear sounds with our ears, but can anyone hear his own Self? So it is with all the senses; the "I" behind all these senses uses them as instruments; therefore, this "I," Self, is not the subject matter of any instrument. Since all instruments depend on it, but it is not dependent on anything, it is the most positive principle on which the positivity, existence, of the organs depends.

In perception of an object, every sense presents its own perception positively, and contradicts the perception of the other senses. For instance, the eye informs us that the Universe is nothing but optical vibration of light and color; the ear informs us that the Universe is nothing but the vibration of various sounds; and so on, in the same way, for all the senses. Mindstuff tells us that the Universe is nothing but the vibration of thought-energy. Here, every sense organ positively presents its perception, and positively contradicts the perception of other organs. Behind these senses and their mutual contradictory perceptions is Consciousness, "I," which unifies them into a meaningful unit. This "I," Self, is the central force of every organ; it directs all organs in their respective activities; it is not perceived by any sense, but it is directly experienced by its own cognition.

## SUTRA NO. 61

यद्भासा भास्यतेऽर्कादि भास्यैर्यत्तु न भास्यते।
येन सर्वमिदं भाति तद्ब्रह्मेत्यवधारयेत् ॥६१॥

YADBHĀSĀ BHĀSYATE' RKĀDI BHĀSYAIR YATTU NA BHĀSYATE.
YENA SARVAM IDAṀ BHĀTI TAD BRAHMETYAVADHĀRAYET.

| | | |
|---|---|---|
| यत्-भासा | Yat - bhāsā | By which light |
| भास्यते | Bhāsyate | Is illumined |
| अर्कादि | Arkādi | The sun, and other lights |
| भास्यैः | Bhāsyaiḥ | By all lights |
| यत् | Yat | Which |
| तु | Tu | Indeed |
| न | Na | Not |
| भास्यते | Bhāsyate | Is illuminated |
| येन | Yena | By which |
| सर्वम् | Sarvam | All |
| इदम् | Idam | This |
| भाति | Bhāti | Shines |
| तत् ब्रह्म | Tat-Brahma | That Brahman |
| इति | Iti | Thus |
| अवधारयेत् | Avadhārayet | One should realize |

Experience to be *Brahman* that by the Light of which luminous bodies such as stars, sun, and moon are illumined; know to be *Brahman* that which cannot be illumined by their lights. The Universe of the body, mind, and senses is illumined by Consciousness alone.

Realize that Self-shining and Self-radiating Supreme Light to be *Brahman* by which all lights of the Universe—sun, moon, and stars-—are enlightened and luminous. All Lights of the universe are illumined by *Brahman*, but their light cannot illumine *Brahman*; hence the Supreme Light by which everything is illumined is called *Brahman*.

"Neither the sun, moon, stars, lightning, electricity, nor fire shines there. *Brahman* shines and everything shines by it. It lights the entire Universe."

*Brahman*, *Ātman*, Truth, Reality is *svayam prakāśa*, that is, Self-shining, Self-radiating, and Self-luminous energy. What does this mean? *Yoga vedānta* defines it as that which is never the object of knowing, acts, or processes, but that which is immediately directly, and inevitably present in knowing, acts, and processes. Without its direct and immediate presence there would be no knowing act, process, or knowledge. Self-luminosity thus means the capacity of being ever-present in all our acts of Consciousness without ever being an object of Consciousness. When anything is described as an object of Consciousness, its character, constituting its knowability, is a quality which may or may not be present in it, or which may be present at which may be present at one time and absent at another. This makes it dependent on some other such entity, which can produce it and manifest it. Thus the knowledge of the perceived objects is in accordance with the training of the perceiver. The same object can be perceived differently by different perceivers. Truly, the Universe is the product of mind.

*Ātman, Brahman*, differs from all objects in that it is never dependent on anything else for its manifestation. It manifests all other objects and itself by its own light. Should Consciousness, *Ātman, Brahman* require another Consciousness to manifest itself, then that might again require another, and that another, and so on, *ad infinitum*. At the time of object-manifestation—such as in hearing, seeing, etc.—Consciousness is pre-manifested and pre-existent; otherwise, there would be no object-manifestation. Even on seeing, hearing, smelling, testing, touching and knowing a thing, one might doubt that one had perceived or known it. Thus practical analysis proves that Consciousness is Self-luminous and Self-radiation energy, for it is prior to any manifestation, and by its Self-manifestation, it maintains the senses, sense experience, and world experience. One should discriminate between pure Consciousness and objective consciousness obtained from the manifesting quality of objects when they are examined, analyzed, and known in the light of Consciousness. Self-luminous pure Consciousness is called Self (*Ātman*) for it stands by itself.

Our present psychological consciousness is dependent on the senses and sensation. According to the degree, quality, and quantity of acuteness and purity of the senses and sensation, Consciousness is manifested. That is why the Consciousness of the dream world is not so systematic as that of the waking state. Psychological Consciousness is completely obscured in sound sleep, for activities of the senses and sensation are lowered below the threshold. In the state of *samādhi*, the senses and sensations are in perfect motion, and by their *tanmātric* motion, tremendous speed, psychological Consciousness realizes its Unity and identity with *Ātman*. However, evolution and involution of psychological Consciousness has no influence on *Ātman*; pure Consciousness does not go through any change. Because it is that which goes through changes, psychological consciousness may be termed qualified consciousness. The real Self of man is identical with the pure, manifesting Unity of all Consciousness. What appears as the perception of the Self as an object of knowledge is but association comprehended under the term *ahaṁkara*, ego-consciousness.

"He in whom the sky, earth, and interspace are woven, also the mind with all the senses and vital breaths, know him alone as the One Self. Dismiss other utterances."

"*Brahman* is the Light of lights. In the state of *samādhi*, this Supreme Light is manifested in human intuition, through *sahasrāram*, where all sensations and motions are joined together, and where *Brahman* is manifested as *nādam*. Meditate on *OM*, *nādam*, as *Brahman*. May you be successful in crossing the ocean of darkness to the far shore of light."

In short, Consciousness, *Brahman*, is that by means of which every sensation, action, and cognition of senses is known, but that which is not known by senses and mind. That is called *Brahman*.

## SUTRA NO. 62

स्वयमन्तर्बहिर्व्याप्य भासयन्नखिलं जगत् ।
ब्रह्म प्रकाशते वह्निप्रतप्तायसपिण्डवत् ॥६२॥

SVAYAMANTARBAHIRVYĀPYA BHĀSAYANNAKHILAṀ JAGAT.
BRAHMA PRAKĀŚATE VAHNIPRATAPTĀYASAPIṆḌAVAT.

| | | |
|---|---|---|
| स्वयम् | Svayam | Itself |
| अन्तः | Antaḥ | Inwardly |
| बहिः | Bahiḥ | Outwardly |
| व्याप्य | Vyāpya | Pervading |
| भासयन् | Bhāsayan | Illuminating |
| अखिलम् | Akhilam | Entire |
| जगत् | Jagat | Universe |
| ब्रह्म | Brahma | Brahman |
| प्रकाशते | Prakāśate | Shines |
| वह्नि - प्रतप्त- | Vahni-pratapta | Red-hot by fire- |
| आयस- पिण्डवत् | Āyasa - piṇḍavat | Like the iron ball |

It is the Supreme, *Brahman* alone, that pervades the entire Universe in every dimension and shines of itself. The individual self, when identified with *Brahman*, begins to shine like *Brahman* in the same way as an iron ball placed in fire inwardly and outwardly begins to glow like fire.

Outwardly and inwardly pervading the entire Universe, *Brahman* shines and radiates by its own light in the same way as electricity, outwardly and inwardly pervading the filament of wire, shines and radiates by its own light.

Outwardly and inwardly pervading white-hot iron, fire shines by its own light and heat; so *Brahman*, as Existence, Consciousness, Reality, and Bliss, permeates the Universe. It illumines the entire Universe and shines of itself as the immanent and transcendent Reality.

## SUTRA NO. 63

जगद्विलक्षणं ब्रह्म ब्रह्मणोऽन्यन्न किञ्चन ।
ब्रह्मान्यद्भाति चेन्मिथ्या यथा मरुमरीचिका ॥६३॥

JAGADVILAKṢAṆAṀ BRAHMA BRAHMAṆO 'NYAN NA KIÑCANA.
BRAHMĀNYAD BHĀTI CENMITHYĀ YATHĀ MARUMARĪCIKĀ.

| | | |
|---|---|---|
| जगत्-विलक्षणम् | Jagat-vilakṣaṇam | Other than the Universe of senses |
| ब्रह्म | Brahma | Brahman |
| ब्रह्मणः | Brahmaṇaḥ | Than Brahman |
| अन्यत् | Anyat | Other |
| न | Na | Not |
| किञ्चन | Kiñcana | Anything |
| ब्रह्म-अन्यत् | Brahma - anyat | Other than Brahman |
| भाति | Bhāti | Shines |
| चेत् | Cet | If |
| मिथ्या | Mithyā | False, unreal |
| यथा | Yathā | As |
| मरु-मरीचिका | Maru-marīcikā | The mirage in the desert |

*Brahman* is transcendental Reality, and the relative Universe in all its aspects is nothing but a manifestation of *Brahman*. *Brahman* is independent of the character of the Universe. Nothing exists in the Universe which is not in *Brahman* and from *Brahman*. If any object of the Universe appears to exist independent of Consciousness, *Brahman*, it is as unreal as a mirage.

*Brahman* is other than the present universe of the senses. Nothing exists that is not a manifestation of *Brahman*. The appearance of the Universe as other than *Brahman* is unreal—like a mirage on the desert. *Brahman* is verily Immortality. *Brahman* spreads forth below and above and in every direction. *Brahman* is indeed this Universe. It is the greatest. "I shall tell you the truth in a nutshell; *Brahman* alone is Real; the world as other than *Brahman* is illusory; man is none other than *Brahman*."

It seems easy to talk and write of the Absoluteness of *Brahman* and of the illusoriness of the world, but it is difficult to comprehend the Real meaning of *Brahman*. How many writers and philosophers have experience of this truth?

The illusory nature of the world cannot be overcome without Realizing *Brahman*. The world is governed by mathematical, Eternal laws; and to declare it illusory is daring indeed. However, it is a fact that *Brahman* is the only Reality, and that the world as other than *Brahman* is illusory. This truth cannot be realized without the Realization of *Brahman*.

To seek Realization of *Brahman* for the sake of desires would mean to manifest the world more and more. As long as a Spiritual purpose is not recognized, *Brahman* will not be recognized, realized. A student should examine his purpose in meditation and in seeking Self-realization. Why do you desire to know *Brahman*? What will you do after knowing *Brahman*? Are you willing and prepared to employ and apply that which will be revealed and received by you for the glorification of Self-realization, and for the benefit of the world? A student of Self-realization does not serve the world in the same sense that other persons do. In serving the world, he will not have the sense of helping others, because there is no otherness. He should understand serving others to be his own service; this is an important part of Self-realization. It would be pseudo Self-realization if one thought to exchange for one's services anything other than love of *Brahman*. In the process of Self-realization, all services should be given without selfish gain, in service to the Supreme. Pride is one sign of dualism which may lead even an advanced seeker of Truth to the world of multiplicity.

In serving the world, a student of Self-realization should treat all as a manifestation of *Brahman*. Regardless of how we keep our house, society, and nation in good order, if we do not understand the motive and purpose of that service, it is just another form of ignorance.

A student should be ready to resign entirely his own selfishness and earthly will, and should earnestly desire to become One with the

Supreme. He who has no such high purpose, who merely seeks higher philosophical knowledge for his personal glorification, so that he may be looked upon as great or enlightened by the world, is not fit to attain identity with *Brahman*. Beneath his pretension, worldly ambition is hidden. The world cannot be overcome by keeping the world in the heart. The multiplicity of the world is not overcome from without, but from within. However pure we may be outwardly, if we are impure inwardly, we are unfit for Self-realization.

Wisdom is not an attainment; it is a discovery, the understanding of our own Self. Man's knowledge and science are like the moon which has borrowed light from the sun. A student of Self-realization is comparable to the sun which has its own light, and is independent of any object upon which it may shine. Thus a *Yogi* comes to the path of the sun from the path of the moon. This is the secret of the paths of the moon and the sun, often described in scripture. The path of the moon is the way of rebirth again and again; the path of the sun is the way of Self-realization.

Such a *Yogi* has no fear of hell and no attachment to heaven. He shall not be intoxicated even by celestial desires other than *Brahman*, the Absolute, because ultimately all these desires will bring him to terrestrial thoughts and desires, and he will not be able to experience this world as *Brahman*. He must overcome all desires, whether they lead to heavenly or earthly majesty because, in either case, the world is present as an obstacle, and *Atman* is not realized.

Everything is given to him who desires nothing. This is the secret law of Nature. Any remnant of desire will cause one to long for the whole. In short, any purpose or desire other than *Brahman* will bring one back to the world. No amount of torturing the brain will bring success in Self-realization, if the purpose and motivation of realization is other than the Self for its own sake.

What is that which stands between individual soul and *Brahman*, between the world and *Brahman*? What is that which does not permit one to realize Truth? That obstacle, that opaque screen, is one's own mind. Although the Soul is a reflection of *Brahman*, owning to its association with mind, the individual soul is under the influence of the mind and senses. As long as the Soul does not leave the company of the mind, it will not be qualified to return to its original state, to *Brahman*. Then alone will perception of the world be dissolved in *Brahman*, the world will remain in one's mind as a mathematical, scientific, and permanent Truth.

The mind too, has lost its original place, form, and power, and is now dominated by the senses. The Soul will not be liberated from the world, unless the mind goes back to its original place. By meditation, return the mind to its original place by the same way that it went out, and keep it steady at its center. The natural way of meditation is not to know many things, but to forget everything. Then you will know everything. Thus, in brief, Self-analysis and meditation is undoing everything (*karmas*) that we have already done.

In search of pleasure and happiness, of which it is naturally fond, the mind jumps from one object to another, becoming energetic and restless. The only way to make the mind steady is to give it a taste of something higher than the pleasure of the world. Once the mind has tasted such serenity, it will be attached forever, and its restlessness will vanish.

The highest happiness is *Brahman*. It is the Eternal radiating energy that has created the Universe. The potential of fire is in wood, but it can neither be seen nor put to any use unless it is first ignited. When two pieces of wood are vigorously rubbed together, fire is manifested and can be used. Likewise, though *Brahman* exists in all, it can neither be seen nor put to use, unless it is first ignited by the friction of meditation on *nādam*. Only then can one experience the world melting into the Self-radiating and Self-shining energy of *Brahman*.

By no amount of external effort, forethought, or intelligence will one accomplish identity with *Brahman*. A man is directly led by *Brahman* to high states of Self-realization. The duty of a Self-analyst is to fulfill the necessary qualifications to be led by *Brahman*; therefore, one should cultivate the following:

1. Love and devotion, *bhakti*;

2. Spiritual strength, *balam*;

3. Truthfulness, *satyam*;

4. Self-discipline, constant and continuous proper use of the senses, *tapah*;

5. Self-knowledge, *ātmajñānam*;

6. Protection of hormonal, chemical, biochemical, and other vital fluids of the body for the manifestation of *Brahman*, *ojas śakti*;

7. Constant practice of *tri-ratnam*, the three jewels, which are:

   a. The development of intuitive knowledge, *prajñā*;

   b. Ethical and moral standards, *śīla*; and

   c. Concentration, *samādhi*.

8. Constant practice of the eight steps of *yoga*;

9. Constant and continuous meditation on *nādam*, *OM*; and

10. Self-surrender to the Supreme.

All experimentation must include the following six systems to check the results and to formulate theory, philosophy, and speculation. These are:

1. Logical and epistemological system, *nyāya*;

2. Ontological, etiological, and etymological system, *vaiśeṣika*;

3. Mathematical system, *sānkhya*;

4. Careful experimentation and observation system, *yoga*;

5. Action and reaction system, including physical, chemical, biochemical, electrical, atomic, nuclear, and psychological, *mīmānsā*; and

6. Formulation of theory and conclusion, *vedānta*.

Later these six systems are developed into systems of philosophy as the way of life. The seeker does not necessarily have to study these systems from the outside, for he will experience them manifesting from his inner Self. He experiences both relative knowledge and Absolute knowledge as the radiation of the Self, when his mind is absolutely free from all thoughts.

Whatever is in the macrocosm is also in the microcosm; therefore, if one can delve within one's Self and experience the Truth of the microcosm, then the macrocosm too will be experienced. Thus One experiences the Oneness of the world and *Brahman*.

At the plane of the eyes, the body is divided into three parts. The part above this plane is the center of Cosmic vibration, and it includes the cortical and subcortical areas in the brain. It deals with Cosmic Existence. The second plane is just the center of the head behind the eyes, and it consists of all sensory stations in the brain. This plane deals with individual existence. The individual "I" communicates with the Cosmic "I" above this plane. Below this plane of the eyes is the plane of the body for physical activities. When the plane above the eyes is vibrated by any means, such as chemical, biochemical, biological, or electrical impulses, then the individual "I" experiences the sensations of peace, tranquillity, and Bliss. When the plane of the eyes is vibrated, the individual experiences the Universe as the artistic manifestation of Consciousness. When the lower centers of the brain are vibrated by impulses, the individual "I" experiences physical manifestations and physical strength, and deals with the physical world.

Self-inquiry, "Who am I?" is different from meditation on: "I am *Śiva*" or "I am he." These are mental approaches; "Who am I?" is the Spiritual approach. In the investigation of Self, "Who am I?" the mind is concerned with cognizing the "I" before it proceeds to know the world or its lord. The quest of Self is the direct method, and it is superior to all other methods. When one goes deeper and deeper in the quest of the Self, the Real Self is found waiting to receive one. Then whatever is to be done is done by that Real Self; the individual has no further hand in it. In the investigation of Self, "Who am I?" all doubts and discussions are abandoned, just as one who sleeps forgets all his cares for the time being.

Everyone is the Self and is indeed Infinite. Yet each person mistakes his body for his Self. To know the Self, there is need of the light of the Self. This light illumines all three planes, physical, mental, and Spiritual. The plane below the eyes is the physical one; the plane on the level of the eyes is the mental one; and the plane above the eyes is the Spiritual plane. The Self can only be of the Nature of light. It lights up both physical light and darknesss, and it remains beyond physical light and darkness. It is said to be light because it illumines everything. Consciousness is the Self of which everyone is aware. No one is ever away from his Self; hence everyone is Self-realized. Realization means getting rid of the false idea, "I am not realized." It is not a new thing to be acquired; it must already exist, for it is Eternal. Once the false notions, "I am the body" and

"I am not realized," have been removed, Supreme Consciousness, Self, remains. This is called Realization. Realization is Eternal, and it exists here and now. Consciousness is pure knowledge. The mind arises out of it and submerges into it. The essence of the mind is Awareness or Consciousness.

There is a constant rain of nectar, but the mind, preoccupied with thoughts, love, hatred, fascination, and other temporal attractions has no time to go in and taste its Bliss. If the mind is upside-down, it will not be filled with the rain of nectar, just as an upside-down jar will collect no water, though it be raining heavily. The mind is like a parachute; it works when it is open. The mind is filled with the nectar of the Supreme Energy of *Ātman* when it is open toward Truth.

Illusions, both subjective and objective, are more a misinterpretation than misperception; thus, due to imperfect knowledge, all information regarding the world is misleading, for it is full of misinterpretation. The present world with the present interpretation is a creation of the mind. Even the description of Reality is no exception to this law. However, the Nature of *Brahman* is not affected in any way by this imperfect knowledge. When a person with defective vision sees two moons, he does not thereby create two moons. The world of appearance with its subjective and objective phenomena, names and forms, which can be defined neither as Real nor unreal, neither as being nor non-being, rests upon imperfect knowledge, *avidyā*. When *Brahman* is realized, the world is transformed into Eternal being which persists without change and transformation. *Brahman* alone is the True and the Real. It manifests itself as the Reality of world experience. That a blind man cannot see the sun is his defect; this will not bring any change in the real Nature of the sun. If, due to imperfect knowledge, men do not recognize *Brahman*, but experience the multiplicity of the world instead, there is no change in the real Nature of *Brahman*. When the Consciousness of non-separateness, "Thou are That," is awakened, the wandering of the mind and Soul, and the subjective-objective division of the world is removed by true and perfect knowledge. In the Absolute sense, the present world does not exist. The world characterized by names and forms is a creation of the mind. If it were absolutely existent, then all efforts toward *nirvāṇam* and enlightenment would be futile.

The Real is defined as the entity not changed by time, not limited by space, and not affected by the law of causality. Anything that passes through time and space, cause and effect, is unreal. The principle of non-contradiction is the criterion of Truth. A straight stick appears bent when in water. Its crookedness in water is as real to the eye as its straightness is to the touch. The wrong judgment of the eye is corrected by touch, which reveals a more constant relation.

What is contradicted is not truth. The dream state and sound sleep are contradicted by the waking state; the waking and dream states are contradicted by sound sleep; sound sleep and waking are contradicted by the dream state. All these states are contradicted by insight into Reality, *Brahmānubhava*. *Brahmānubhava* is the highest Truth, because it is not contradicted by any other knowledge or experience.

*Yogis* do not question the psychological perception of the world, but they question its interpretation. The psychologically-perceived Universe is not denied and neglected, but its perception as other than *Brahman* is denied because the sense of otherness and multiplicity is illusory and is due to ignorance. This ignorance has no Absolute Existence; it is an inexplicable state of mind, which ultimately vanishes in *Brahmānubhava*, experiencing of *Brahman*.

Since the beginning of human existence, man's drive for knowledge and understanding has created principles, dogmas, and theories about the origin of the world, the purpose of human existence, the goal of life, the origin of cosmic phenomena, the meaning of good and bad, sin and virtue, and thousands of other things which he thought important. To a great extent man's theories, philosophy, religious thoughts, and plans are often directly harmful to others, and indirectly to himself. This is the consequence of slovenly thinking due to limited experience, thinking that he cannot tolerate the challenge of logic and science. Man has fought against unfavorable situations, fate, illness, suffering, and death with ineffectual means; and thus has used his energy uselessly and harmfully. In attempting to change fate and destiny by magic and prayer, and in attempting to solve his problems, he created a mental God in his own image, and then created a demon to oppose the image. Man has divided against himself. There is little difference to be seen between primitive inner life and modern inner life. Selfishness and ulterior motives play an important part in the center of a man's thinking, although they may be unknown to him.

The goal of meditation is to ascertain the Truth regarding the world, and to discard untruth from life. For this purpose, the evolution of intelligence, and the development of knowledge and its adaptation, assimilation, and accommodation, are extremely important. Man is striving for *nirvāṇam* and liberation, but he cannot discriminate between freedom and bondage. Can one obtain freedom without the development of wisdom and intelligence? Can a man develop intelligence and learning without a firm determination to renounce prejudice and traditional bad habits? Gods and demons, good and bad, merit and demerit, purity and sin, happiness and unhappiness, all are his own creation and image. There can be no imposition of judgment on others when, in reality, there is no valid knowledge of the world.

To understand the evolution of intelligence in space and time, cause and effect, is not easy. It is not enough to know that man is born. An intelligent man should be interested to know where he was before he was born, and where he will be after death. Heaven and hell are terms without specific meaning for a particular man. One must know how sensation is transformed into motion, and how motion is transformed into sensation. One must utilize logic and intuition in one's speculation and formulation of ideas. Man knows nothing about his existence and the Reality of the world. He lives on certain information handed down to him by religious practices, faith, belief, and other sources; consequently, he has lost the use of his sense and wisdom. Strangely enough, he questions his own experience, if it is contrary to tradition and belief!

Actually man is in conflict with himself. How can a man be happy when fighting with members of his own family in the same house? Man tries to live happily in the home of the mind and sensory-motor intelligence, while denying the senses and their experiences, and while ignoring the Cosmic forces responsible for creation, sustenance, nourishment, and dissolution of his body. Man needs to understand the best and exact use of his body, senses, and mind. When the senses and mind are trained properly through Self-analysis, and when there is manifestation of higher intelligence, then he feels that the Universe of the senses is nothing but *Brahman*. A man cannot know about himself anything besides sensation and motion; he lives on information presented by his senses and mind. Whatever the senses give him, he accordingly feels a degree of happiness or unhappiness. If the senses give him sensations of birth, suffering, or death, he feels so. If they inform him of *nirvāṇam* and liberation, he is liberated, because he directly perceives and feels so. Therefore, one must be careful to evaluate his sense, sensation, motion, and emotion. One should meditate until he experiences the absolute manifestation of intelligence and sense, so that he feels the world to be nothing but *Brahman*.

The keynote of Self-analysis is perception of the "I." The meditator should ask, "What is that in me which never deviates even for a moment? Am I not positively 'I am'?" This cognition of "I" generates knowledge of the past, present, and future. The seeker will find that it is "I," Consciousness, in himeself that is One and changeless. From childhood to old age, everything is changing but the "I." He who experiences the "I" has experienced Absolute God.

## SUTRA NO. 64

दृश्यते श्रूयते यद्यत् ब्रह्मणोऽन्यन्न तद्भवेत् ।
तत्त्वज्ञानाच्च तद्ब्रह्म सच्चिदानन्दमद्वयम् ॥६४॥

DRŚYATE ŚRŪYATE YADYAD BRAHMANO' NYAN NA TAD BHAVET.
TATTVAJÑĀNĀC CA TADBRAHMA SACCIDĀNANDAMADVAYAM.

| | | |
|---|---|---|
| दृश्यते | Dṛśyate | Is seen |
| श्रूयते | Śrūyate | Is heard |
| यत्-यत् | Yat yat | Whatever |
| ब्रह्मणः | Brahmaṇaḥ | Than Brahman |
| अन्यत् | Anyat | Other |
| न | Na | Not |
| तत् | Tat | That |
| भवेत् | Bhavet | Is |
| तत्त्व-ज्ञानात् | Tattva-jñānāt | Due to knowledge of Truth |
| च | Ca | And |
| तत्-ब्रह्म | Tat - Brahma | That Brahman |
| सत्-चित्-आनन्दम् | Sat-cit-ānandam | Pure Existence, pure Consciousness, pure Bliss |
| अद्वयम् | Advayam | Non-dual |

Whatever is sensed, perceived, and experienced is nothing but the manifestation of *Brahman*. The Self seems to be divided in and among all, while in essence it is indivisible, Eternal Existence-Knowledge-Bliss; and it is the "I," *Brahman*.

The Universe that is sensed and perceived—seen, heard, smelled, tasted, and touched—is nothing else but *Brahman*. With the increasing manifestation of Absolute Intelligence and insight into Reality, the threshold of the senses is expanded, and the sense-perceived universe is transformed into the Absolute Existence-Knowledge-Bliss, and subjective-objective experiences are transformed into non-dual *Brahman*.

Seekers of Truth should follow the path of Truth, says Lord *Buddha*: "Do not accept anything on mere hearsay (i.e., thinking that thus have we heard it for a long time). Do not accept anything by mere tradition (i.e., thinking that it has thus been handed down through many generations.) Do not accept anything on account of mere rumors (i.e., by believing what others say without any investigation.) Do not accept anything just because it accords with your scriptures. Do not accept anything by mere supposition. Do not accept anything by mere inference. Do not accept anything by merely considering the reasons. Do not accept anything merely because it seems acceptable (i.e., thinking that as the speaker seems to be a good person his word should be accepted.) Do not accept anything, thinking that the ascetic is respected by us (therefore it is right to accept his word.

But when you know for yourselves these things are immoral, these things are blameworthy, these things are censured by the wise, these things when performed and undertaken conduce to well-being and happiness—then do you live acting accordingly."

Do not depend on others for liberation and freedom, but depend on yourself. To depend on others is negative; to depend on oneself is positive. Be your own island to protect yourself from the ocean of misery, suffering and death. One, like a scientist, should believe in nothing but facts; and these facts are presented by one's internal and external Nature.

When right knowledge of *Brahman* is reflected in the perceptual mechanism, *buddhi* through constant Self-analysis in *nirvikalpaka* or *asamprajñāta samādhi*, sensations of the sensory organs reach to the level of Cosmic sensation; thus the sensation of separateness and otherness disappears, one's individual existence is transformed into Universal existence, and one sees *Brahman* everywhere.

Ignorance is protective like a mother; it is transformed into *Brahman* upon Self-realization. Without ignorance, man would know the suffering of the entire world in addition to his own suffering. Due to the cumulative suffering, he could die. Ignorance protects him until the attainment of right knowledge.

After such attainment, he has not only knowledge, but also

omnipotent power to protect himself. From the standpoint of *Brahman*, ignorance and its products, subjective-objective multiplicity, are nothing but *Brahman*. Whether man knows it or not, whatever he sees, hears, smells, tastes, and touches is *Brahman*. One should continue constant meditation and Self-analysis until this Oneness is realized.

Right knowledge is Self-luminous. In the Absolute sense, there is no such thing as consciousness of Consciousness. This Self-evident and Self-luminous character is not fully reflected in our perceptual mechanism due to our psychological prejudices. The Nature of Utlimate Reality does not depend on human notions and opinions. It depends only on itself. To say of a dummy that it is either a dummy, or a man, or something else is not stating its truth. That it is a dummy is the truth, since it conforms to the nature of a dummy. When psychological consciousness and senses reach to the level of Ultimate Consciousness and Ultimate sensation, the world which appears in the state of ignorance as other than *Brahman*, is realized as a manifestation of non-dual *Brahman*.

Is there anything in this Universe which is without motion? Motion, *prāṇa*, is the fundamental property and inherent Reality of every organic and inorganic entity. Is there any motion which is without sensation, consciousness? *Brahman* is the Ultimate source of all motion and sensation.

There are three ways of knowing Reality:

1. Sense experience presents the perception and knowledge of the sensible qualities of the Universe, the external world.

2. Epistemological, ontological, etymological, mathematical, and logical reasoning give us knowledge of both the external and the internal, but in an indirect way through principles, laws, concepts, and symbols.

3. Intuitive knowledge is immediate and direct. In intuitive knowledge the knower and the known are one and identical. To know Reality is to be Reality. Knowledge of the Self, *Ātman, Brahman*, is an example of intuitive knowledge.

Neither sense experience nor reasoning give immediate insight into Reality. Sense experience is modified and mediated by the senses, for it comes through the medium of the sense organs. Logical reasoning depends on the person who uses it; his projection cannot be avoided. In any case, there is conclusive knowledge, but no direct identity with knowledge. For instance, a physiologist knows physiological action and reaction indirectly; a chemist, a biochemist, and a biologist know chemical, bio-chemical, and biological action and reaction indirectly; they know but they themselves do not feel them.

After enlightenment, one becomes aware of *Brahman* in the same way that one becomes aware of love, anger, hunger, or other feelings—directly—by experiencing it as his own Self; thus Self-knowledge is inseparable from Self-existence. Though Self is the All-pervading Reality, it cannot be perceived by those who have not developed intuitive knowledge. As no one can eat or sleep for another, and no one can take drugs to remove another's sickness, so no one can experience the Self, "I," for another. Everyone has to experience his own "I" as the Eternal and Immortal principle of this Universe.

## SUTRA NO. 65

सर्वगं सच्चिदात्मानं ज्ञानचक्षुर्निरीक्षते ।
अज्ञानचक्षुर्नेक्षेत भास्वन्तं भानुमन्धवत् ॥६५॥

SARVAGAṀ SACCIDĀTMĀNAṀ JÑĀNACAKṢUR NIRĪKṢATE.
AJÑĀNACAKṢUR NEKṢETA BHĀSVANTAṀ BHĀNUM ANDHAVAT.

| | | |
|---|---|---|
| सर्व-गम् | Sarva-gam | All pervading |
| सत्-चित्-आत्मानम् | Sat-cit-ātmānam | Existence-Consciousness-Reality of Self |
| ज्ञान-चक्षुः | Jñāna-cakṣuḥ | The eye of wisdom, intuitio |
| निरीक्षते | Nirīkṣate | Perceives |
| अज्ञान-चुक्षुः | Ajñāna-cakṣuḥ | One whose vision is cover by ignorance |
| न | Na | Not |
| ईक्षेत | Īkṣeta | Perceives |
| भास्वन्तम् | Bhāsvantam | Shining |
| भानुम् | Bhānum | The sun |
| अन्धवत् | Andhavat | Like a blind man |

The Self-realized man experiences Existence-Consciousness-Bliss everywhere and in every object of the Universe. The ignorant man does not experience the presence of *Brahman*, just as a blind man does not perceive even the shining sun.

Eternal Existence, Consciousness, Reality, Bliss of *Atman* is realized only by those who have developed intuitive knowledge by meditation and Self-analysis. As the sun cannot be seen by a blind man, so *Ātman* cannot be realized by those who do not have intuitive knowledge, although it is present everywhere in its Eternal Radiance.

Intuitive knowledge should not be confused with non-philosophic intuition. Intuitive knowledge is not confined to the narrow region of the little self. It is developed by progressive meditation. As intuitive knowledge more highly develops, so does the individual self. The more the individual self develops, the more it can absorb and identify with Reality, and the greater is the intuitive knowledge of Reality. Intuition is not anti-intellectual; it is super-intellectual. It is not below reasoning; it is beyond reasoning.

This intuitive knowledge cannot be obtained by faith or belief, nor by studying holy books and repeating religious formulae, nor by depending on others' perfections; it is progressively developed by constant meditation with an open heart and mind. Prejudice in any form—whether it be religious, social, political, national, cosmological, or philosophical—is inimical to the mind, and it should be thoroughly eradicated from one's thinking.

In investigation of Truth, ideas of theism or atheism have little value. Theists have faith and belief in God, but they have not seen God. Atheists deny the Existence of God, but they have not investigated all of inner and other Nature. Agreeing with something, when you do not know, is as indefensible and misleading as denying something which you definitely know.

However one attends meetings regularly and faithfully, one will not develop intuition without practice and application of those principles in life. Without practice one will fail the final examination of life, just as a student who attends university classes regularly, but neglects to do his homework will fail. Preparation for life, meditation, Self-analysis, and application of natural laws in one's life are like doing homework. Other things such as listening to lectures, attending meetings, and reading books are like attending schools and universities. Each has its own signficance.

The aim of meditation and Self-realization is to know the real Nature of one's Self, and the Nature of the Universe, and to become One with Reality. One must develop access to intuitive knowledge, *jñāna-cakṣu*. The study of man is the study of the Cosmos. Individual soul is the unit for study and experimentation.

There are five organs of sensation and five organs of action. All these organs are under the control of mind. Here the term "mind" does not mean the fragment, the conscious mind, but the integral mind including conscious, subconscious, and superconscious aspects. Such mind controls the entire body, all systems, all actions and reactions, including physical, chemical, biochemical, biological, atomic, and nuclear. Each cell of the body has its own cell mind, as each man has his individual mind. The harmonious working of all cells brings normal hormonal powers, which in turn bring the power of *ojas*, psychic power. This power of *ojas* revitalizes the mind to harmonize the motor and sensory organs. As plans without the power of money will fail, so plans of the mind are doomed to failure without psychic power. There are two classes of *ojas*:

1. *Para ojas* is responsible for the life principles. On its destruction, death is certain to occur. Its main office is the heart, and through cardiorespiratory motions, it helps the mind to control all motions of the cells and the entire body.

2. *Apara ojas* is constantly in *tanmātric* motion, through the circulation. On its deficiency or destruction there are various physical and mental diseases in the body.

By means of *ojas*, psychic power, the mind works with the senses for acquisition of knowledge of the external and internal environment. Knowledge is not possible if the power of *ojas* is not with the mind.

In order to know the physical environment, the mind should be concentrated on physical phenomena; and its impressions and stimuli should reach the psychic center in the brain for their interpretation. To know the internal environment, the mind should be concentrated on internal impressions and stimuli, which will be interpreted in the psychic center of the brain.

By recalling and reciting, the mind brings the development of the cells and the body. In the psychological plane, this is called memory. This process of reciting and recalling is going on continuously. Thus the physical universe comes into contact with the physical body.

The conscious mind is midway between matter and the Soul; this mind can be displaced from one idea to focus on other ideas for its sublimation. Displacement from lower ideas and sublimation of the mind to higher ideas by concentration is the object of *Yoga*. *Yoga* teaches the methods to control the mighty waves of the mind, and to subdue them completely to the primordial Consciousness, which is operating eternally through every perceptual mechanism.

Recitation of *OM*, with concentration, leads the mind to Awareness of *nādam*, the melodious word within, which makes the mind aware of the more subtle Universe. This concentration deepens as one goes within from subtle to subtler regions of Nature; thus individual mind comes progressively into contact with the Universal mind.

The Universal mind is reflected through *śirobrahma*, cerebrum and cerebral cortex, while the individual mind operates on the body through *ājñā cakram*, subcortical areas.

By still further concentration, with the power of *ojas*, one has access to intuitive knowledge, *jñāna-cakṣu*. This intuitive knowledge gives the power of dissociation of the Soul from all mind and matter. This concentration is superior because Consciousness goes beyond the gravitational attraction of matter and the senses.

The Ultimate cannot be apprehended through sight, speech, or other senses, nor through penance, prayers, charity, or philanthropic and meritorious deeds. When man's mind is purified by the above-mentioned activities and others, he becomes fit for meditation. After long practice of meditation, he obtains intuitive knowledge, *jñāna cakṣu*. By this light of the Self he experiences ultimate Reality and becomes Reality; thus intuitive knowledge is the knowledge of identity, direct and immediate perception.

*Yoga* does not recognize physics without metaphysics, or metaphysics without physics; it is the missing link between them. Self-realization through the *Yoga* system is a mathematical, methodical, systematic effort to attain Perfection through control of the elements of human nature, physical and metaphysical, biophysiological and psychobiological. The physical body, chemical, biochemical, and biological forces, active will, understanding mind, and psychic Energy are to be brought under control to overcome the dichotomy of body and mind. Human mind has other perceptive faculties than those served by the five senses.

Self-realization is the process of Self-purification. Although all obstacles in the path of Self-realization are superficial, a meditator has difficulty in overcoming them. A meditator should examine his mental states, where he is, what he is, and what he ought to be; thus he gradually and progressively leads himself from a lower to a higher state.

There are innumerable progressive states in meditation. Understanding the following three general classifications will be helpful. These classes include all the innumerable progressive states:

1. *Piṇḍa*, *kṣara*, is the classification of gross physical matter with the limited reflection of Spirit into matter necessary to this state. This is the first resting state for beginners.

One's life depends on this limited admixture of *Puruṣa* and *Prakṛti*. Matter is dominant here. This material-Spiritual state includes all physical and material solar systems with their planets and satellites. Our solar system is one in which our earth is one planet of several, and our moon is one satellite of many in the solar system. Billions and trillions of solar systems are known to astronomers, and are but a small portion of the grand total of the *piṇḍa* or *kṣara* region. This entire *piṇḍa* region is nothing but a speck floating in the sky of the *Brahmāṇḍa*, Infinite space, region. All physical solar systems move in an endless procession within *Brahmāṇḍa*, and are sustained by it. This world of *piṇḍa* is perishable, and so are its products including matter and Spirit. The wise student, after realizing the transitory nature of the *piṇḍa* state, reaches into the second state, *Brahmāṇḍa*.

2. *Brahmāṇḍa* is the state of highly and tremendously moving Cosmic Energy. It is mostly Spiritual, but is mixed with highly refined matter. It is a Spiritual-material region, and its inhabitants are happy beyond the conception of human mind. They are relatively emancipated Souls. *Brahmāṇḍa* is vast in extent, and beyond the thought of human mind. All solar systems shine in *Brahmāṇḍa*, space, like shining and radiating *aṇḍas*, eggs. This is the state of Supreme Energy of *Brahman*. When a student realizes it, he reaches into the last state of Perfection called *nirvāṇam*, *Brahma sthiti*, *satya lokam*.

3. *Satya lokam* is the state of Absolute *Brahman*, unmixed with matter. It is intelligence, love, joy, and Energy. On reaching this state, the seeker knows not death, change, or imperfection. From it all other regions are derived; by it they are sustained; and into it they ultimately enter.

In the state of *piṇḍa*, the physical Universe, Spirit, and matter are *kṣara* because they are in the ocean of everchanging Cosmos. In *Brahmāṇḍa*, Spirit and matter become *akṣara*, Eternal Spirit, unchanged and immobile, the immutable in the mutable. When the seeker reaches this state, his Soul realizes its immutable Nature, Cosmic motions become the motion of the Soul, the sense of duality departs from Consciousness, and Consciousness reaches its Eternal Existence.

These two, *piṇḍa* and *Brahmāṇḍa*, *kṣara* and *akṣara*, physical and metaphysical, are not irreconcilable opposites. *Ātman* is both one and many, the Eternal unborn and the Cosmic streaming forth.

Beyond these two states is the state of *Brahman*, which transcends and permeates both. This Ultimate state of *Brahman* is attained upon overcoming the states of *piṇḍa* and *Brahmāṇḍa*, physical and metaphysical, through progressive Self-purification.

Total existence can be divided into three aspects:

1. Physical aspect of the Universe, constantly in change;

2. Individual consciousness, Eternal but qualified and modified with constant change in which it is involved. It is called the individual "I"; and

3. Eternal and unqualified by any change, the Cosmic "I." It is the Real "I" of all individual "I's." It is written in *Bhavagad Gītā*, "I am the Self of All beings, seated in their heart, O Gudakesa. I am the beginning, the middle, and also the end of All beings."

Thus God is not only centered in the heart of All, but He is also the "I" of all individual "I's." The fact is that *Brahman* is All; *Brahman* remains indivisible and is ever-realized. Man does not know this fact, although it is the very thing he needs to know. Knowledge means overcoming the obstacles, which conceal the Real "I." There cannot be numerous "I's"; the Real "I" is one for All. It is reflected in the mind as the individual "I" in the same way as the one sun appears to be multiple due to its reflection in many mirrors.

## SUTRA NO. 66

श्रवणादिभिरुद्दीप्तज्ञानाग्निपरितापितः ।
जीवस्सर्वमलान्मुक्तः स्वर्णवद्द्योतते स्वयम् ॥६६॥

ŚRAVAṆĀDIBHIRUDDĪPTAJÑĀNĀGNIPARITĀPITAḤ.
JĪVASSARVAMALĀNMUKTAḤ SVARṆAVAD DYOTATE SVAYAM.

| | | |
|---|---|---|
| श्रवण-आदिभिः | Śravaṇa - ādibhiḥ | By hearing, etc. |
| उद्दीप्त- | Uddīpta | Kindled |
| ज्ञान-अग्नि- | Jñāna-agni- | In the fire of knowledge |
| परितापितः | Paritāpitaḥ | Heated |
| जीवः | Jīvaḥ | The individual soul |
| सर्व-मलात् | Sarva-malāt | From all impurity |
| मुक्तः | Muktaḥ | Freed |
| स्वर्णवत् | Svarṇavat | Like gold |
| द्योतते | Dyotate | Shines |
| स्वयम् | Svayam | Of itself |

By hearing, thinking, and meditating, the light of the Self is kindled. Once this light of Self is kindled, the individual "I" becomes free from all impurities. It begins to shine forth as the Universal "I," in the same way as gold shines when it is purified by fire.

The fire of knowledge kindled by hearing, thinking, meditating, and directly perceiving, burns all impurities of the individual; and *jīva*, the individual Soul, freed from all impurities, shines of itself like gold purified by fire.

Self-realization is an inner and an outer process. There are four stages, each dependent on another chronologically:

1. *Śravaṇam*, hearing and reading;

2. *Mananam*, thinking and reasoning. After hearing and reading, one should start logical and philosophical reasoning on these matters to have some ideas for experimentation.

3. *Nidi-dhyāsanam*, experimentation in concentration, contemplation, and meditation to obtain the state of *Samādhi*;

4. *Sākṣātkārah*, direct perception, is identity with Truth.

Internally one should listen to the sound current, and one should know that it is *Brahman* itself reaching into the realms of mind and matter, or *piṇḍa*, the physical world, in a perpetual stream of Consciousness. It is not heard by the physical ears; it is manifested in the perceptual mechanism. It may be heard in many parts of the brain and head simultaneously and, in an advanced state, every cell of the body begins to project this sound current. In a further advanced state, the inner and outer worlds simultaneously and, in an advanced state, every cell of the body begins to project this sound current. In a further advanced state, the inner and outer worlds simultaneously are perceived in the ocean of sound current.

At first, *nādam*, sound current, is feeble and variable in tone and tune, but as one continues listening to it and reasoning on it, it becomes more distinct and more musical. Finally, all physical sounds are transformed into it. On reaching the third state of *nididhyāsanam*, concentration, contemplation, and meditation, it attracts the Soul upward. This attraction is indescribable; *nādam* attraction cannot be compared even with electromagnetic attraction, for the latter is mere physical attraction. In figurative and mythological language, it is called *Kriṣṇa*, attraction, with a melodious flute, *nādam*.

The stream of Consciousness runs upward to meet its source and master, its own Reality. The stream of Consciousness going from the higher world to the lower world, is called *dhārā* (*dhā* + *rā*). When the same stream of Consciousness rises from the lower world, it is called *rādhā* (*rā* + *dhā*). This electrical stream of Consciousness is transformed from *dhārā* to *Rādhā*, and runs up to discover its Ultimate

Source and master, Ultimate Reality, the vibrating Eternal electromagnetic ocean of music. This vibrating *nādam* is the Ultimate Source of the rising Consciousness; thus it is called *Rādhāsvāmi*, master of *Rādhā*, or *Rādhākriṣṇa*. In figurative and mythological language, it is *Kriṣṇa* with his consort *Rādhā*.

This *nādam* purifies the mind, and enables the Soul to attain higher perception. After a few months' practice on *nādam*, a seeker realizes an awakening of Superconsciousness, *Kuṇḍalinī*, and the development of supernatural powers never before realized. With love, knowledge, and practice, he now traverses all the regions of *Brahmāṇḍa* and stands in the radiant region of Consciousness.

Reaching the fourth state, inner *sākṣātkāra*, subjective identity, he now transcends *piṇḍa* and *Brahmāṇḍa*, the world of manifestation and the world of Energy, and reaches the *Rādhā-svāmi-dhāma*, the abode of *Brahman*.

All of this is achieved by constant practice. The achievement is accomplished in the light of full Conscousness and perfect memory. Achievement of this state is the Ultimate goal of *Yoga* and philosophy.

In the purification of the mind, *jīva* is compared to gold. Fire does not create gold, but burns its impurities, so that the gold shines by its own lustre. Likewise, the fire of Self-analysis and meditation removes obstacles and impurities, so that *Ātman* shines by its own light and radiance. Like gold, the inherent Nature of *Ātman* is Self-luminosity, Self-light, and Self-radiance.

The entire process of meditation may be summarized in three terms of investigation:

1. *Prāṇa*, primal force, which has produced the vast Universe;

2. *Praṇavam*, *nādam*, which is the Ultimate Source of the Universe; and

3. *Caitanyam*, which is the leading Conscious Energy of the Universe. When Conscious Energy with the primal Energy, the Energy of *prakṛti*, is focused on the sound current, *nādam*, one attains identity with *Brahman*.

*Jīvatman* and Soul are other names of *Ātman*. It is a reflection of *Brahman*. In other words, the Soul has descended into the body from the highest plane of *Brahman*, and is entangled here by the three *guṇas–satoguṇa, rajoguṇa*, and *tamoguṇa*; the five *tattvas*–solid, liquid, gaseous, light, and the ethereal state of Nature; the ten *indriyas*–five sensory and five motor organs; and the mind. It has developed such a strong tie with the mind and material forces related to it that, in its present condition, it cannot free itself from these bondages.

The body is inner bondage. Family, national and international relationships constitute outer bondage. The Soul has now no recollection of its Cosmic form. It has become a citizen of a particular country, and has forgotten its Universal citizenship. The Soul is really a citizen of every planet and every solar system. One must take Consciousness back to its Real Source, in order to free oneself from the suffering of the world.

How can one take his Consciousness back? The following method is inspiration for meditation.

All Nature is electromagnetic vibration, and life is the crown of all vibrations. Motion is the fundamental property of all living beings and living tissues; there is no motion without sensation. Here sensation means Consciousness.

The motion of the heart is the manifestation of Eternal life. This motion of the heart initiates the motion of the lungs; and these motions initiate motion in all cells of the body, and these cells initiate all actions and reactions–chemical, biochemical, biological, and psychological. Each and every cell of the body is a vast factory of chemicals, where components are created to further manifest life; thus cardio-respiratory motion is the leader of all life activities and all motions. It is life!

*Yogis* advise one to start meditation on this primal source of life and Consciousness in the body. The heart is playing the main part in motion, while the brain is playing the main part in sensation. They depend on each other. The heart is the organ of unity, and the brain is the organ of multiplicity. Through meditation on the heart, electrical phenomena lead Consciousness to the motion and sensation of the cells; and the motion and sensation of the cells lead to molecular motion. This molecular motion leads to atomic motion, which in turn leads to electronic, *tanmātric*, motion of life.Thus in higher perception, the electronic motion of individual existence leads one to Cosmic motion.

Mighty Cosmic forces are manifesting their motion through the motion of the heart. Its motion is the representative for Cosmic forces. This Truth is realized through meditation when the body is deeply relaxed and kept free from all voluntary motions, mental and physical. One gradually and progressively reaches the state of Cosmic motion and Cosmic sensation, Consciousness. He begins to feel a mighty, homogeneous, eternal ocean of life and Consciousness, and the individual existence becomes like a transmitter and receiver of that mighty motion and Consciousness.

The electromagnetic attraction and supra-electronic vibration of *OM* present more difficulty in description than in realization. This entire Universe begins to melt into the ocean of electricity, for the Universe is really a potential form of electricity, which appears to an ordinary man as a collection of mass. This electronic ocean of *prāṇa* is constantly melting into the ocean of *ākāśam* ether, which in turn is melting into the ocean of Consciousness. This ocean of Consciousness is in its own radiance with its own dazzling and shining light. When this state is realized, the individual becomes free from all bondage, and is identical with this mighty wave of Consciousness. This All-vibrating, mighty wave of Consciousness is manifested in the heart.

Meditation is the suspension of all thoughts, so that the meditator can experience the original Source of all thought. As long as thoughts are rushing one after another in the mind, one cannot experience their original Source. Holding the mind on the "I"-principle, "Who am I?" all thoughts are expelled. Continuous practice of such meditation gives the mind the necessary strength to enter into its original Source.

## SUTRA NO. 67

हृदाकाशोदितो ह्यात्मा बोधभानुस्तमोऽपहृत्।
सर्वव्यापी सर्वधारी भाति भासयतेऽखिलम् ॥६७॥

HṚDĀKĀŚODITO HYĀTMĀ BODHABHĀNUSTAMO' PAHṚT.
SARVAVYĀPĪ SARVADHĀRĪ BHĀTI BHĀSAYATE' KHILAM.

| | | |
|---|---|---|
| हृद्-आकाश- | Hṛd-ākāśa | In the firmament of the heart |
| उदितः | Uditaḥ | Rising |
| हि | Hi | Indeed |
| आत्मा | Ātmā | The Self |
| बोध-भानुः | Bodha-bhānuḥ | Sun of knowledge |
| तमः-अपहृत् | Tamaḥ-apahṛt | Destroyer of darkness |
| सर्व-व्यापी | Sarva-vyāpī | All-pervading |
| सर्व-धारी | Sarva-dhārī | All-sustaining |
| भाति | Bhāti | Shines |
| भासयते | Bhāsayate | Causes to shine |
| अखिलम् | Akhilam | The entire Universe |

*Brahman* shines as "I" in the heart of every being. When the identity of the individual "I" as the Universal "I" in one's heart is awakened, it is experienced as the sun of knowledge, which destroys the darkness of ignorance, *Ātman*, *Brahman*, pervades All, sustains All, reveals the Universe of the senses, and reveals Itself.

Omnipresent, omnipotent, and omniscient *Ātman*, the sun of motion and Conscousness, arises in the firmament of the heart. When *Ātman* is realized in the Ethereal ocean of the heart, it destroys the darkness of ignorance. It is manifested as motion of the heart and Consciousness of the brain, although it is All-pervading and All-sustaining. It illumines All and shines in its own radiance.

The history of thought moves imperceptibly. When motion is highly imperceptible, it seems to lose its main characteristic of changeability, and appears to be a mass of inert matter. The electromagnetic waves of sunlight are of high velocity and imperceptibility; consequently there is a visible perception of a motionless ocean of light.

High motion seems to go beyond the limits of time and space, cause and effect. For example, if a man wishes to travel from Montreal to New York City on foot, the trip may take ten days. If he sends his message by telephone, it will take but a moment. By telephone from Montreal to New York, he talks as though he and his friend are face to face. Here the motion of electricity is so high and imperceptible that one feels the phenomena of no motion at all. The motion of the mind has the highest imperceptibility. Its motion transcends all physical motions. Due to its high motion, it seems to be motionless. Distance and nearness, within and without, having no meaning in high velocity.

In *yogic* meditation, if one goes beyond the motion of the mind, one will transcend the world of mind and causality, time and space, cause and effect. Such a highly moving Consciousness will be everywhere, simultaneously. Naturally birth and death, pain and suffering, cannot touch this Consciousness, because they are creations of causality and mind.

How will such a highly moving Consciousness manifest through the motion of the heart, brain, and mind? It does not need to manifest; it is present everywhere, in everything. Consciousness, *Brahman*, *Ātman*, has no feet, but its motion is inexpressibly fast; it has no ears yet it hears everything; it has no hands yet it performs all actions and reactions of the Universe. Without a tongue, it enjoys all taste; without a voice, it speaks eloquently; without eyes, it sees All; without skin, it touches everything; and without a nose, it savors every odor. So marvelous in all ways are its performances and acts that none can describe the greatness of *Brahman*, *Ātman*. This highly inexplicable Supreme principle is manifested through the motions of the heart, brain, and mind as "I."

This mighty Consciousness, *Brahman* in which all worlds find rest, is manifested in *samādhi* in the center of purified *cittam* mindstuff. *Cittam*, figuratively the mother of Consciousness, *Ātman*, contemplates with rapture the wondrous beauty that captivates the heart of Sages. Ethereal motion, the lovely and charming ocean of beauty and sense perfection, pervades everywhere. How can one pray to and worship this Consciousness, when it is everywhere? The worshipper and his entire Universe, including the moon and stars, are swept away by this principle. Who can believe that this mighty Consciousness, whose creation is the entire Universe in which innumerable solar systems move like electrons in the atom, can take birth in the womb of wisdom? It is a Truth which cannot be realized except in *samādhi*.

To say that this Consciousness is Reality is to say that it is different from the phenomenal, the spatial, the temporal, and the sensible. It is what is assumed as foundational.

Concentrating the mind on *nādam*, sound current, contemplating its Energy, meditating on its Nature and focusing Consciousness with full attention on its various melodies, tones, and tunes, one realizes the Oneness of one's Existence, and the Existence of the Cosmos. *Ātman*, *Brahman*, is vividly felt in the heart which sustains the body, senses, and mind. One feels the Oneness of one's *Ātman*-Consciousness which pervades the entire body, senses, and mind and sustains them—and *Brahman*—which pervades the entire Universe and sustains it.

## SUTRA NO. 68

दिग्देशकालाद्यनपेक्ष्य सर्वगं शीतादिहृन्नित्यसुखं निरञ्जनम्।
यस्स्वात्मतीर्थं भजते विनिष्क्रियः स सर्ववित्सर्वगतोऽमृतो भवेत् ॥६८॥

DIGDEŚAKĀLĀDYANAPEKṢYA SARVAGAṀ ŚĪTĀDIHṚNNITYASUKHAṀ NIRAÑJANAM.
YASSVĀTMATĪRTHAṀ BHAJATE VINIṢKRIYAḤ SA SARVAVIT SARVAGATO' MṚTO BHAVET.

| | | |
|---|---|---|
| दिक्-देश-कालादि | Dik-deśa-kālādi | Direction-space-time |
| अनपेक्ष्य | Anapekṣya | Independent |
| सर्व-गम् | Sarva-gam | Omnipresent |
| शीतादि-हृत् | Śītādi - hṛt | Destroyer of cold-heat, etc. |
| नित्य-सुखम् | Nitya-sukham | Eternal happiness |
| निरञ्जनम् | Nirañjanam | Without blemish |
| यः | Yaḥ | Who |
| स्वात्म-तीर्थम् | Sva-ātma-tīrtham | Temple of his own Self |
| भजते | Bhajate | Worships, praises |
| विनिष्क्रियः | Viniṣkriyaḥ | Renouncing selfish actions |
| सः | Saḥ | He |
| सर्व-वित् | Sarva-vit | Omniscient |
| सर्व-गतः | Sarva-gataḥ | All-pervading |
| अमृतः | Amṛtaḥ | Immortal |
| भवेत् | Bhavet | Becomes |

That *Brahman* is independent of time and space, cause and effect; is omnipresent, omniscient, and omnipotent; is the destroyer of the pairs of opposites such as love and hatred, pain and pleasure, heat and cold; and is the giver of Eternal happiness. He who, renouncing all ulterior motives and selfish activities, in the Temple of his heart worships that *Brahman*, I, becomes All-knowing and All-pervading, and attains immortality here in this very life.

He who serves the world without ulterior motives and selfish desires; he who meditates on *OM*, the Supreme, in the serene, sacred, constantly shining and radiating Temple of his mind; he who renounces all selfish activities, becomes All-knowing, All-pervading, and immortal by attaining identity with *Brahman* which is beyond cause and effect, space and time; which is omnipresent, omniscient, and omnipotent; which is the destroyer of ignorance and dualism; which is the giver of Absolute beauty, Existence, Consciousness, and happiness.

The aim of Self-realization is prosperity in the physical plane and *nirvāṇam* in the Spiritual plane. The whole process of Self-realization may be summarized in two classes:

1. Analysis of the nature of knowledge; and

2. Analysis of the nature of nescience.

*VIDYĀṀ CĀVIDYĀṀ CA YAS TAD VEDOBHAYAṀ SAHA,*
*AVIDYAYĀ MṚTYUṀ TĪRTVĀ, VIDYAYĀMṚTAM AŚNUTE.*

He who simultaneously knows the nature of knowledge and ignorance, passes over death by means of *avidyā*, nescience, and attains *nirvāṇam*, liberation, by means of True knowledge.

All material knowledge, science, action, and prayers other than Self-realization are to purify the mind. They are helpful because by them man overcomes his death, and prepares his mind for incarnation of the Supreme.

*Anitya-aśuci-duḥkha-anātmasu, nitya-śuci-sukha-ātmakhyātiravidyā.*
(Yoga Sutras of Patañjali, 2-5)

According to this aphorism of *yoga*, the first phase of *avidyā*, ignorance is to behave in the transitory world as though it were Eternal, to feel immortality about the mortal body, to believe that the created Universe, which we experience everyday, has been going on since Eternity and will not perish, or that the gods keep the same body at all times by Spiritual power.

The second phase of *avidyā* is to regard as pure the things which are impure, e.g., the body of the opposite sex, falsehood, theft, and other things.

The third phase is to regard as pleasure-giving the things which are painful, such as sensual indulgence.

The fourth phase is to regard as Spiritual the things which are carnal.

These four kinds of wrong notions are *avidyā,* nescience. The opposite of ignorance is knowledge, i.e., to know non-eternal things as non-eternal, Eternal things as Eternal, impure as impure, pure as pure, pain as pain, pleasure as pleasure, non-spiritual as non-spiritual, and Spiritual as Spiritual. *Vidyā*, knowledge, consists of knowing a thing exactly as it is, and *avidyā*, nescience, consists in knowing a thing differently from what it is.

The Ultimate aim of life is the realization of Self. This means realizing the Real. The Nature of Reality is Existence, Consciousness, and Bliss without beginning or end. This Reality can be realized only in the Temple of one's heart. Relative knowledge depends on the trinity of the knower, the process of knowing, and the knowable; but the knowledge of *Ātman* transcends this triad. The triad is only an appearance in time and space, while Reality lies beyond it. The triad is like a mirage; it is the result of ignorance. The word "ignorance" is not used in a literal sense, but in a philosophical sense. All knowledge of the relative universe is called ignorance; knowledge which reveals the Real Nature of I, Self, Absolute God, is called knowledge.

Now a question arises: if this individual "I" is an illusion, then who projects this illusion of "I" within us? The answer is that it is the Real "I"; and the Real "I" will cast off the illusion of the individual "I." A Self-realized being does not see any contradiction or paradox in this. The Absolute God remains permanently Absolute; but it is the mind which apparently splits this "I" into multiple personalities.

As a matter of fact, Self-realization also is a figurative term. Persons understand, in the state of ignorance, the non-self to be the Self, and the unreal to be the Real, and that they have to come out of this unreal self by means of Self-realization. The Self is pure Consciousness; there is no activity of human life which can be performed by unconsciousness; thus it is Consciousness which is realizing itself. Self-realization is not limited to the world of time and space; a Self-realized person comes to know the Universe in all its phases, past, present, and future. Without exception, any person in the past, present, or the future can only express himself through the word "I"; hence, he who knows the "I," knows the Universe relatively and transcendentally. Since the "I" is the center of every being, he who cognizes this "I" becomes the Self of All beings, and is free from birth and rebirth. It is the mind which passes through constant changes:—birth, growth, decay, and death,—with its products, body and senses. Consciousness, I, which is behind the panorama of body and mind, does not go into any change. When the identity of "I" with the body, mind, and senses is removed by means of Self-analysis, one experiences Eternity. *Mokṣa,* liberation, does not mean obtaining something new; for the Self, I, remains Eternally as it is, was, and shall be. It is the identity of this "I" with the body, mind, and senses, that produces the feeling of birth, growth, decay, and death. Through Self-realization, Consciousness is released from its identity with body and mind, and it is enlightened in its Real Nature, which is *Sat-Cit-Ānanda*, eternal Existence-Consciousness-Bliss.